The
Moral & Spiritual
Crisis in Education

p. 78

... how an education might facilitate
the quest for what is holy.

the educator as prophet p. 105

ON TRUTH p. 113 →
NON VIOL - p. 115
LOVE - p. 117

CRITICAL STUDIES IN EDUCATION SERIES
EDITED BY PAULO FREIRE & HENRY A. GIROUX

EDUCATION UNDER SIEGE
The Conservative, Liberal & Radical Debate Over Schooling
STANLEY ARONOWITZ & HENRY A. GIROUX

CRITICAL PEDAGOGY & CULTURAL POWER
DAVID W. LIVINGSTONE & CONTRIBUTORS

LITERACY
Reading The Word & The World
PAULO FREIRE & DONALDO MACEDO

THE POLITICS OF EDUCATION
Culture, Power & Liberation
PAULO FREIRE

WOMEN TEACHING FOR CHANGE
Gender, Class & Power
KATHLEEN WEILER

BROKEN PROMISES
Reading Instruction in Twentieth-Century America
PATRICK SHANNON

EDUCATION & THE AMERICAN DREAM
Conservatives, Liberals & Radicals Debate the Future of Education
HARVEY HOLTZ & ASSOCIATES

THE MORAL AND SPIRITUAL CRISIS IN EDUCATION
A Curriculum for Justice & Compassion in Education
DAVID PURPEL

POPULAR CULTURE & CRITICAL PEDAGOGY
Schooling & the Language of Everyday Life
HENRY GIROUX, ROGER SIMON & CONTRIBUTORS

The
Moral & Spiritual Crisis in Education

A Curriculum for Justice and Compassion in Education

INTRODUCTION BY HENRY A. GIROUX AND PAULO FREIRE

David E. Purpel

CRITICAL STUDIES IN EDUCATION SERIES

BERGIN & GARVEY
New York • Westport, Connecticut • London

Library of Congress Cataloging-in-Publication Data

Purpel, David E.
The moral & spiritual crisis in education : a curriculum for justice and compassion
in education / David E. Purpel : introduction by Paulo Freire and Henry A. Giroux.
    p. cm.—(Critical studies in education series)
Bibliography: p.
Includes index.
ISBN 0-89789-153-8 (alk. paper)
ISBN 0-89789-152-X (pbk.: alk. paper)
    1. Public schools—United States—Evaluation. 2. Education—United States—Aims
and objectives. 3. Social justice. 4. Moral education—United States. I. Title.
II. Title: Moral and spiritual crisis in education. III. Series.
LA217.P87   1989
370'.973—dc19   88-16602

Library of Congress Catalog Card Number: 88-16602
ISBN: 0-89789-153-8
      0-89789-152-X (pbk.)

First published in 1989

Bergin & Garvey, One Madison Avenue, New York, NY 10010
An imprint of Greenwood Publishing Group, Inc.

Printed in the United States of America

The paper used in this book complies with the
Permanent Paper Standard issued by the National
Information Standards Organization (Z39.48-1984).

10 9 8 7 6 5 4 3

Contents

Acknowledgments   *vii*

Preface   *ix*

Introduction   *xiii*

1   The Current Crisis in Education: Professional Incompetence or Cultural Failure   *1*

2   Recent Educational Reform: Delusions and Trivialization   *14*

3   The Moral and Spiritual Crisis in American Education   *28*

4   A Religious and Moral Framework for American Education   *65*

5   Education in a Prophetic Voice   *100*

6   A Curriculum for Social Justice and Compassion   *121*

7   Issues of Curriculum Planning, Design, and Implementation   *138*

Bibliography   *166*

Index   *169*

Acknowledgments

It is, of course, impossible to acknowledge fully all those who have helped and supported me in this effort. Surely family, friends, colleagues, and students have given much to me in their energy, encouragement, ideas, and criticisms. I will always be indebted to my first real teacher—Don Oliver—who overwhelmed me with his genius and who, much to my surprise, encouraged me to think that I had something to say. There are other colleagues who have been significant teachers for me—certainly Jim Macdonald, Ralph Mosher, Henry Giroux, Bob O'Kane, Fritz Mengert, and Svi Shapiro are among them.

I am happy to acknowledge the vital importance to the work of this book of the research leave granted me by the School of Education and the University of North Carolina at Greensboro. The Graduate School at UNCG also provided valuable assistance in the preparation of the manuscript. The development of my writing was also greatly helped by my participation in the Coolidge Colloquium, particularly through my interaction with Ben Beliak and Carol Ochs.

I very much appreciate the careful and thorough editing provided by Carolyn Steele and the editors at Bergin and Garvey. Joyce Sloop and Becky Blomgren read an early draft and gave me helpful reactions. A special thanks to the loving, patient, valiant, and tireless way in which Jeannette Dean has prepared the manuscript.

Preface

This is in many ways an extraordinarily exciting time for educational theorists and yet in other ways it is a particularly dreary and bleak era. The dreariness and bleakness is not very hard to locate, since they are what emerge from current mainstream educational dialogue, particularly the language of so-called educational reform. This discourse is not only trivial and distracting; it is marked also by a singular lack of imagination and daring. The criticisms made, the solutions offered, may be important insofar as they affect current policies and programs, but they hardly stir us with wonder and awe. Beyond this hum and drone, however, there is the roar of high excitement involving enormous possibilities and dangerous risks.

I speak of two roars—the first has to do with the enormity of our present cultural, political, and economic crisis and with it the incipient possibility of catastrophe. The second general realm of energy and excitement is in the world of ideas which is bursting with ever increasing vitality and brilliance. Virtually every scholarly and professional field is awash with significant controversies, challenges to existing canons, emerging paradigms—some of which have led to whole new areas of inquiry and new research modes. Clearly, some of this excitement is evident in the field of educational theory as we see qualitatively different discourses emerging from the invigorating effects of the newer insights, theories, and critiques. I believe that we in education do in fact need to re-conceptualize mainstream educational discourse. More precisely, we need to quicken the pace of these efforts already begun in the seminal work of such educators as

Paulo Freire, James Macdonald, Henry Giroux, Maxine Greene, William Pinar, and Michael Apple.

It is my hope that this book contributes to the effort to develop a more liberating discourse on the intimate relationships among the society, culture, and education. Furthermore, I want very much to facilitate the process by which we can understand and act on the ways in which our schools might at the very least not increase the probability of social disaster. I continue to have the faith that schools can go even beyond that point and can actually contribute to the creation of a more loving, more just, saner world. My efforts toward this goal focus on the possibilities involved in enriching educational theory with a moral and religious discourse. More particularly, I have tried in this book to make a case for the necessity for educators to affirm moral and educational commitments. I believe that there is an urgency not only to be critical, not only to deconstruct, debunk and unmask, but also simultaneously to affirm, commit, and advocate. I try in this book to confront the problematics of moral affirmation in the context of confronting the problematics of avoiding moral affirmation. I come away from these efforts more convinced than ever that we as educators have special responsibilities in this unique moment to risk positive commitment in addition to risking negative criticism. Indeed, I have come to see that one effort is not complete without the other.

The book is organized into seven chapters; the first two chapters examine on the nature of recent and current mainstream educational discourse particularly in its trivial, vulgar, and technical character. These chapters present a number of explanations for this state of affairs including a discussion of American anti-intellectualism and the fears of education. They conclude with the position that what is most lacking in current educational discourse is the inclusion of the moral and religious dimensions of society and education.

In chapter three I present a moral analysis of the current culture in a series of paradoxes and conflicts that reflect both the dangers and possibilities inherent in our present consciousness. It is an analysis that focuses most directly on middle-class life, in part because I believe that the middle class has both political and economic power and high educational potential, i.e., is in position to inform its power with a moral and religious vision. I address in this chapter the enormous conflicts, contradictions, and divisions within our society, as well as our pride in pluralism and diversity. It is my strong belief that we both need and are capable of creating an overarching belief system (I call it a mythos) that can accommodate both our affirmation and skepticism of them.

In chapter four I spell out such a moral and religious framework or vision that speaks to meaning, purpose, and ultimacy. It is a framework that borrows from two ancient traditions, the Socratic and the Prophetic and two current theological movements: Liberation Theology and Creation Theology. The major emphasis, however, is on Prophecy, conceptualized as the voice that in Walter Brueggemann's phrase combines "energy and criticism" and a consciousness which, says Abraham Heschel, "has the ability to hold God and man in a single thought." Prophecy holds us to our deepest commitments, chides us when we do not meet them, and provides hope for us when we think we cannot.

The fifth chapter describes how educators might internalize this voice and thereby provide themselves with purpose and direction. The chapter concludes with a credo focusing on the goal of education being that which facilitates love, justice, community, and joy.

The concluding two chapters deal with how a curriculum primarily directed at social justice and compassion might look. The chapter includes a list of specific educational goals and objectives, and the book ends with a discussion of issues of implementation and of overcoming sabotage and cooptation.

I certainly hope lots of people read this book, and if they do I certainly expect that there will be criticisms and disagreements. I hope and expect that there will be questions and eyebrows raised. I expect that flaws will be found in my reasoning; that some will point to contrary findings; and that some will find my analysis insufficient and unpersuasive. Such criticism is legitimate and required, just as vital if not more so that the work itself, and can only serve to advance our understanding. What I ask of critical readers, however, is that they not only point out faulty analysis or misreading—this surely must be done—but that they also address the issue of affirmation in general and the particular affirmations I make. This is because my strongest hope for this book is that it will stimulate others to reflect on and engage in the struggle involved in clarifying our convictions. My challenge to critics is to confront the question of what it is that we are working hard to make happen. If the convictions are unclear as stated, how and in what ways ought they be clarified? If they are insufficient, which should be added, which should be deleted? If credal statements are more problematic that liberating, what should we say about developing evaluative criteria for judging cultural and educational policy? I look forward to this dialogue and to continued excitement and vitality in educational theory for I continue to have faith that education can indeed help us to overcome the demons.

Introduction

by

Henry A. Giroux and Paulo Freire

We must abandon completely the naive faith, that school automatically liberates the mind and serves the cause of human progress; in fact, we know that it may serve any cause. [It] may serve tyranny as well as freedom, ignorance as well as enlightenment, falsehood as well as truth, war as well as peace, death as well as life. It may lead men and women to think they are free even as it rivets them in chains of bondage. Education is indeed a force of great power, particularly when the word is made to embrace all the agencies and organized processes for molding the mind, but whether it is good or evil depends, not on the laws of learning, but on the conception of life and civilization that gives it substance and direction. In the course of history, education has served every purpose and doctrine contrived by man [sic]. If it is to serve the cause of human freedom, it must be explicitly designed for that purpose.
George S. Counts[1]

You must know who is the object and who is the subject of a sentence in order to know if you are the object or subject of history. If you can't control a sentence you don't know how to put yourself into history, to trace your own origin in the country, to vocalize, to use voice.
Nelida Piñon[2]

There is a volatile debate in social theory taking place over what constitutes the relationship among knowledge, power, desire, and subjectivity. Within the humanities, social sciences, and educational

xiii

theory there is an ongoing criticism being waged over the ideological nature and social function of the canons, the status of grand theories, the boundaries that define disciplines, the meaning of history, and the role of intellectuals. In the reaches of higher education, the major thrust for reform has come from the various discourses of poststructuralism and postmodernism. Declaring war on the categories of transcendence, certainty, and foundationalism, exponents of contemporary social theory have reconstituted the meaning and method of critical inquiry and radically challenged the dominant modes of authority and social practice. In fact, many of the new critical voices have forcefully proclaimed that there exists no "objective reference point, separate from culture and politics, available to distinguish truth from ideology, fact from opinion, or representation from interpretation."[3]

What is particularly valuable about this new mode of critical inquiry is its insistence that interpretation cannot be situated outside of ideology, that is, outside of the considerations of power, historical struggle, and human interests. The importance of this work, especially for educators, is reflected in its powerful dismantling of the resurgent discourse of the New Right,[4] whose claim to objectivity and scientism in defense of its policies has been revealed as inextricably enmeshed in the language of ideology, politics, and power. While acknowledging the important contributions of postmodern social theory, it is also crucial to recognize its serious limitations. For instance, it has not sufficiently addressed the central issue of how identities and subjectivities are constructed within different moral experiences and relations, nor has it pursued with enough analytical rigor how power produces, accommodates, and challenges not simply the discourses but also the material relations of dominant political life. In other words, it has failed to develop a substantive ethical discourse and public morality that is necessary for overcoming existing forms of exploitation and subjugation. In addition, its methods of analysis and critique have not been posed as pedagogical issues. Thus, as a mode of critique, much of what constitutes postmodern social theory has not fully appreciated the critical value of engaging its methods of analysis and inquiry as forms of pedagogical practice that bring into critical relief the relationships that obtain among teaching, knowledge/texts, and learning. One result has been that this work has had only a minor influence among critical educational theorists or within the educational reform movement presently being debated in the United States and elsewhere.

Now, as before, the debate over the reform of public schooling in the United States is being principally set by the right wing. The emphasis on character education and moral fundamentalism currently trumpeted by New Right critics such as William Bennett and Chester Finn, Jr., have served primarily to legitimate forms of authority and social discipline that undermine the very principles of democratic community and social responsibility. Similarly, this ideological thrust has been instrumental in framing the public questions related to how one should conceive of ethics, power, and history in present-day social reality and what role these should play as part of the language of educational reform. For example, public schooling and higher education are analyzed by New Right critics within what could be called a crisis of authority approach, one which abstracts equity from excellence and social responsibility from achievement. Central to this view is the claim that what constitutes the crisis in schooling is the breakdown of traditional forms of authority and moral regulation. Concerns such as those expressed above by George Counts have been largely subverted by the New Right in the current debates over schooling.[5] Under the guise of attempting to revitalize the language of morality, right-wing educators and politicians have, in reality, launched a dangerous attack on some of the most fundamental aspects of democratic public life and the obligations of socially responsible, critical citizenship. What has been valorized in this ideological discourse is not the issue of reclaiming public schools as agencies of social justice and critical democracy, but an elitist view of schooling based on a celebration of cultural uniformity, a rigid view of authority, an uncritical support for remaking school curricula in the interest of labor-market imperatives, and a return to the old transmission and acculturation model of teaching.[6]

The current crisis in educational reform is more than a crisis of authority to be resolved primarily through the language of means and technique— developing better ways to promote the same old content and social relations—it is, in fact, a crisis of morality and political nerve. This is evident both in the New Right's attempt to subordinate questions of ethics and power to the discourse of authority and rigid social discipline and in its attempt to reconstruct history as part of a wider political project. In this case, history is fashioned within a particular interpretation referred to by Christopher Lasch as arising "from a need to forget."[7] Lost from this perspective are the voices and struggles of oppressed groups fighting to transform the ideological and material conditions which support forms of subjugation and exploitation. It is a history without a language of moral responsibility, a history characterized by an impoverished civic discourse that celebrates freedom as a form of possessive individualism and treats the concept of democracy as if it were at odds with the notion of community and the call for collective social possibilities that enhance rather than demean civic and public culture. In its right-wing version,

history is offered up as narrative cleansed of social conflict and struggle, reconstructed around the tenets of a mythical past dominated by
republican virtues such as those expressed in the McGuffey Eclectic
Readers and in an insular reading of the traditions of Western civilization.[8] Of course, there is more at work here than the abuse of history;
there is an ideology and politics that denies the importance of forms
of pedagogy that allow people to speak out of their own histories,
cultures, experiences, and traditions.

In *The Moral and Spiritual Crisis in Education*, David Purpel takes
up the challenge presented by poststructuralism and postmodernism
and the threat to democracy and schooling currently posed by the
New Right. He begins with the assumptions that educational reform
cannot be debated or understood outside of the space of politics and
social power and that central to the language of reform is the need
to rethink and remake our social meanings and social relations as
part of our effort as public intellectuals. From this stance, Purpel not
only criticizes the New Right's attempt to undermine the democratic
and moral dimensions of schooling, he also brilliantly argues for the
rebirth of a moral culture from which to reconstruct and reconnect
the spheres of politics, ethics, and education.

For Purpel, the reform period of the last decade exemplifies in its
language and philosophy not simply the narrow political and economic interests of the Age of Reagan; more lamentably, it points to
the emergence of a public philosophy which in its refusal to confront
the basic moral paradoxes and contradictions that shape the ongoing
relations between public schooling and the wider society constitutes
a crisis of democracy and moral courage. In Purpel's terms, educational discourse has been trivialized through its neglect of larger social
and political issues along with its willingness to define the task of
reform as a technical rather than ethical, social, and cultural enterprise. If Purpel were to stop here his message would be important
but far from new. What is both unique and inventive about his analysis
is that he not only convincingly argues for the importance of recog-
nizing the crisis in education as a crisis in meaning, but he defines
what he thinks should be done about it both in terms of reconstructing
a new public philosophy of education and in developing a set of
pedagogical practices consistent with such a vision. Similarly, Purpel
steps outside of the existing Left and progressive analyses of schooling
by aiming both his criticism and programs for reform at a much wider
audience than that usually addressed by current radical school critics.
In this case, Purpel speaks both to and against the attitudes and beliefs
frequently held by the middle class in this country. Rather than limiting his message to the marginal and excluded, Purpel has chosen
to speak to the issues, attitudes, and values that are familiar to main-

stream Americans. He does this in order to widen the possibility for change and to clarify how the challenge of empowerment is not restricted to the disenfranchised and disadvantaged.

Drawing upon a wide variety of theoretical resources and traditions, Purpel combines the languages of critique, hope, risk, and vision in offering new possibilities for the direction of public schooling and for the examination of political and moral responsibilities that both shape and result from our various interventions as administrators, teachers, students, and parents. Purpel's voice is not that of the technician, ideologue, or prophet. It is the voice of the engaged intellectual reflecting on his or her own historical presence and that of the institutions and social practices that position and engage one's work as a committed and caring educator and parent. Purpel seeks to recover the notion of the public good and make it a central aspect of teaching and education. But he is not content merely to deepen our understanding of the importance of ethical and social responsibility; he also succeeds in linking the enterprise of critical understanding to forms of teaching and social relations that ground our ideologies and visions in emotional attachments and spiritual concerns. In other words, Purpel provides theoretical dimensions to his public philosophy of education that are often missing from some of the most radical and critical approaches to education. He accomplishes this by situating the ideological meanings, ideals, and language of public responsibility and virtue in a politics of compassion and hope that makes all of us more attentive to the experiences and emotions of pain, joy, suffering, and human connectedness. If Horkheimer wants us to stare into the face of history in order to recognize both the suffering and possibilities it offers us, Purpel argues that we do this and more. He wants to create social practices and pedagogical relations that allow us once again to realize ourselves as historically connected subjects. Teachers, in Purpel's vision, do more than transmit meanings; they enact the role of social and moral agents of change; they uncover, reproduce, and produce forms of learning and social relations based on those often repressed memories, stories, and dreams that allow us to analyze and embrace schooling as part of a wider politics of solidarity, caring, and joy.[9]

In Purpel's work we see fleeting images of the compassion and pedagogies of Gandhi, Jesus, Martin Luther King, Rosa Luxembourg, and others who lived out their beliefs—and in some cases died defending them—as part of a political and pedagogical struggle that refused to separate learning and justice from compassion and hope. We know of few books that make explicit in such compelling and engaging terms both the foundation of a critical and emancipatory vision of schooling and the pedagoical practices that give it shape and substance. In many respects, this is a book that gives new meaning to linking a democratic vision with a politics of practice, that makes concrete without being dogmatic what it means for teachers and other educators to struggle with purpose and dignity. This is a risk-taking and pathfinding book that will be appreciated by all who recognize the importance of education as part of the wider practice to know, to learn, to care, and to struggle for a more just and better world.

NOTES

1. George S. Counts, *Education and the Foundations of Freedom* (Pittsburgh: University of Pittsburgh Press, 1962), p. 62.
2. Nelida Piñon, "La contaminacion de La Languaje: Interview with Nelida Piñon," *13th Moon 6* 1(2): 74.
3. Gary Peller, "Reason and the Mob: The Politics of Representation," *Tikkun* 2(3): 30.
4. For an analysis of the notion of the New Right as part of a new political, cultural, and ideological formation, see Harvey Kaye, "The Use and Abuse of the Past: The New Right and the Crisis of History," *Socialist Register 1987*, eds. Ralph Miliband, Leo Panitch, and John Saville (London: The Merlin Press, 1987), pp. 332–64.
5. For a short but insightful analysis of this issue, see Steven Selden, "Character Education and the Triumph of Technique," *Issues in Education* 4(3): 301–12.
6. For an extended discussion of these issues, see Henry A. Giroux, *Schooling and the Struggle for Public Life* (Minneapolis: University of Minnesota Press, 1988); see also Stanley Aronowitz and Henry A. Giroux, "Schooling for Less: Literacy in the Age of Broken Dreams," *Harvard Educational Review* (forthcoming); Peter McLaren, "Culture or Canon? Critical Pedagogy and the Politics of Literacy," *Harvard Educational Review* (forthcoming).
7. Christopher Lasch, Introduction to Russell Jacoby's *Social Amnesia* (Boston: Beacon Press, 1974), p. viii.
8. This is evident in the speeches, books, and commentaries made by right-wing spokespersons such as William Bennett, Chester Finn, Diane Ravitch, and John Silber.
9. Peter McLaren, *Schooling as a Ritual Performance* (London: Routledge & Kegan Paul, 1986).

1

The Current Crisis in Education: Professional Incompetence or Cultural Failure?

The prophet is engaged in a battle for language, in an effort to create a different epistemology out of which another community might emerge. The prophet is not addressing behavioral problems. He is not even pressing for repentence. He has only the hope that the ache of God could penetrate the numbness of history. He engages not in scare or threat but only in a yearning that grows with and out of pain.

Walter Brueggemann The Prophetic Imagination

BACKGROUND: EDUCATION AND SOCIETY

Historians are fond of reminding us that the notion of a cultural crisis, as reflected in serious criticism of current educational practice, is hardly new. Indeed, they are able to furnish quotations dating back hundreds, perhaps even thousands, of years that provide an astonishing resonance with contemporary displeasure, anxiety, and even horror over the present and future prospects of our educational system. That there have been crises before ours does not by itself demonstrate that our current sense of alarm is either overly harsh or needlessly worrisome. We are, I believe, very much in a cultural, political, and moral crisis and hence, ipso facto, in an educational crisis. Indeed, it is imperative that we confront the nature of this crisis or, more accurately, that we attend to how a number of critical, cultural, and educational issues and problems are perceived and interpreted. I prefer the word "crisis" to "problem" or "issue" or "concern" because I very much share the view that we as a culture, nation, people, even as a species, confront enormous and awesome threats to our most cherished notions of life, including life itself. The dangers of nuclear war, starvation, totalitarianism, and ecological disaster are as real as they are menacing, and not to view them as problems of immense magnitude and consequence is to contribute to their seriousness.

I consider this book as an educator's response to this crisis. Obviously, an educator is more than an educator and this seemingly trivial point can serve as a metaphor for the inevitable and intimate relationship between education and culture. In point of fact, many educators have presented their professional work in a detached, technical manner as if the educator were *not* more than an educator. A major theme of this book, then, is the critical importance of educators' broad responsibility for the state of the culture as it relates to their specific responsibility for the quality of the "educational program."

The current crisis among other things has served to enhance the highly suspect conception of the educator as a technical expert. It is amazing that in the face of a truism that borders on cliche—that education and culture are significantly interrelated—a great deal of the actual work done by professional educators is being done with minimal or superficial social/cultural analysis. It is not that educators are not to some degree aware of the significance of social and cultural context or of the importance of social goals and aims to the educational process. The difficulty is that when most professional educators examine the social setting they tend to use the very narrow and limited perspectives of the accessible present and of vocational preparation and economic need. The current situation is but the latest instance of the phenomenon of the trivialization of educational issues. Hence, in the mid-1980s we face the possibility of major political and economic revolutions in the Third World, nuclear war, mass hunger, nuclear proliferation, a stagnant or at best uncertain economy, and a very uncertain job market. We are also in the midst of a great many exciting and fundamental intellectual debates on so-called new paradigms and breakthroughs in various academic and professional areas. Yet, in the context of both enormous problems and incredible intellectual ferment, what constitutes the focus of mainstream educational concern? Apparently, such issues as closer evaluation of teachers and students (e.g., merit pay, competence tests, periodic testing) prayer in the classroom, "middle schools," "creationism" *vs.* evolution, and public aid to private schools. This extraordinary chasm between profound challenge and trivial response helps to frame two major questions for this chapter: How can we explain the continuing phenomena of the trivialization of educational discourse? What would constitute an appropriate and meaningful point of departure for a more serious educational conversation?

THE TRIVIALIZATION OF EDUCATION IN AMERICA

When I speak of trivialization I refer to two major phenomena of educational discourse—the evasion or neglect of larger, more critical topics and the stress put on technical rather than on social, political, and moral issues. Ironically enough, the discourse on the trivial nature of education can be quite intelligent, elaborate, and sophisticated, and indeed we have seen enormous human energies focused on such relatively minor issues as merit pay and the efficacy of homework. This is by no means to say that laborious and painstaking study on organizational and pedagogical issues is not required but rather that such intense effort would be better channeled toward the *most* important social and cultural concerns of our time. To put it bluntly, it is the fundamental assumption of this book that given the elements of our political, economic, and cultural crises, educational discourse must focus on the urgent task of transforming many of our basic cultural institutions and belief systems. Responses that are at best ameliorative have the danger of deepening the crisis by further strengthening social and cultural policies and practices that endanger our deepest commitments. If we accept the basic proposition that we must make some drastic changes in our culture to forestall disaster and facilitate growth, then clearly educational institutions must be a part of that process. However energetic and imaginative, efforts that ignore or deny this necessity are eligible for "trivial" status.

The recent flurry of educational reports do not, for example, reflect or propose anything approaching a fundamental reconceptualization of the schooling process, much less anything in the way of a serious social/cultural critique. Instead they suggest relatively minor reforms directed at amelioration rather than transformation. It is indeed ironic that these reports are highly critical of the intellectual excellence of schools and yet themselves offer relatively superficial responses to the roots of the problem they identify. Even more significantly, none of the reports speak to the necessity for fundamental cultural and social changes even though it is well understood and accepted that schools reflect more than they shape policies and beliefs. The public is once again given the distinct message that schools and education can make serious changes without parallel changes in the basic conception of schooling and in cultural beliefs. Hence, attention is directed to the more modest issues of class electives, schedules of testing, length of school year, and mode of funding rather than to issues of moral numbness, spiritual alienation, social injustice, nuclear armaments, and terrorism.

I do not subscribe to the nostalgic school of educational history that speaks of a fictional time when the culture recognized education as a vital and critical activity, when teachers were highly respected, and when educators were people of vision and daring, endowed with learning, sophistication, and wisdom. On the contrary, serious scholarly and systematic analysis of public education in America is still relatively rare and recent, and very little of that has become part of public awareness. Although there is a significant serious literature on education, the number of contemporary genuine educational gurus, leaders with profound insight and educational vision, is quite small. Indeed, an important assumption of this book is that American dialogue on education, with a number of very important exceptions, has been narrow in scope, technical in nature, and naive in quality.

Surely much of this is due to the intellectual and moral dilemmas implicit in the complex questions about the nature and purpose of education. The term "education" has been defined and examined in a myriad of ways and from innumerable perspectives, resulting in genuine perplexity and unsettling uncertainties—it is a field fraught with conundrums, puzzles, mysteries. It is an area that has been addressed by virtually every major social, political, and philosophical theorist over the centuries from Plato to Rousseau to Machiavelli, from Marx to Dewey. However, the public dialogue on education in America rarely touches upon major theoretical alternatives but rather focuses on the much narrower possibilities within the perspective of existing practices. Even within this fairly narrow range there is a great deal of confusion, complexity, and controversy on the nature of the conventional educational model. Even under the superficial educational discourse we are unclear and unsure about our priorities. For example, should we emphasize vocational in contrast to general education? Should there be sex education or citizenship education in the curriculum? In addition, the public has an enormous number of unrealistic, if not contradictory, expectations for the schools. We want our schools to discipline our children and support and encourage their independence; we want our children to learn to love their country, to honor and respect authority and tradition, and we want them to develop initiative and critical thinking; we want the schools to help students at least deal with, if not overcome, their difficulties with nutrition, health, sexuality, death, morality, interpersonal relations, the maturation process, and sibling rivalry; we want the schools to provide community for the student and to be a focus of community life for adults; we want the schools to teach students how to participate in sports, to be musical, to sew, cook, clean, do woodworking, printing, to paint, sculpt, and dance; we want some decent place to send our children so that adults can work (or play) without worrying about them; we want the schools to provide psychological, vocational, and social counseling to our children; we want students to be evaluated intellectually, socially, psychologically; and we want to know how they rank with other students and what their prospects are. We want the schools to provide opportunities for exercise, celebration, play, hobbies, eating, ritual, friendship, and competition. And so on.

Obviously, we cannot have, and do not want, all of these things—

nor do we want or can we have them in equal degrees of intensity and importance. This plethora of expectations certainly speaks to our confusion and uncertainty, but there is a deeper dimension to the confusion that has to do with the wider moral, political, and social aspects of these "educational" issues. Although there is some attempt to have public dialogue on what major social concerns underlie these concerns for students as individuals, much of it has been connected to current economic and foreign policy (e.g., competing with Russians and Japanese) or to moralistic concerns (e.g., book censorship and sex education). Parents are faced with the highly complex and frustrating challenge of trying to figure out simultaneously what is "best" for their individual children at this particular moment *and* how to participate in a discussion on what constitutes sound educational policy for the society. As a profession, we have not provided these people with very much in the way of conceptual and analytical tools to engage in this challenging and paradoxical dialogue.

It is clear that important public dialogue on the relationship between education and meaning over the years has *not* generally been conducted widely and intensely. We educators have for the most part been able (willing) to separate our concern for education from our discussion of our most serious and profound matters. What is the meaning of life? How do we relate as a family, nation, people? What is a just and fair way of distributing rights and responsibilities? How do we make appropriate moral choices? The irony here is that such questions are quintessentially reflective ones—areas that require knowledge, insight, understanding (i.e., an educated mind). However, we tend in our fragmented and highly differentiated society to equate education with particular institutions and processes which are, if at all, only vaguely linked to deeper social, cultural, economic, and political matters.

A central question that must be addressed is why this dialogue has not expanded into broad public discussion—that is, why have intellectuals, politicians, and other members of cultural leadership maintained such a conventional attitude toward education? A clue to this phenomenon can perhaps be found in the complexities of the culture's ambivalence toward education. For example, given what we have just said about the enormous demands and expectations that we have for education, it is rather extraordinary that we provide so little in the way of resources to support this enterprise. Working conditions for public and private educators at the elementary and secondary levels are absolutely shocking. Compared to other educational institutions (colleges and universities) and to corporations, salaries of teachers and administrators are very low, opportunities to grow intellectually and professionally are extremely limited, and resources are slim and of low quality. Americans are supposed to put enormous faith and trust in education (which they do by and large), which should mean that they need to put enormous resources into the process (which, by and large, they do not). Many would say that this is a financial problem, that the cost of providing a first-rate education for everyone is staggering, too much even for our economy. I find this difficult to accept in a nation which is able to spend billions upon billions on a military budget which is not only marginally productive but downright dangerous. The question then is not so much how we can get more funds for education but why it is we have such a low standard for what appears to be a commitment to provide high-quality education. Perhaps that can be explained as a failure to realize what would constitute the conditions for a truly excellent educational environment for all.

Somewhere along the line we as a culture accepted general standards of the school budget—for example, classes should be around thirty, with twenty or twenty-five considered extraordinary; teachers should teach between twenty-five and thirty hours per week (as opposed to nine to twelve hours for university professors); students should go to school for five or six hours per day (unlike college students who divide their twelve to fifteen hours per week in more flexible and individual ways). It is not clear how these standards came to be accepted, but the question is why the public has not seriously challenged these appallingly low standards. As usual, the answer to question like this is probably a combination of inertia, lack of awareness, conscious acceptance, as well as deception, delusion, and avoidance. Yet, one uncomfortable possibility comes to mind, namely that we are perhaps suspicious of the intellectual process itself, and the acceptance of low standards represents our impulse to restrain the educational process.

It is certainly not a new idea that America has a significant tradition of what has been called "anti-intellectualism." America's support for schools is not the same as support for education, or at least for education defined as the development of the mind. As a culture we retain, along with our reverence for learning, a scorn, if not a suspicion, of it. The terms "intellectual" or "idealist" are more often used in our culture as epithets than as compliments. We seem to be more proud of our technical virtuosity, our engineering genius, and our pragmatic, problem-solving stance than we are of our theoretical and speculative consciousness. We value the new, the useful, and the applied as reflected in Henry Ford's classic putdown of reflection, "History is bunk." This is surely not to say that the technical, the applied, and the pragmatic are not themselves worthy of instruction, nor that they do not have significant educative potential. It is to say that our strong emphasis on the pragmatic and applied at the cost of significant concern for the abstract, theoretical, and speculative does speak to a less than total commitment to a serious, thoroughgoing, and richly textured education for all people.

Part of this reservation toward serious education can be said to be rooted in our traditional aversion to elitism and aristocracy. Our history includes a consciousness which associates people of "higher" learning with those who assume a sense of moral and human superiority; we are apt to reject the notion that such people deserve a higher station in life by dint of their intellectual excellence. Such an aversion is surely compatible with our traditions of democracy, equality, and skepticism. However, the fact remains that what is abhorrent here is that only a few have such an education and that people with such an education feel entitled to more privileges than those without this education. Surely, the proper response to the fear of elitism is to demand higher quality education for all and to be skeptical if not resistant to any special claim for preferential treatment. If certain education does give people certain powers (and it surely does), then it can be seen not only as having pragmatic meaning but moral and political significance as well. Therefore, in addition to the scorn for education by some, which probably is founded in a consciousness of ignorance, naïveté, and isolation, there is the lesser known fear of education by the dominant culture, more likely founded in a rather sophisticated and thoughtful realization of the power of education. Presumably those who are *not* "well educated" fear and scorn the "well educated" because of their alienation. In like manner, many of those who are "well educated" are aware that their dominance is in part related to the powerlessness that is derived from a lack of education. Differences in educational potency become models of providing for political and moral differentiation.

Another aspect of the value and power of education lies in the possibility that this power could be used for both good and bad, or more specifically the power could be used to challenge existing institutions and power arrangements. Education, if one is to believe educators, has enormous power which not only has the effect of esthetic exhilaration but of inducing fear. The most powerful metaphor of this paradox is seen in the remarkable trial of Socrates in the fifth century B.C.E. which literally reflects the life and death significance of education. Although Socrates tries rather disingenuously to soft-pedal the importance of simply asking people to clarify what they are saying, his prosecutors are very much aware of the potential of such a process to undermine a contemporary and entrenched cultural consciousness. It is important to note that literally hundreds of Athenian citizens voted to execute Socrates, that this was a *community* decision and not one imposed by a tyrannical and feared ruler. Undoubtedly, there were a variety of reasons for this action, but the very fact that the charges were presented to the community as a serious threat to the public welfare represents the recognition of the basic vulnerability of the status quo to serious reflection and examination.

This recognition persists today, albeit in somewhat more subtle form. Our society certainly does not legally execute people who ask us to reconsider our basic assumptions and to critically examine our culture. Although we are fearful of such people, and sometimes people like Abraham Lincoln, Malcolm X, and Martin Luther King are assassinated for insisting that we reexamine our way of being, more often that fear is masked by scorn, avoidance, and self-deception. It is indeed difficult to maintain the paradox of both valuing and fearing education, particularly when the only way to resolve the paradox is to address the underlying moral issues. Serious education, therefore, has a way of forcing continual confrontation with our basic moral commitments and, more unnerving, with our failures to meet those commitments. Such an education is not reflected in a curriculum focused on diplomas, certificates, and credentials.

This returns us to the phenomenon of the fragmentation and isolation of education in our culture; we continue to sidestep moral paradoxes when we talk about education apart from the moral considerations of the kind of culture we wish to create. This is a way of avoiding conflict but at the price of irrationality, mediocrity, and madness. When we talk of education we are simultaneously talking about culture; when we propose changes in education, or when we propose not making changes, we are making moral statements. The people of Athens knew this as did the communities which made the teaching of reading to American slaves a felony. This obvious, usually unspoken, moral relationship is at the heart of such issues as school segregation, tracking, grading, and selective admission. The silliness (or hypocrisy) of calling these issues "educational" rather than cultural or moral reveals our culture's discomfort with making moral choices.

The issue of "grading" is particularly instructive in this matter. I believe that most teachers regard grading (as opposed to evaluation) as an obstacle to the learning process. It is very difficult, and probably impossible, to develop procedures for giving grades that are valid, reliable, fair, and efficient; students come to worry more about grades than meaning; and both teachers and students respond to these problems by developing techniques (e.g., multiple choice tests, cramming, memorizing) which are at best distracting, and at worst counterproductive to serious learning. The concern for grading produces anxiety, cheating, grade grubbing, and unhealthy competition. However, even though grading may be at best of dubious value "educationally," it is absolutely vital to a culture that puts enormous stress on success, achievement, and individuality and to a system that requires social and economic inequality. The critical issues of grading are not primarily technical (though there are certainly such problems within the particular field of evaluation and grading) but moral and cultural. To value grading is to value competition and to accept a society of inequality and a psychology that posits external behavior rather than internal experience as more important. Grading is primarily a technique for promoting particular social, moral, and political goals, and it is those goals which should be debated rather than the technical and misleading questions about the value of essay *vs.* objective testing or whether to use grade point averages or standardized tests as the basis for college admission.

To raise the question of our culture's commitment to equality by critically examining so-called educational issues like grading is, of course, parallel to what led to the tragedy of Socrates' trial. There is a kind of conspiracy of silence, a tacit recognition, or what has been called "structured silences" about the intense relationships between moral/social concerns and formal education. The political question has always to do with who benefits from such an arrangement. It is clear that those who benefit at least in the short term are mostly those in power and those who represent dominant institutions and ideas. (Included in this group are, alas, educators who have little real power in the larger culture but are fearful of losing their modest power within the educational establishment. It also includes educators who have bought into the existing arrangements by still insisting that they are "educators" rather than politicians.) It is my contention that one way to avoid conflict and change in the basic cultural structure is to deflect such dialogue into discussion of technical problems. Professional educators have developed a concept called "educational policy" or "educational issues" which enables (or disables) us to trivialize and depoliticize cultural and moral issues into technical or partisan debates.

For example, educators spend enormous amounts of energy researching issues around the topic of equal educational opportunity. There is considerable research being done on the financial, sociological, and psychological aspects of the nature of the inequality and how to overcome unfair differences in educational opportunity for various groups and individuals. Programs like Head Start, magnet schools, and equalized financing of education are designed to respond to these problems, and with such programs come controversy and disagreements. Fundamental to these controversies is a deeper issue involving the basic question of who should and can be truly educated, who deserves the full development of their reflective and creative potential. To do technical studies on research on how to ameliorate the problems within existing arrangements serves to obscure and deflect the more basic moral and spiritual issues. Complex as they are, the technical problems are of relatively minor importance compared to the questions of our social and cultural vision. It is very likely that underlying the technical controversies are much more profoundly serious differences on the basic question of who is educable and who ought to be educated. Such differences cannot be overcome by technical studies or partisan debates for, they run to far deeper roots in our psyche.

It is my belief that perhaps the most significant dimension in the conservative/progressive continuum revolves around the matter of faith in the educability of humanity. At one end of the continuum is the faith that only a very small number of people can be expected either to be well educated or to deal with this education in a responsible manner. This is the position that holds that many if not most people are so selfish and vulgar that they would use the wisdom of the ages only for personal and short-run advantage and thereby undermine the fragile social structure. Hence, the position arises that we are better off with most people being acculturated and socialized, with only a carefully selected and prepared minority being able to deal responsibly with the ambiguities and sophistication of serious learning.

At the other end of the continuum is the idea that all people are capable and desirous of living a life of meaning and that all can be educated to be free and responsible. This is the position that refuses to accept inherent inequality of people; those individuals who show contrary evidence are said to be victims of an oppressive system and of false consciousness. It therefore becomes the task of educators to provide the conditions under which all people can express their full human potential. This basic difference in assumptions about the human condition represents a historic and continuous struggle between fundamentally different consciousness and orientations toward human nature and destiny.

What this means is obviously that when we talk about education the stakes are very high—we are talking ultimately about the basic and most important questions of human existence. To trivialize education by obsessing on technical or superficial, symptomatic concerns is not only illogical but harmful: it distracts us from the responsibility to engage in serious dialogue on how the educational process can facilitate a world of love, justice, and joy.

A particularly tough, anguishing, hair-pulling, brain-bending debate on education revolves around the question of freedom—that is, how much faith do we have in free expression and free inquiry as opposed to the kind of faith that leads to a view of education as acculturation? Many see the prime function of education as the transmission of the culture and the preservation of its values. One difficulty with this view is that our culture contains many institutions and value systems, some of which are in conflict. Our culture, for example, has a tradition which speaks to major, even violent, change (e.g., the American Revolution and the Civil War), in spite of the understanding that when we stress the importance of transmitting the culture what we really mean is stability and continuity. The schools are yet another locus for the drama of acting on impulses toward both liberty and order. Generally speaking, organized education (schools, colleges) is oriented toward acculturation and order even though there are individual pockets where there is greater stress on full inquiry and liberty. I do not wish to simplify or polarize this issue—it is by definition impossible to talk of education without cultural considerations or without the necessity of preserving certain cultural values. It is, however, possible to speak of an education virtually and wholly in terms of acculturation and socialization. It is not a matter of choosing between acculturation and education but of choosing a path where we can educate about what our culture is while helping to redefine it. Education involves some combination of affiliation and skepticism, a concern both for boundaries and for the crossing of boundaries. Formal education is thus both parent and child of culture—they shape and reflect each other, even as both may share the same contradictions and anomalies. This is not to say they are the same. Many cultural values and institutions are not reflected in educational institutions. For example, there are greater opportunities for free speech and expression in certain cultural spaces than in the schools.

Most significant for our purposes is the importance of locating the unique and special responsibility and character of an educational institution. This book will directly speak to these issues, and with an orientation that many will find wanting or unacceptable. Such disagreement is not only inevitable but necessary and desirable. However, I believe that every educator must as a minimum necessity for professional and cultural integrity make clear the moral, political, social, and cultural perspective of his or her educational ideas on policy practice. The public and the profession ought to (and I believe does) require educators to be thoughtful and reflective enough to realize the relationship between educational practice, policy, theory, and social, moral, political, and cultural issues. Furthermore, as public servants/leaders, educators owe it to the public to reveal their theoretical and ideological perspectives as a kind of truth-in-advertising principle. It is time for educators to end their naivete and coyness about their social and moral principles, not only as part of their professional ethic but as a way of deepening and enriching the quality of public dialogue on education.

These strike me as minimal expectations of educators, namely that they be able and willing to articulate the social, political, and moral principles, ideas, and ideals as well as the theoretical and experiential knowledge that inform their ideas on educational practices and policies. However, these are only minimal requirements, for what our society needs from its educators is not only the ability to understand but the ability to lead—we need, in addition to knowing about and reflecting on their orientations, to be able to choose from them. This requires not only knowledge and understanding by both the public and the educational profession; it also demands courage and wisdom. All concerned must be able to choose and act on *wise, sane,* and *sensible* orientations to education, an action which as we have already indicated is tantamount to making important moral decisions on the quality and nature of the culture. Educators must confront their awesome responsibilities and must give up their retreat into the myth of political neutrality based on a pseudoscientific conception of their work. Education surely requires knowledge of the learning and maturation process, knowledge of content, language skills, rhetoric, technique, and interpersonal relationships. However, these are necessary but not sufficient requirements for a true educator. What is required in addition to this knowledge and these skills is a commitment to a vision of who we are and what we should be. An educator without such a commitment is like the person who is all dressed up with no place to go. An educator, like other professionals, needs tools and skills but must have the wisdom to use these in such a way that courage and passion are inevitable and graceful.

Although these are general expectations of educators, I must speak to the particulars of the specific realities of this moment. This is yet another critical moment in history—a time of enormous crisis, a time of great hush and anticipation. Shall it be war, destruction, desolation, and disaster, or shall we have peace, abundance, and freedom? We are faced with immense problems and opportunities—we are in another of Dickens's "best of times, worst of times" eras. At a time of great peril, in a moment when we realize humanity's gigantic capacity for horror, greed, callousness, cruelty, and stupidity, we also are experiencing the human capacity for brilliant creativity, we are in touch with the extraordinary possibilities of human nature and the opportunity to create true human community. Technology has not only provided us with hydrogen bombs and nuclear waste but also with the possibility of the global village.

Surely, there is intense and fundamental disagreement about the nature of our problems and how to solve them. There does seem to be a consensus, however, that as a culture, indeed as a species, we face very serious problems and that fundamental changes (either to radically new or radically old forms) will be required to overcome or at least substantially ease these problems. It is certainly not a time for "business as usual" nor a time for avoidance and self-deception. It is a time to make commitments and to root these commitments in faith, trust, hope, and energy. It is a time for all of us to engage in this titanic struggle, and as educators we must accept our part of this struggle and seek to establish our commitment and reiterate our faith in what part the educational process can play in transcending the current crisis.

2

Recent Educational Reform: Delusions and Trivialization

[E]ducators, as well as other middle-class moralists, underestimate the conflict of interest in political and economic relations, and attribute to disinterested ignorance what ought to be attributed to interested intelligence.... There is no educational process which can place any class in possession of all the facts or cause it to appreciate all the feelings which activate another class.

Reinhold Niebuhr, Moral Man and Immoral Society

Despite all the hoopla and passion of the educational reform movement, I believe that the differences in classroom curriculum and pedagogy between the public educational system of the 1980s and that of the recent past reflect modest differences in emphasis and cannot be said to be fundamental. We grant that these differences are significant and have considerable impact on students, teachers, and the culture; yet it is also vitally important to note the persistence and continuity in the structure and content of American public education. Contrary to some folklore, for example, the 1960s were not a time of widespread radical changes in public education; permissiveness, anarchy, and experimentation were not rampant or even widespread. There were a number of modest, liberal (not radical), highly controlled attempts at ameliorating arbitrary, rigid, and unexamined practices, but the changes adopted were well within existing frameworks of traditional goals and objectives of the in-place system. Such "reforms" as "minicourses" did not challenge the notion of requirements or the importance of disciplines but only represented minor organizational and conceptual approaches to how these requirements were to be met. The premises of the "open classroom" included acceptance of traditional classroom goals (the three Rs, science, social studies) and differed from conventional schooling basically on issues of pedagogy and organization. Indeed much of the reform efforts of the 1960s represented serious efforts at increasing the academic and intellectual potency of the traditional school curriculum (most particularly in the science and math area).

What became ultimately threatening to the culture about the 1960s movement (including its manifestations in education) were the few programs that did have deeper social and political significance. These were programs that connected to and highlighted issues of existing social and economic inequalities, particularly as they affected the poor and the nonwhite (e.g., open admissions and preschool programs). Another threat emerged from programs that seemed to threaten the conventional power structure of the schools (e.g., community involvement, school integration, student rights, and alternative schools). Although all of these movements started with a fairly modest goal—improving the quality of the local schools—the dominant culture soon realized that the implications of some of the proposed changes were particularly serious and far-reaching.

It is true that the 1960s saw the emergence of a significant challenge to how schools were to be governed and controlled and whose interests were to be served. What was not seriously challenged in the numerous reform efforts and community struggles, however, were the basic goals, purposes, and curriculum of the existing educational system. People argued rather about who was to get a particular program and demanded that the existing program be put in the hands of more proficient and qualified practitioners, and argued that this was more likely to happen for more people if the political apparatus were changed to allow for community accountability. The major issues, therefore, were much more narrowly political than broadly educational, more concerned with the who and the how than with the what of educational policy and practice.

The results of these movements are well known. Even though there are important residues of these efforts, the combination of the political backlash and a serious economic recession has worked to wipe out many if not most of the very modest and mild changes of the 1960s. We now live in a time of great economic uncertainty after experiencing mass layoffs, high and continuing unemployment, serious international competition, the weakening of unionism, and the serious erosion of governmental concern for human welfare. Our consciousness has reverted and regressed to one involving scarcity, survival, competition, and stagnation. The language of growth, potential, daring, and challenge has become muted: a sense of infinite possibility has been replaced by timidity, expansiveness by caution, long-range thinking by the bottom line, visions by quotas.

In the wake of all this has come the renewal of harsh economic and social competition in which the metaphor and mythology of organized sports and war have been used to glorify, extol, and legitimate an ideology of "opportunity," which comes down to mean a winner-loser culture. In such a culture we congratulate ourselves for helping people to compete fairly (if not equally), for creating the conditions for the competition to be held and for offering enormous rewards to the "winners." Unfortunately, it also means that we continue to both produce and ignore the "losers." Freedom has come to mean license for the powerful rather than liberation for the weak; equality is seen as the privilege of competing rather than the right to dignity; individualism has come to mean greed rather than moral autonomy; and community has come to be oriented around terms of class rather than terms of humanity. At its worst, it is a time of revenge and reaction, and, even at its best, a time of rejection of tacit understandings involving compassion and support of the poor and weak. The dominant ideology of the moment, however, contains its own contradictions: freedom in the marketplace but not in the bedroom; relaxation of consumer protection, reduction in public legal services, curtailment of environmental controls, and the regulation of public utilities, but a steady increase in intellectual and moral intimidation through heavy doses of piety and sanctimony. There is more censorship of ideas and less of an attempt to check greed; our current administration values freedom of the marketplace more than freedom of ideas.

It must be remembered, however, that there are significant countervailing forces, some of which can be seen, as I mentioned before, as the residue of the 1960s. There is enormous energy that is at least latent, as reflected, for example, in popular music and dancing, and there is the continuing impulse for real freedom, as well as resentment about the arbitrariness, impersonality, and coldness of our modernized, computerized, high-tech culture. What has so far kept these impulses under control is the fear and uncertainty about jobs and security, fears which have been manipulated and fanned by the hardline attitudes of government and industry toward unions, social security, unemployment insurance, and other social programs supported by taxation.

In the context of a failing economy, energy has been diverted away from equality and justice to personal survival. As indicated in Robert Bellah's *Habits of the Heart* (1985), culturally we have been increasingly attracted to a consciousness of individual well-being, which also became heightened during the 1960s and, ironically enough, has been given new legitimation and energy under the banner of free enterprise and so-called supply-side economics. What had, and has, been referred to as narcissism and self-indulgence in matters of taste and morals is transformed in the economic sphere into the exercise of individual initiative, freedom, and creativity. This reinforcement of the individual acting alone (which has among its origins existential and phenomenological thinking) as the primary unit has in the 1980s intensified competition and anxiety about survival and advancement. The operative metaphor has changed from making the pie bigger or being happy with equal shares of the pie to how to have the biggest piece of a shrinking pie.

This is expressed in educational communities primarily by an even greater emphasis on the pragmatic and functional nature of schools—extraordinary emphasis on job training, meeting the needs of industry, and the school's relationship to American foreign policy. This emphasis is hardly new—we will remember that among the early major pieces of federal aid to education in the 1980s was the National *Defense* Education Act. What is different is the matter of emphasis and the nature of the trade-offs this new emphasis has meant. What has been given less emphasis, for example, is education for personal development. There is less concern for the arts, less demand for critical and creative thinking, less rhetoric about human growth and developing potential. Another casualty is the school's strong association with the preservation and importance of democracy—less concern about citizenship education, student responsibilities, and student governance. Instead, there is an almost obsessive concern for productive competition and selectivity.

The code word for this renewed energy for using the school to sort and weed is "excellence," and the basic technique for implementing the policy is testing. Excellence and testing have become two sides of a coin minted to exchange a once popular coin of equality and justice for the classic gold standard of hierarchy and privilege. "Excellence" has through a relentless process of reification and reductionism come to mean high scores on normative standardized tests. Many politicians have been shrewd enough to pick up on this phenomenon and have pushed this technique by employing the rhetoric of excellence and the magic of testing as a way of making and fulfilling promises. Politicians can and do demand that the "quality" of education be raised—this is something everyone applauds, particularly when there is the promise that this can be done without increased taxation or costs. *And*, both educators and politicians can demonstrate and prove that the quality has in fact been improved.

The process, absurd as it is, is simple enough. Give students and teachers a test, teach them how to pass the test, and Eureka! the test scores go up—which the public is told means that excellence has been achieved. What is particularly painful about this cynical travesty is the degree to which professionals in education, sociology, and psychology participate in such nonsense even when they know or should know better. These professionals participate, indeed contribute to and shape a public dialogue in which education is reduced to a concern for passing tests of dubious validity, thereby bypassing the serious and perplexing questions of what should be taught, for what reason, and for which model of humanity and community. By avoiding these serious questions professionals not only trivialize their work; more importantly, they neglect their responsibility to focus public dialogue on central issues.

This means that the dominant culture and the dominant professional community have committed themselves to facilitating the conception of the school as a place where students compete and where they may expect to learn the necessary requirements for economic and social advancement. This concern for acculturation does not necessarily exclude but certainly distracts us from serious reexamination of our basic premises. It does not reflect a commitment to moral or esthetic excellence or a commitment to nourish the imagination or the idealism of our students. It represents a powerful affirmation of the cultural status quo, and because of this the schools are criticized for their inability to sufficiently meet the demands and values of the dominant culture—namely, individual achievement, success, political and economic continuity, and national strength. The changes that are being urged are designed for more efficiency, sharper focus, and more directed energy at meeting predetermined (and largely unexamined) specific, concrete learning goals. This focus is perhaps best expressed professionally in the strength of the "effective schools" concept and the strong interest in the instructional approach called "time on task." Politically, this emphasis is expressed in the widespread use of competence tests, which basically are techniques designed for continual monitoring and control of teachers and students.

These ideas are, in part, borrowed from industrial language and techniques—"quality control," "accountability," and "the bottom line." They also employ many concepts from logical positivism, such as the idea that the educational process is to be divided and broken down into constituent, observable, measurable parts which are used as criteria for selecting techniques and methods, as well as a basis for evaluation (control).

Schools are criticized for wasting time by not focusing energy on instruction; they are criticized for not having finely discriminating measures of teacher and student productivity; and they are criticized for not setting high enough standards. The proposed remedies include merit pay for teachers based on the notion that not only should the more productive teachers be rewarded, but that merit pay will provide incentive for teachers to increase their productivity. Other remedies call for closer, more frequent testing based on more sharply and concretely defined outcomes and clearly delimited expectations. Again, there is inherent in these proposals a tacit acceptance of the conventional curriculum, although there are some who speak more openly about a need to "return" to the traditions of academic excellence. However, these ideas, although they at least extend beyond technique, usually come down to the rejuvenation of very superficial, conventional courses in American history, science, English, foreign language, and mathematics, which stress knowledge, retention, homework, and mastery of material rather than a serious effort at developing intellectual curiosity and gaining insight into significant ideas.

Here again we meet the paradox of the trivialization of American education, for the analysis I have just presented reflects both a superficial, if not vulgar, response to the issues, as well as a response that emerges from intense interest in the issues. How can such a sophisticated culture have schools of such low quality (in the culture's own terms) in the first place, and second, how is it that even after increased study and awareness the culture persists in conceptualizing the crisis in such trivial and mechanical terms? There seem to be two interpretations. The optimistic one is that such superficial development represents insufficient attention, awareness, and application of reason, intelligence, and creativity. This is the thesis that underlies Silberman's *Crisis in the Classroom* (1970), where he characterizes American education as "mindless." I say this is optimistic because such a reality is amenable to change: the schools could be improved if they were more "minded," if educators put more thought, reflection, and care into them. There is, however, an alternative interpretation— that the so-called problems of the schools are not accidental and inadvertent. Indeed, there is a way in which the schools can be said to be a huge success in that they accomplish very well what the culture "really" expects them to do, namely to acculturate, socialize, sort, and indoctrinate.

This is not to say that there have not been serious critiques of American education. The most significant of these criticisms of education, alas, have not had an impact on the culture, although they are of stunning power and insight. Over the past two decades a whole generation of scholars has emerged that, although writing in several fields (sociology, history, and curriculum), has constituted a major revisionist perspective of education. These writers include, among many others, Michael Apple, Jonathan Kozol, Henry Giroux, Maxine Greene, Michael Katz, James Macdonald, William Pinar, and Paulo Freire, who write from different perspectives and have significantly different points of view. However, they represent a broad consensus that can be characterized as follows: (1) the schools represent a powerful force of social, intellectual, and personal oppression; (2) the reasons for such oppression are rooted in the culture's history; (3) they represent a number of deeply held cultural values—hierarchy, conformity, success, materialism, control; and (4) what is required for significant changes in the schools amounts to a fundamental transformation of the culture's consciousness.

Some of this criticism has adopted the use of the term "the hidden or tacit curriculum" which refers to the values, attitudes, and assumptions toward learning and human relationships reflected in the school's policies and practices. A major theme of this criticism deals with the school's role in "reproducing the culture," in sorting out the candidates for class and caste system through its various testing and classification systems. The school's hidden curriculum also includes ways in which students learn to be obedient and passive, to work at meaningless tasks without complaining, to defer their pleasure, to value achievement and competition, and to please and respect authority figures. It is in the hidden curriculum that these social critics find cultural manifestations of sexism, racism, and elitism. The new criticism is not directed at technique, organization, and curriculum in instrumental but rather in symbolic terms. For example, the low salaries and dreadful working conditions for teachers are not seen as a kind of neglected agenda item, a problem requiring patience and understanding, but rather as aspects of a demoralized and weak teaching force that is a required part of the basic structure of our culture. It is, in this analysis, in the culture's interest to have schools that do *not*, structurally and purposely, promote excitement, a critical capacity, or creative potential.

Paulo Freire (1970, 1973) is perhaps the most eloquent and best known of these writers. Writing from the perspective of a Latin American culture beset by enormous inequalities and colonial oppression, Freire has vividly demonstrated the intimate relationship between human freedom and an informed and critical literacy. Indeed, he says that attempts to prevent people from acquiring these critical skills is tantamount to a "violation" of the human spirit and, hence, are acts of "violence" (1970:74). The "mindlessness" school of criticism would say that the fact that a very large number of Americans do not have significant verbal critical skills (Kozol 1985:4) is a function of neglect, or insufficient funding, or inadequate techniques. Revisionist critics see the poor quality of American education as functional and consistent with what is, at best, an American ambivalence toward education, and, at worst, a conscious effort to maintain the existing class structure. The major issue for Freire is explicitly that of human liberation, and he deals with issues of technique in the perspective of the struggle for human liberation. In mainstream educational criticism the concern is on technique itself with little or superficial reflection on what the technique is to serve. The point of revisionist criticism is to sort out "the hidden curriculum," the implicit, tacit, indirect functions and goals that these techniques basically serve.

Whether we agree or not with the revisionists, we owe them immense gratitude not only for the brilliance of their individual analysis but more broadly for providing the language and possibility of discussing education in nontrivial terms. These writers have made explicit the immense importance of the issues involved in education and offer the culture an opportunity to reconstitute the nature of its dialogue in this area. It is also important to point out, however, that they are members of the same culture as everyone else and, therefore, subject to the same opportunities and limitations. What I mean to say is that these sharp criticisms can also be seen as reflections of the culture: they represent the articulated concerns of a much wider and more representative group of people than a handful of educational theorists. These writers not only provide hope but also reflect deep concern and hope in the wider culture.

Let us shift for a moment to a broader cultural focus, in order to establish a contrast between public consciousness of broad social concerns and its response to the particular case of education. I wish to return to issues raised in the beginning of this chapter where I made reference to the incredible problems and opportunities that confront us in the last moment of the twentieth century. It is above all else a time of heightened consciousness, a time when more people are more aware than perhaps at any other time in history. Our young people in particular are more psychologically hip, they have traveled more, have experienced more; they are more sophisticated about technology, drugs, the mind, the spirit, and are much more aware of the possibility for catastrophe. The culture includes not only a horror list of problems but a matching list of programs, activities, and opportunities to raise consciousness about these horrors. We surely know a great deal more about pollution than we once did—and certainly we are more aware of the relationship between the environment, nutrition, and health; in particular we have become more sensitive to the real possibilities of disaster having experienced some "real" ones— such as Vietnam, the Thalidomide tragedy, and Bhopal disaster, as well as those like Chernobyl and acid rain that terrify in an unclear way. It is very difficult to be a genuine paranoid in these times. We have become more suspicious, much more cautious, more likely to be skeptical about what our political leaders tell us after all the lies and deceit of Vietnam, Watergate, and Irangate. We have come into a consciousness of crisis and uncertainty, and in that consciousness we are edging closer to a stronger sense of the interrelationships among the elements of the crisis. We are taking on an ecological way of thinking and beginning to see not only how big business, big labor, and big government interrelate but also how university research is related to the military, how child abuse is related to poverty, and how the status of women relates to our economic structure and our epistemological beliefs. Surely, this consciousness is felt more strongly by some than others, and clearly it would be fatuous to suggest that anyone has arrived at a full degree of awareness of our situation. However, it is clear that there is stir or unease in the culture, a sense of unsettlement and dissatisfaction in the awareness of serious worries about the future.

This kind of cultural unrest is also directed at education, and I believe that there is a latent sense of parallel fundamental concern about our basic educational structure. The tragedy is that most of our educational leaders and virtually all of our political leaders have chosen to conceptualize those concerns into the trivial terms that we have discussed. The revisionists have, I believe, succeeded in accurately reflecting these latent concerns, and their work stands in very sharp contrast to mainstream conventional discussion on education. The public is trying to grasp what is fundamental to life, liberty, and the pursuit of happiness, and in response educators give them more standardized tests; the culture yearns for meaning and hope, and the schools suggest more homework and a longer school year. The world teeters on the edge of a new holocaust, and our leaders urge us to consider merit pay. Surely, we need and deserve more than nostalgic trips, pseudoscience, and school prayers to meet fundamentally new problems with fundamentally new approaches. This, above all else, is not a time for timidity, self-deception, or magical thinking. If we are to take education seriously, it means we are taking cultural concerns seriously. If we take cultural concerns seriously within the context of education, then what is required is far more structural change than the mainstream leadership is suggesting. To this extent, I believe that our current crop of educational and political leaders is out of touch with the culture's basic needs, fears, and concerns or, even worse, they have chosen to ignore the culture's impulse to transcend their parochial, short-term, narrow vision of personal success and achievement.

Thus, there would seem to be another general interpretation of why the culture has chosen to trivialize our current educational crisis, and that is because the culture is not so much mindless or clever as it is ambivalent. In this interpretation both Silberman and Freire are right in that the culture is only in part aware of what it is doing in the schools and perhaps at a preconscious level is not fully pleased with how these efforts are focused. What we are talking about is confusion, as well as ambivalence: as a culture we have the impulse for both charity and greed; we value justice and hierarchy; we treasure community and individuality. The culture has developed clever and effective ways of deceiving itself into thinking that it can do all of these things, that it can have its cake and eat it too. However, given the heightened awareness within our culture, we have doubts—pangs of guilt, episodes of uncertainty, periods of confusion about who we are, where we came from, and where we are going. This severe confusion is magnified in a time when for many people God is not accessible, and neither are the stable and reassuring guidelines of a cherished church, government, or philosophy. The educational establishment has done us all a disservice by refusing to connect our serious and fundamental cultural malaise to educational issues. Instead it is proposing solutions to other problems, problems that are neither real nor serious but at least serve as problems that fit the available solutions. Our primary task in education is not to throw out premature, distracting, and obfuscating solutions to ill-conceived problems but is instead to clarify the questions that are of most worth. These questions can help educators develop appropriate responses, but they must be questions rooted not in the existing arsenal of the education establishment but in the most vital concerns of the culture's and individual's search for meaning

Our era has been described as "the age of anxiety" and has produced a number of gloomy descriptors and concepts—"alienation," "anomie," "angst"—it is a time when we have been challenged seriously to confront suicide and the death of God. It has been called a time of spiritual and moral crisis—a time when words like "anxiety," "despair," and "absurdity" are part of everyday vocabulary, a time when suicide rates rise and when self-help books and organizations proliferate. A whole generation of psychological phobias and obsessions has been spawned—drug and chemical addiction, anorexia, compulsive gambling, and even serious new diseases (herpes, AIDS). The most popular response to the lack of meaning and the emptiness of life seems to be one of a highly intensified personal hedonism: an orgy of individual gratification in the form of consumerism; heavy reliance on sex, drugs, and music for release and distraction; a never-ending pursuit of still greater heights of pleasure—the best ice cream, the deepest orgasm, the most powerful and fastest automobiles. *The Guinness Book of World Records* has become a metaphor for the mindless pursuit of excess and vulgarity.

When one considers this kind of crisis and how the schools have responded to it, one would have to conclude that the schools are intellectually and morally bankrupt. A "soft" version of this indictment is based on a notion of bankruptcy by definition; if education is bankrupt, then the evidence of the culture's failure, ipso facto, reflects the failure of the educational process. This is still another case of the interpenetration of culture and education, where the loss of cultural meaning *is* the loss of educational meaning, and vice versa. The "harder" indictment of education's bankruptcy has to do less with symptoms and more to do with the likelihood that education has not merely failed to stem the erosion of meaning but has been a significant contributor to it. If education *is* important, if we are to take it seriously, then we must accept logically the proposition that education has serious consequences. Indeed, when we think of education as significant we are bound to consider it as a part of the solution to the cultural crisis. Typically, however, criticisms of the schools have been closer to the soft end of the dimension in that schools are typically criticized for failing to attend to certain major issues (e.g., the moral or esthetic dimension, a global consciousness) or to be unwitting instruments of some social policy (e.g., racism, elitism, sexism).

A major exception to this general rule is the criticism that comes from the political and religious Right. Their criticism does indeed take the educational system seriously, for they point their accusing fingers at the schools as active and conscious agents of what they call secular humanism, an ideology of godlessness and materialism. The Right (as the Left) sees the schools as an important ideological battleground and (as the Left) rejects the notion that the schools can be value-free and ideologically neutral. In fact their criticism is that the school's attempt to be value free or to "clarify" values is itself an ideology, one involving the "idolatry" of science and secularism. This is not to say that the political and religious Right have a single consistent and coherent view in this area since, for example, they have serious differences among themselves about the importance of the traditional academic disciplines, particularly science, in the curriculum. It is not altogether clear whether they mean to change the overt course of study (as they have spoken out only in the area of evolution and "obscene" books), but they do call for prayer in the schools, the active recognition of America as a Christian nation, and the teaching of (rather than teaching about) certain traditional values like respect, humility, obedience, piety, and hard work.

Although the professional educational community has tended to write off this movement as parochial and extremist, the criticisms of the Right merit serious consideration on a number of counts. First of all, their diatribes against so-called secular humanism, however simplistic and crude the analysis may be, do reflect a deeper awareness of the hidden curriculum than is usual in our culture. Like their ideological counterparts on the Left, the Right rejects the conception of the schools as innocent or bland centers of learning striving to be apolitical, neutral, fair, and objective. Both the Left and the Right have helped us to see more clearly the political nature of the nonpolitical stance, the morality of moral relativism, and the ideology of objectivity. More specifically, the Right has stumbled onto a reality that embarrasses those who like to think of the public schools as divorced from religion. They are accurate insofar as they remind us that our culture is in part defined by an active and lively religious tradition, and they are insightful insofar as they (as well as others) point to the strength of a vivid albeit tacit, civil religiosity often expressed in the schools (e.g., the veneration of democracy and patriotism and the celebration of rituals such as Thanksgiving and Memorial Day). Of course they are less sensitive to the traditions and realities of religious diversity and pluralism and less than open to the possibility of education and religion as having critical functions to play. Nonetheless, the harsh and strident criticism, which ironically enough is far less sophisticated and scholarly than the equally harsh and less strident criticism of the Left, gets far more public attention than afforded to the Left and has confronted educational leaders with a serious challenge. This criticism has put the schools in virtually a "put up or shut up" situation. If the Right is wrong, then what *do* the schools stand for? If they are not godless, are they committed to any cosmology? If they reject "secular humanism," when do they do this and on what basis? Can the schools continue their claim to be innocent, nonpolitical, nonmoral? (To do so would be tantamount to admitting to vacuity.) If the schools are not to operate in a political and moral vacuum, then can they describe and affirm their informing and energizing principles? I do not believe that the school establishment is prepared to meet this challenge because it does not have a well-developed language in which to respond. The primary language is the technical and bureaucratic one of control, task, and engineering; the school establishment has only a vague understanding of the language of ideology, religion, and meaning. This is a language deficiency of serious proportions with important consequences to our society, for it is a language that shows increasing signs of revival.

Another important dimension of the "thunder from the Right" is the powerful and popular base which supports these criticisms. It is one thing to ignore a local crank or even a national "extreme" group, but the time has surely gone by when we can afford to dismiss the New Right (religious or otherwise) as ephemeral or faddish. Important as it is to register the emergence of this phenomenon, it is of a greater importance to note its more basic rather than superficial aspect. We need to be in touch with the concerns, needs, and impulses of these as well as other movements and be less obsessed with their solutions or proposals. I believe that there is much more opportunity for consensus on what the important problems and questions are than on the solutions. However, whether or not consensus is possible, we must attend to the legitimacy of those who are passionate and seek to at least understand and empathize with the source and nature of the passion.

I am persuaded by Harvey Cox's argument that this passion can be seen at least in part as a *cri du coeur*, as the anguish and pain about our modern industrial nuclear computerized world. In *Religion and the Secular City*, Cox (1984) points out that the liberation theology movement in Latin America and the Moral Majority movement in the United States have, in addition to their obvious major differences, a number of common characteristics. Both are active political movements which work within religious boundaries, and both work outside the conventional political apparatus. Most important, Cox asserts, is that they both (along with several other movements, notably the women's movement) represent rejection of modernism, that cluster of values centered on materialism, science, individuality, and consumerism which constitutes the basis of Western ideology. Both represent characteristically very different responses, but both represent *serious criticism* of the fundamental structure of contemporary society. Both are grass roots operations having built on popular unrest and dissatisfaction, and both have prospered by articulating that deep sense of cultural disease into a program. Cox goes on to speak more broadly about the renewed interest in religion and the question of the connection between politics and religion. His basic conclusion is that although there was a time in history when religion had to yield to secular forces, this is a time in history when the secular society needs *religious criticism*.

> *"Secularization," one of the most severely chastised children of modernity, is also the unappreciated offspring of the prophets, including the prophet of Nazareth, who railed against religiously sanctioned injustice with as much fervor as any anticleric. At its best, such secularization was once a sturdy strand in the history of human freedom. It was a legitimate response to the illegitimate use of the sacred for demeaning purposes. It spoke with the same voice that cried out through heresies, witches covens, popular agnosticism, and even, at times, atheism. If it eventually went to excess and produced its own pseudosacral devices—the goddess of Reason in Paris or the tomb of Lenin in Red Square—this means only that external vigilance is still the price we pay for the freedom God intends for all people. If freedom once required a secular critique of religion, it can also require a religious critique of the secular." Cox (1984:170–71)*

The notion of religion as social criticism is fully developed by a number of contemporary scholars (e.g., Ackermann 1985; Soelle 1974; Croatto 1981; Segundo 1976) and is a concept that intersects with education seen also as a critical function. Indeed, the essence of education can be seen as critical, in that its purpose is to help us to see, hear, and experience the world more clearly, more completely, and with more understanding. Education can provide us with the critical tools—critical reading, critical thinking, critical seeing, critical hearing, and writing—that enable us to understand. Another vital aspect of the educational process is the development of creativity and imagination, which enable us not only to understand but to build, make, create, and re-create our world. Crucial to these processes are critical dimensions, standards to be employed in both the critical and creative processes, and frames of reference which give energy and direction to the criticism and creativity. We are here talking about a vision that can illuminate what we are doing and what we might work to achieve. Such a vision needs to inform all aspects of our life, and naturally that includes education; in the case of education, it can also be said that the vision, in turn, is shaped by educators.

The questions of what our vision is and should be are in fact the most crucial and most basic questions that we face. They generate the complex and perplexing questions of how these visions are to be determined and reflect the conflict among competing groups eager to inform the vision with their particular wisdom. Fundamentally, the language of this vision belongs to the moral and religious family of language, for it is the function of moral and religious language to provide the essential dimension of education—the language of meaning. Our cultural crisis is a crisis in meaning, and this crisis can therefore be seen basically as moral and religious; we need to see the crisis in education as not primarily problems of technique, organization, and funding but as a reflection of the crisis in meaning. The educational bankruptcy is based on both its failure to ease this crisis and its success in contributing to it. We therefore propose to examine the true educational crisis with the language of meaning, by examining the moral and religious dimensions of our culture as reflected in our educational policies and practices.

3

The Moral and Spiritual Crisis in American Education

[R]eal criticism begins in the capacity to grieve because that is the most visceral announcement that things are not right. Only in the empire are we pressed and urged and invited to pretend that things are all right—either in the dean's office or in our marriage or in the hospital room. And as long as the empire can keep the pretense alive that things are all right, there will be no real grieving and no serious criticism.

Walter Brueggemann The Prophetic Imagination

We have thus far posited a number of basic assumptions to this analysis, including the intimate interrelationship between culture and education; the view that education should serve primarily to facilitate the struggle for meaning; that the key educational strategy is to nourish the critical and creative consciousness that will contribute to the creation and vitalization of a vision of meaning; and, finally, that the failure of the educational system is both cause and effect of a crisis in the culture's capacity to synthesize a coherent moral and spiritual order. We wish to explore the nature of this moral and spiritual crisis more deeply, particularly as it is reflected in educational policies and practices. We claim nothing like a definitive or even thorough exposition of the mood, mores, or attitudes of the culture—our goal here is much more modest. Our purpose is to suggest the broad boundaries of the culture's moral stance, a prospect which, of course, runs the risk of oversimplification and datedness. We take this risk because we believe such an analysis is critical to any examination of the educational process and, thus, we proceed with the confidence that such an overview is needed and with the caution that it is likely to be flawed and incomplete.

MODALITIES OF AMERICAN CULTURE

This is surely not the place to attempt an exact and thorough description of the American socioeconomic class structure and cultural landscape, but it is appropriate for us to sketch out our assumptions about major influences in American culture. We will be focusing primarily on the attitudes and values of an inchoate but bounded group that has been given several names—middle class, mid-America, the bourgeoisie, mainstream America. We will be addressing those attitudes and behaviors that generally characterize what is considered to be norms of American middle-class life—that which is legal, accepted, legitimate, routine, normal, and popular, what is considered to be part of "common sense," "normal expectations," and "popular culture." We are excluding in this particular analysis that which is considered esoteric, countercultural, socially deviant, and eccentric.

We focus on this aspect of American society for several reasons. First, we believe that it is obviously an influential and powerful force in the culture, albeit it is also one that is itself significantly manipulated by other cultural forces and groups. Secondly, it is a force/group in which I and almost all other professional educators have membership, and, thus, its examination can to some degree allow for self-reflection. In addition, this group has energy, intelligence, resources, and the capacity to make choices and changes given its relatively secure socioeconomic position. It is a group that has great potential for deeper education and, indeed, may be the only major group that has both the potential power and inclination to transform the culture.

Even though values and beliefs of this group cut across social, cultural, and economic groups, this consciousness is much more likely to be dominant in the middle class. Other cultural, political, and social groups are surely strongly affected by these belief systems, but their unique situations allow for significant variation and deviation from this consciousness. One group, if there is such a group (and I believe there is), consists of the supremely powerful and rich, a group very much isolated physically and culturally from mainstream America except in its exploitation and manipulation of it. We exclude them not because they are not important and powerful (indeed they are enormously so) but rather because, frankly, we are neither interested in, nor capable of, developing an educational strategy that might significantly affect their consciousness.

For other reasons, we will not fully address in this chapter the belief system of marginal and countercultural groups—the alienated, the poor, and the disenfranchised. Let me quickly say, however, that the book's central concern is in fact the plight of these people—they are the victims of a set of attitudes and values that are rooted in other sources. These are the oppressed of whom Freire (1970, 1973) has written so passionately and whose oppression is made all the more poignant when some of these oppressive norms and behaviors are internalized by the oppressed themselves. A major goal of this book is to develop ideas that can serve significantly to liberate these people from poverty, bigotry, and alienation; a major educational strategy for us is to develop an education aimed at those who tacitly and often overtly support those policies and programs that serve to keep the poor and powerless poor and powerless. An absolutely fundamental tenet of our social and educational orientation is the supreme importance of liberation for all—liberation from hunger, disease, fear, bigotry, war, ignorance, and all other barriers to a life of joy, abundance, and meaning for every single person in the world. Our efforts are directed at the mind-sets, values, and attitudes that are not directed at this kind of liberation and that are amenable to transformation by educational means.

This indeed is the most significant aspect of the consciousness that we wish to reengage educationally—that is, the cultural modalities we speak of include an impulse to "do good," to want to live a coherent life of ultimate meaning. I am excluding from my consideration the consciousness of evil, again because as an educator I simply do not know how to respond to people who knowingly and willingly try to keep people from being free. I operate on the assumption that there is a vast and influential group in America who would very much like to choose a way of life that is right, just, and loving. Part of the reason this group has not been fully able to make such a choice has to do with the power of elitist and powerful groups (who perhaps represent evil), and no doubt part of the reason comes from choices that middle America has made. However, it is my firm belief that these choices represent confusion and frustration more than they represent a desire to hurt and oppress. Confusion and frustration are indeed areas in which the educational process is relevant. When we look at our problems as rooted in evil and sin, then the only alternative to despair is prayer; but when we are able to see them based more on confusion, then we can put our hope in education. What this chapter is designed to do is to explicate the confusion, which adds up to a confusion about our losing struggle to choose a creative rather than a destructive life. It is a confusion that emerges from value conflicts and from the paradoxes and dilemmas inherent in the effort to inform what we do with deeply felt moral principles.

I have chosen to present this broad conception of the nature of this confusion in the form of a number of discrete yet clearly overlapping dyads of value paradoxes. These will be discussed more as dilemmas than as easy changes, more in dialectical than dualistic terms, more as points on a continuum than as either/or considerations. However, my purpose will not be to blur moral and value choices but rather to indicate that although certain values are clearly to be preferred, their choice usually involves legitimate and attractive conflicts with other choices. At the risk of redundancy, I wish to point out that these are problems that permeate American culture and that manifest themselves in educational settings, in addition to other sites.

PARADOXES AND CONFLICTS IN AMERICAN CULTURE

Individuality/Community

The first of these value dyads is perhaps the most basic and serious single cultural issue facing us, namely the matter of individuality/community. This issue has to do with our impulse to define, maintain, and nourish both a self and group identity; we are interested in being unique, autonomous, independent, and in having a strong and well-defined ego, and at the same time we seek strong human and symbolic relationships in which our identities are connected with those of others. Not only is there an impulse to seek group, interpersonal, and symbolic identity, but we also recognize the social character of our lives: whether we like it or not, we are interdependent, have symbiotic relationships with others, and are by nature socially defined.

There is by now a vast and persuasive literature that reinforces the strong consensus that ours is a generation dominated by individuality, self-gratification, and narcissism (e.g., see Lasch 1979; Bellah 1985; Sennett 1977). It is also a time, not surprisingly, when there is great loneliness and when a myriad of new techniques to help people develop relationships has emerged, such as singles' bars, computer dating, support groups, and the like. The great emphasis in the desperate pursuit of individual gratification can be seen in the grim status of the divorce and suicide rates. It is also seen in the increase in competition, greed, and crime, and in the decrease in concern for the poor and powerless. The concept of "welfare," for example, has come to be a term for pariahs and slackers; public support for the unfortunate has come to mean government interference, and unemployment has come to an unfortunate but necessary consequence of reconstructing a more efficient economy.

By individuality we mean here not so much the development of autonomy and independence as much as a egocentricity, a belief that the individual is the basic and most important unit of decision making. There is a sense here that from the perspective of self-gratification, self-fulfillment, self-help, and self-advancement, concerns for group, family, or culture, are irrelevant or threatening. Group is seen not so much as stifling but as a setting for individual competition in which the group provides hierarchical norms. This stress on individuality is by no means free of its conformist aspects—indeed the culture demands that individuals compete, that they strive for winning over and beating others; and that achievement in a broad but ultimately bounded realm constitutes success. The acquisition of materials, feeling good, and a sense of achievement become the common standards for individual pursuits.

This emphasis strains our commitment to the development of traditional community and shared values in spite of the fact the our traditions are full of images designed to provide for a sense of common concerns and common struggle. The Declaration of Independence, the Constitution, and the Gettysburg Address, for example, speak of nationhood, peoplehood, brotherhood; of union, common purpose, and common destiny. We presumably value family and neighborhood; we are nostalgic about celebrations involving powerful bonding rituals: Christmas, the Fourth of July, Mother's Day, and graduations. Our politicians continue routinely to use the rhetoric of patriotism, of our common heritage, and of the special opportunities and blessings of the American people.

The schools, however, play a more powerful role in stressing an individual rather than a common vision. Individual success and achievement are greatly emphasized, as seen in the increasing stress in normative grading and correlatively in our obsessions with the idea of "cheating." Although we are aware of the individuality of knowledge, of the value of group study and interaction, and the importance of students sharing their ideas, we actually discourage these educationally sound practices because they interfere with the practice of individual grading. Students are, in fact, urged to compete with each other in the classroom—entrance into certain tracks or programs (e.g., reading groups, college track, gifted and talented programs) is competitive and limited, as is college admission through standardized test scores and course grades—as well as outside the classroom in such activities as team sports and cheerleading. However, the irony here is that it is in the athletic rather than the academic programs that one is far more likely to find serious concern for cooperation, interdependence, and the intimate relationship between the team as a whole and the individual. The emphasis in community on the sports program is, however, mitigated by at least two considerations: first, the sports program often supports the "star" orientation in which superior individual achievement often attains far more attention than that of the team; and second, the stress remains on winning and surpassing another team. In fairness, there still remain the ethics of sportsmanship, which, at least theoretically, affirms a community of competitors.

The insight that schools' prime educational approach consists of students trying to please teachers by getting the "right answer" is one which also reveals how students are put in a position of competing with each other on who can most please teacher. Individual students are singled out for praise or vilification so as to indicate their individual efforts and achievements or lack thereof. Students are said to earn their stars or smiling faces or detention notices or reprimands, not so much as students functioning within a cultural and social setting but as solitary figures acting as independent agents oblivious to each other and mindful only of being "fair" to competitors. This, no doubt, is appropriate preparation for the conventional world of real estate, stockbrokerage and professional sports. However, it is highly inappropriate preparation for an interdependent world in which the sense of justice, community, and compassion should be the overriding considerations.

Habits of the Heart, by Robert Bellah and associates (1985), documents the culture's inability to articulate its impulse for a conscious-ness that transcends concern for self and its losing struggle to find a larger meaning grounded in common and shared beliefs and experiences. In their study of current views of middle-class Americans toward self and group, they found

> *all the classic polarities of American individualism still operating: the deep desire for autonomy and self-reliance combined with an equally deep conviction that life has no meaning unless shared with others in the context of community; a commitment to the equal right to dignity of every individual combined with an effort to justify inequality of reward, which when extreme, may deprive people of dignity; an insistence that life requires practical effectiveness and "realism" combined with the feeling that compromise is ethically fatal. The inner tensions of American individualism add up to a classic case of ambivalence. We strongly assert the value of our self-reliance and autonomy. We deeply feel the emptiness of a life without sustaining social commitments. Yet we are hesitant to articulate our sense that we need one another as much as we need to stand alone, for fear that if we did we would lose our independence altogether. The tensions of our lives would be even greater if we did not, in fact, engage in practices that constantly limit the effects of an isolating individualism, even though we cannot articulate those practices nearly as well as we can the quest for autonomy. (1985:150–51)*

We thirst for true community, for a broader context to individually struggle and share authentically our joys, confessions, and heart-breaks. When we go to school, we are taught mostly to learn to be alone, to compete, to achieve, to succeed. The emphasis on individual achievement is not uniform in the schools since there, as elsewhere, the concern for community also gets expressed however modestly and infrequently. Schools sponsor parent groups and choral societies;

they have school rallies, school songs, try to raise school spirit, speak sometimes of a school's tradition. They also try to support alumni groups and speak of the character of a group or student ("This year's junior class is really special"), and in times of distress the school community is often mobilized to express its collective concern. It is certainly not that the schools, like the culture, are not mindful of a social identity, but they clearly put much more emphasis on our personal identity, especially as it relates to our obsession with personal success and achievement. This brings us to our second major value paradox—that how much our culture has come to blur worth with achievement.

Worth/Achievement

This particular value configuration represents, I believe, the core of our moral crisis and anguish, for it reflects a glaring contradiction between our most deeply felt moral conviction—that which affirms the essential dignity of each person—and our most widespread social policy—that which demands that each person must achieve (i.e., that each of us has to earn our dignity). Our most revered symbols and credos continue to urge us to love ourselves, our neighbors, and even our enemies; they tell us that all people are created equal, that we are born with certain inalienable rights, that we are all God's children, that we all have a spirit or soul within us, that each one of us is precious and sovereign. These profound expressions are elaborated and exhorted in every aspect of our culture—in homes, in the media, and yes, even in schools these sentiments are accepted as part of our faith—at least in rhetoric. In addition, we have a popular psychology that urges us to be considerate of the feelings of others and that values empathy and a sense of well-being for everyone. After all I'm O.K., you're O.K., and we're O.K. Well, that is not quite how it works or otherwise we would not need to be continually encouraged and urged to take on that outlook. We are having to be prodded to think that you and I are O.K. because we live in a culture that does not say that we are O.K. until and unless we demonstrate that we can do something well that is valued. In a word, we live in a world where personal dignity is not inherent and inalienable but is negotiable and problematic. Some would even say that in schools we need to "motivate" students to strive for this dignity, and to use dignity as a reward (i.e., in exchange for achievement).

However, it is not just that many educators see reinforcement theory as a useful psychological construct or see extrinsic motivation as a "reality" of our being. The question that lies underneath the widespread use of the reward-punishment approach to learning is partly one of wondering why we are so strongly attracted to this way of being. The answer, I believe, lies in part in our insistence on hierarchy and privilege and the necessity for having clear criteria and justification for that hierarchy of privilege. Our democratic principles involve a rejection of the notion of ascribed hierarchy (i.e., privilege that comes with birth or position). As a people we congratulate ourselves not for rejecting privilege but only for redefining the conditions under which people may have privileges.

This has led us to a tacit acceptance of a notion of "deserving"— namely, a set of connections which, at least implicitly, legitimates inequality on the basis that it is deserved or merited. The mainstream culture has in fact legitimated a number of conditions under which it approves more justice for some than others—for example, those who work hard, those who have strong educational backgrounds, and those who have particular professions (medicine, law, professional music, professional sports). We are a culture that simultaneously celebrates equality and inequality, community and competition—one that rejects the notion of any person as having special privileges as immoral and unfair and yet at the same time actively creates and legitimates possibilities for this to occur.

It has been pointed out that a major shift in emphasis occurs at the point where children begin to go to school in earnest, and that is the difference in stress on affiliation and achievement. Presumably, families, while surely concerned with achievement, accept, support, and nurture their members *because* they are members (i.e., they belong). The constitutive rules of the schools are somewhat different in that achievement becomes the basic condition for acceptance. Students learn very quickly that the rewards that the schools provide— grades, honors, recognitions, affection—are conditioned upon achievement and certain behaviors of respect, obedience, and docility.

This is not to say that the schools are monolithic and rigid in the areas in which they demand students to achieve, although the increasing stress on normative and standardized testing indicates a clear direction toward uniformity. Indeed, thoughtful, kind, and sensitive teachers often express their flexibility and progressiveness by widening the arenas of achievement. Such teachers will say in effect, "I so much want Cedric to have a good self-image which I know he can get if only he could be proud of what he did. Now, mind you it doesn't have to be in things like math or history—it could be in art or sports or woodworking, and I'm going to continue to look for whatever it is that Cedric can excel at."

We tend to applaud and glow when we hear such a sentiment expressed, and surely it is a well-intentioned impulse, one which expresses a teacher's strong dedication and willingness to strive to help a student find fulfillment and a sense of well-being. However, such a sentiment and our approbation for it reveals cultural standards for both fulfillment and a sense of well-being. It is, in fact, a sentiment that underscores our obsession with achievement and success, since what it says is that we do not care what Cedric does as long as he does *something well*. This standard indicates that a necessary if not sufficient condition for fulfillment and strong self-image is achievement and the ability to excel in a particular realm of achievement. This would indicate an ethic of conditioned love: we will love you if you achieve. Presumably the more enlightened of us have a longer list of the significant areas of achievement, but we still must achieve. Moreover, our worth is really not inherent, not sovereign, not inevitable, but continuously subject to trial, examination, and evolution. It is also possible and likely that the list of what areas are significant enough to achieve in will change, so we will have to be alert to shifts in the cultural requirements for dignity.

This harshly severe demand has clearly exacerbated injustice, pain, suffering, confusion, and doubt about our ideals. Each of us, I suspect, harbors quietly, if not secretly, the convictions that "we and our loved ones are as good as anyone else," and yet we constantly engage in practices designed to demonstrate that we are "better than." This conflict and contradiction is destructive, self-fulfilling, and has the capacity to feed on itself—that is, the more we engage in the madness of demanding that we prove that we are deserving, the more it becomes entrenched and "inevitable."

Schools present students and the larger school community with the notion that an integral and vital aspect of school life involves the pursuit of dignity, and they take on responsibility for setting the conditions for this pursuit—for the competition of who will have how much dignity. This means inevitably that some people will emerge with *lots* of dignity and some with very little. This means, ironically and at the risk of reductionism, that the schools' job includes, however unintended, that of identifying those who are of little or no worth. It is not only that schools are competitive and that they encourage their students to succeed and excel each other, but at an even more basic level they represent in their being and practice this deadly equation of achievement with worth. It is a notion which is so pervasive and routine that it is hardly even noticed, much less questioned. Because their rhetoric of intellectual and academic excellence resonates so strongly with what we think of as noble aspirations, schools actually add a particularly strong legitimation to what is, at base, a serious variance with our deepest moral and spiritual convictions. In fact, schools are criticized by enlightened members of the upper-middle class (including so-called radicals) for not sufficiently stressing academic, or intellectual, or esthetic "excellence"—a code name for more intense competition.

This reflects the depth of the culture's commitment to the values of success and achievement. It is rare to see serious social, cultural, and educational critics confronting the issues of hierarchy based on intellectual and professional abilities and achievements. This would indicate a very strong if not always articulated support for hierarchy, for privilege and ranking, but presumably one based on intellectual achievement. Are "smart" people any more deserving than "dumb" ones? Are brilliant poets any more entitled to privilege than conventional ones? Why do we single out a group for "graduating with honor"? Does this mean that those who are not in this group are without honor? Why do we have minimum grade point averages as conditions to participate in certain activities? The schools mirror the culture by giving its admittedly meager but powerfully symbolic rewards to those who achieve more than others. Again, the mark of a so-called progressive school is not necessarily that it rejects achievement but that it extends the realm of areas worthy of recognition— for example, the hardest working, the student who has made the most progress, or the most congenial. All of this rests on a firm and presumably unshakable conviction that dignity and worth are to be earned. And yet this conviction, however strong and widespread, must coexist with our immense and overwhelming yearning for unconditional love—our intense desire to love others, be loved by others, to love others for who they are rather than for what they do or have.

Equality/Competition

The political consequences of the stress on individuality, competition, personal achievement, and success include an erosion of our traditional commitment to social equality. The 1930s and 1960s movements mark our more recent attempts to make this commitment real and vital. We have a strong tradition of activism for social and economic equality in which literally thousands of people have shown their willingness to risk and lose a great deal (including their lives) for these causes. We have, of course, also struggled with the dilemmas engendered by the situations in which equality can conflict with freedom. Over the course of time, various groups have worked out arrangements and understandings which, at least politically, have tried to overcome these difficulties by an overriding concern for equality and justice. Tax policies, trade unions, professional associations, social welfare programs, unemployment insurance, minimum wages, collective bargaining, affirmative action, open admission, consumer protection policies, and pollution controls can all be said to restrict individual freedom, but they are intended to provide more freedom for more people whose own freedom is limited by unnecessary barriers. Our overriding concern for social justice and equality and our impulse to be compassionate have enabled us, for the most part, to accept and tolerate practices which might not please us in our individual and private consciousness but which resonate with our social identity.

However, it seems the 1980s are a time when these arrangements and understandings are no longer accepted as a framework for social policy. We seem to be going back to a neo-Social Darwinism, where the play of the free market will in the long run overcome anomalies and inequities. In part, the new conservatism can be seen as the continuing backlash to the 1960s, to the fear and threat engendered by what was perceived to be moral excess and, perhaps more significantly, serious efforts to alter the power structure. The 1960s social policies added to their concern for providing basic material necessities—income, education, food, housing—a new item on the agenda, a major concern for community political development. Many groups, hitherto powerless and rendered invisible and harmless by their powerlessness, were given the secrets of how their latent power could be developed. The 1960s were, if nothing else, a time when collectivity was both celebrated as a virtue and utilized as a powerful agent for change. The poor, the minorities, and the neighborhoods were organized, as were various middle-class constituencies—school groups, support groups, groups of the afflicted (those dealing with the ravages of mental illness, retardation, physical handicaps, and the like). In fact, it was probably the politicization of many middle-class Americans, who perhaps for the first time experienced, either themselves or through relatives, officially sanctioned horrors (e.g., the draft and police brutality), that had the greatest impact on the areas of greatest immediate political changes—the passage of civil rights legislation and the ending of the war in Vietnam. What threatened the power structure was not the number of individual hippies or freaks but rather that what might have remained a series of fads or a relatively harmless release of exuberance had been transformed into a movement. This movement, though varied, had a number of common themes, particularly collectivity, community, solidarity, peoplehood, and all aspects of and paths to dignity, freedom, and autonomy.

Interestingly enough, two significant policies on the military draft illustrate the ultimately destructive, distracting, and divisive powers of competition and individuality. The first of these policies is the one which gave exemptions to college students, clearly a way of providing the middle class with a significant advantage. This policy also reinforced the edge that came to those who so successfully competed that they were admitted to colleges and were also able to meet the academic requirement of maintaining matriculation. Those "smart" and "wealthy" enough to be in college were seen as less appropriate for military service. The second policy which I believe cleverly undermined middle-class resistance both to the Vietnam war and to an aggressive U.S. foreign policy was the elimination of the draft and its substitution with an all-volunteer professional army. Given economic realities, this effectively made the army appealing mostly to those unable to make it in the civilian economy—the poor, the disadvantaged, the minorities. Taken together, these policies provided mechanisms of competition and division that had serious consequences; they were policies that forced people to think individually rather than collectively, to think of the consequences of acting on the basis of personal freedom rather than on the basis of social equality.

The political rhetoric of both parties in the 1984 election campaign (with the exception of Jesse Jackson) shows a common theme of individual competition. Some candidates stressed the concept of opportunity, which is only a way of having competition that is made "fair" by equalizing opportunities to participate in the race for dignity. It is also a rhetoric that implicitly accepts the inevitability of scarce resources, and accepts that discipline and self-restraint are in order because, if anything, the resources and goodies will soon be even scarcer—fewer jobs, less government involvement, more "overqualified" people competing with each other. Our economic policy, such as there is one, seems to accept as inevitable and desirable the need to enter the postindustrial era, which, among other things, involves even more efficiency, more cost-effective controls, less reliance on human labor, and avoidance of long-range commitment to higher wages. We are told that we are in a time of painful transition, that we have economic troubles largely because the high wages we pay make us unable to compete with countries where people work much harder and earn much less. We are also told that our federal deficit contributes to the economic crisis and that the roots of this defect are mostly in our social welfare or "entitlement" programs. This has led, among other things, to the most serious efforts by industry, with the active support of the government, to weaken if not break unions and professional associations since the 1920s. Current economic conditions have allowed many companies to use the stick of replacing unionized workers with nonunionized workers quite willing and eager to work, even if it means at lower wages.

Much of the culture now accepts our economic situation as serious and highly shaky, and in this atmosphere of fear and anxiety the stress on competition and personal freedom is seen as both an intellectually sound economic policy of social salvation and a harshly realistic way of responding to the cruel necessities of personal and family survival. We have once again been put in a situation where we are driven to make a choice, however theoretically unnecessary, between equality and justice for all and survival for me. I believe that most of us find it hateful to confront such a choice, or at least that is my hope. I fear that there are those who may not resent this conflict because they have come to rationalize the competition not as corrosive to equality but as actually contributing to it in the long run. An even greater fear is that this seemingly technical argument about the best way to achieve equality masks an increasing indifference to the pain and suffering that are the concrete consequences of significant social inequality.

CARING: COMPASSION AND SENTIMENTALITY

The concern for social equality can be said to be a correlate of the human impulse to be caring, to be concerned about the welfare of others to the point of helping and nurturing them. We are a caring people, a contention which can be seen in the intense concern parents have for their children, and for that matter, as Willard Gaylin (1978) points out, we seem programmed biologically to be sensitive to the vulnerability of children. Our culture, in fact, accepts a sense of deep caring as a natural and desirable aspect of family life; deep caring is not seen as an exotic and unrealizable ideal within the family structure but as an inevitable dimension and a key defining aspect of the family.

The schools have traditionally encouraged the concept of caring in a variety of ways: organizing food drives for the needy; arranging for ways to comfort classmates who are ill or have suffered family loss; encouraging concern for others when the safety and well-being of others is involved, such as conduct in the cafeteria, hallways, and auditorium; and in the emphasis on caring as a positive value in the context of academic classes (e.g., as shown in the popularity of novels by Charles Dickens in English courses). However, the stress on competition and individuality narrows and undermines this impulse to care and nourish. Indeed, the culture and the schools have had to develop techniques to become immune to the kind of caring that might deflect us from competition and the pursuit of individual success and achievement. We have come to find ways in which indifference is valued—it's good to be "cool," to be stoic, to avoid feeling guilt. We have bought into a psychology that urges us to consider that we are responsible individually for our feelings and behavior, that we are responsible only to ourselves and cannot be held responsible for others. While this may at one level enhance (properly) our own responsibility, this attitude can, at another level, serve to reduce the sense of our interdependence and our opportunities to help and support others.

When we call cooperative and collaborative acts of research and study "cheating," we insist that students take individual responsibility for what they claim to know. Students are neither asked to take very much responsibility in helping other students to learn, nor are they encouraged to note how their gains are often at the expense of their classmates. In addition, playing the competitive game of schooling means in part not allowing one to feel sorry for the losers since losers are also competitors. To show sympathy for them would give one's competitors support and might sap one's resolve and determination to win.

Surely, students are likely to encounter the realities of human poverty and hunger and to study formally the whys and wherefores of the problems. When such matters are studied, it is typically with an emphasis on understanding the issues, gaining insight into them, and almost always on agreeing that it would be good to untangle the complexities in order to help these wretched people. However, schools are usually reluctant to encourage students to develop deep emotional attachment to the issues or to dwell on the moral obscenity of these situations. Teachers are very reluctant and careful not to "induce guilt" but rather to develop the distance that can allow one to have a sober and thoughtful understanding. In any case, where schools do organize an annual fast day or encourage the social studies curriculum to deal with hunger and poverty, they often do so as simply one more "interesting" activity. There is seldom, if ever, a story of a school or university that sets as one of its prime continuous and long-range goals the cultivation of human caring and concern.

The tragedy of this policy is to truncate the human spirit, especially that part that yearns for connection and involvement. We as humans do and want to care and have shown a glorious tradition of responding heroically and selflessly in times of need. However, with our need to compete; with the feeling that our brothers and sisters may be barriers to our race for the scarce resources; with the recognition that a person in trouble is a less formidable rival for dignity, and that caring for others may infantilize them and hook us; and with the knowledge of the problems that come to well-meaning people who do get involved (e.g., law suits, the victimization of good Samaritans by robbers, police, et al.), the answer seems to be to "stay cool," to remain aloof, skeptical, and to avoid being swept away by the emotions of grief and pity. For one thing, such emotions will cloud our judgment, develop false expectations that we can rescue others, and distract us from our path.

It is no surprise, therefore, that we hear of relationships without love, of joyless sexual activities becoming the norm for both men and women, of the sharp increase simultaneously of the use of surface pleasantries (e.g., "Have a nice day") and the reluctance to make serious human commitments of the kind exemplified by a deep sense of caring. We yearn to care and to be cared for; yet, we work on developing callousness to these yearnings and in so doing deny ourselves, for as Abraham Heschel says, "The opposite of freedom is not determinism but hardness of heart" (Heschel 1962:191). When we shut down our impulse to care, we interfere with one of the very most precious essences of what it means to be human.

This is not to say that our culture is without "feelings." Quite the contrary, for we have seen a veritable explosion of feelings, and discussion, analysis, and explanation of feelings continue to be a major focal point of modern thought and concern. We are a culture that has learned to be in touch with our feelings, to express them, to consider them as real and vital aspects of being human, and above all else we have learned that it is important that we feel "good." Bellah's *Habits of the Heart* (1985) and Lasch's *The Culture of Narcissism* (1979) spell out the lengths to which we as people will go to extend this value of personal well-being, as indicated by how we as individuals feel about our individual selves. The issue I wish to address here is the direction and locus of these feelings rather than the issue of the validity of feelings themselves. I believe we are beyond the point of actively avoiding and denying the reality and power of feelings, but we are still very much wrestling with issues related to their boundaries, to their relationship to other moral, political, and religious considerations.

Matthew Fox, in his *Spirituality as Compassion* (1979), has articulated an important distinction in this regard, between compassion and sentimentality. *Compassion* to Fox represents an acknowledgment and celebration of interdependence which results in action directed toward the "reign of pain." In contrast, Fox sees *sentimentality* as representing feeling by itself, alone and determinedly separate from any sense of responsibility. In this analysis Fox is able to provide insight into the political and moral nature of states of feeling so that we can see that feelings can and do have an effect on human relationships. Sentimentalism certainly reflects feelings, but they are self-indulgent feelings, perhaps feelings without form or meaning or as Fox quoting Ann Douglas puts it, "sentimentalism is politically rancid" (1979:5).

Compassion, as here defined by Fox, acknowledges the social reality of connectedness, the political reality of human relationships, and the moral impulse to care and nurture. Compassion is feelings with moral meaning; its literal meaning of "suffering with" reveals profound understanding of the nature of being—that it is likely to involve pain and suffering, that the burdens are particularly severe when one is alone, and that it is part of human nature to share the burdens and efforts to ease them. It is the cluster of feelings that energizes our intellectual conceptions of justice as well as the expression of our deepest urges to love. Not to feel the connections with social and moral concerns is to locate the emotions we have in reaction to other people's woes in self-oriented, self-directed, ego-centered sentimentality. Fox puts it this way: "Sentimentalism is not only a block of social justice and a thorn in the side of love—justice—it is in fact their opposite.... It actually interferes with the natural flow of energy outwards that all persons are born with" (1979:5–6).

I have already indicated why we can expect to find lots of sentimentality in the schools and precious little compassion. Given the heavy stress on competition, individuality, achievement, and personal success, any emotions of concern are likely to be of a more sentimental nature. Surely, the school community will express its sorrow at a student's misfortune—they will likely send notes, flowers, even mobilize schoolwide or classwide expressions of concern. The coach will surely empathize with the pain of an athlete's injury and the teacher will say that the punishment he/she is inflicting is hurting teacher more than student. The administration surely sympathizes with the difficult living conditions (divorce, unemployment, illness, etc. of some students and they will surely wince and shake their heads, as well as shrug their shoulders, when confronted with the pain and horrors that form the basis of these students' lives.

However, rules are rules, standards are standards, reality is reality—we didn't make these rules and standards, nor did we create this reality—life must go on, and it's possible that your teacher doesn't understand that you fell asleep in class because you worked the third shift. But it's up to you to find a way—have you tried talking to your teacher? Have you thought about getting another job? You have to learn to cope—after all when I was your age....

The stress on individual achievement in school is the same for individual failure and pain: it's *your* problem and *you're* going to have to deal with it. The emphasis on sentimentalism is the emotional dimension of individuality, privatism, and competition in that it seriously deemphasizes mutuality, interdependence, and the human origin of culture. Sentimentality allows the underlying problems to go unchallenged (e.g., why do some students have to make difficult choices between an education and economic survival?) by privatizing the feeling and locating the source of the problem in the person in pain. This distancing erodes social responsibility ("Yes, sometimes life isn't fair, so just go ahead and stay after school even if the punishment isn't fair"); encourages powerlessness ("Yes, I see your point, I feel bad that your teacher flunked you, but my hands are tied"); and engenders alienation ("Yes, I can feel your enthusiasm for music and that's very nice, but one has to establish priorities"). Here again we experience the phenomenon of conflict, of how we find ourselves in a place we did not plan or expect to be. We as people both value compassion and are compassionate—we do care for and with each other and we respond to those who extend their concern for us. At times of crisis, we yearn to help, to ease pain, and are often frustrated by the difficulty or impossibility of doing anything. The sense of impotency in the face of suffering reflects in a vivid manner the depths of what it means to be powerless, for one feels rage, guilt, and dehumanization when one is not afforded the opportunity to participate in the healing process when one is denied the responsibility to help other people's lives become whole.

RESPONSIBILITY AND GUILT

We want to be responsible but not to feel guilty. Responsibility involves the celebration of social connections; guilt involves the pain of social demands. When we act responsibly, it means that we are (in Heschel's [1962] conception) "responding" to the human condition of interdependence and the mutuality of our interest, and hence responsibility is seen as the ability to respond to the challenges and demands that arise from that social consciousness. We have learned, however, to be wary of a phenomenon called "guilt," which is the term applied, apparently, to an inappropriate response to social demands. Feeling guilty is bad because it makes us feel bad when we really do not have to feel bad. To act out of guilt is considered unhealthy and counterproductive since it engenders anger, resentment, and depression. No doubt there is the very real possibility of a pathological response to every human situation and it is clear that many people have been unnecessarily immobilized by neurotic responses to issues related to social and moral expectations. The danger that I see is that the concern for the individual's feeling "good" is so powerful that it has led to an overreliance on the phenomenon of guilt as a mechanism to avoid responsibility. One way of avoiding distasteful, entangling, absorbing, and risky responsibilities is to rename the impulse involved. By psychologizing moral issues we can transform our inclination to view these tasks as rooted in our our moral impulse to an impulse that is rooted in a concept of guilt. This allows us to do what is "psychologically healthy" ("We mustn't act out of guilt") at the risk of not taking on a task that is considered morally right ("It is your responsibility to take on this task").

The school says, "It is your responsibility to work hard and get high grades and not to feel guilty if your friend flunks the course." The school says, "It's right to feel a sense of responsibility for the starving Ethiopians but you won't be able to help them if all you are really feeling is guilt." The school says, "Yes, it's a shame your friend won't be able to play because of her injury, but feeling guilty won't help." The school says, "It is not professional to complain about another teacher—you sound like you're projecting your guilt." The school says, "I don't know anything about college admissions—don't ask me to deal with your guilt trips." The guidance counselor says, "Maybe you feel guilty that you're getting good grades and that your friend is flunking out."

The culture and the schools have made a great deal of the dangers and perils of acting out of guilt because it is unhealthy to do so. They have done far less about speaking to the consequences of moral irresponsibility; they seem less concerned with the "illness" of avoiding the consequences of mutuality than with the "illness" of personal anguish. Perhaps the school ought to set itself to the task of helping people to sort out their legitimate responsibilities and contribute to the development of the intellectual, psychological, and spiritual resources required to respond in a way that is fulfilling and meaningful. For not only do we strive to be responsible, we waver at the risks and burdens involved. Part of this wavering can be seen as having educational rather than strictly psychological significance: part of the reason we sometimes avoid our responsibilities is that we lack the clarity and the skills appropriate to exercising those responsibilities. We do not have to learn the impulse to be responsible, but we do have to be encouraged to accept the related challenges; moreover, we do have to learn how best to respond to this most human of all impulses—to be my brothers' and sisters' keeper.

AUTHORITY/POWER/COERCION

With responsibility comes the opportunity and necessity to exercise power with all its risks, uncertainties, and dangers. Power in itself, and in its inevitability and ubiquity, is neither good nor bad. It is a force like fire and wind which is necessary and natural with as much capacity for life as for death. The moral and spiritual boundaries are the truly critical dimensions of power since it is they which give power its meaning. Power can be seen as equivalent to the capacity to make decisions; one can then examine the issues surrounding the conditions under which this capacity is exercised. Perhaps the most significant of these conditions is the one which deals with the basis of the decision and, more particularly, with whether, or to what degree, the decision is based on some legitimate authority or is simply a function of coercion.

Let us refer to this distinction as one of authority as opposed to coercion, authority being used here to refer to some shared set of principles as to what constitutes the true, the good, and the beautiful. We are not talking here of agreement on specific issues but rather agreement on what generally constitutes acceptable criteria for a proper decision, be they very general criteria like empirical verification, logic, reason, research, or somewhat less abstract frameworks like Freudian theory, Marxism, Christianity, or Keynesian economics. What is crucial in this general attitude toward decision making is a reliance on general principles that have wide acceptance, and so it can be said that when we make decisions in this mode, we are trying to persuade and influence through mutually accepted moral, intellectual, professional, or spiritual criteria.

Those who make decisions based on coercion brush aside these considerations and, instead, simply impose their will by dint of their power, whether it be direct brute power or the more indirect coercive power which implicitly stands behind people who have been chosen not to exercise authority. Presumably, if one refuses to go to school, one will confront sooner or later the full force of the police and the courts. This mode is classically expressed by Thrasymachus in Plato's *Republic* when he proclaims that "Might makes Right" (1985:35). (Socrates's response that reason makes right is an equally apt expression of decision making as authority.) This distinction is crucial to understanding the significance and meaning of education as representing the hope and faith in authority rather than coercion. The point of education is to present and critically examine various approaches which claim authority. We need to learn about these claims, to know their language, grammar, and presuppositions, and to learn about another set of claims designed to help us evaluate and judge claims (i.e., critical theories). The educated person hopes to decide and act on an informed basis, as one informed by a circle of authority of what is considered to be acceptable principles of morality, science, and art.

Surely, we are a people who value authority over coercion. We certainly want decisions made fairly, sanely, and wisely rather than arbitrarily, and clearly we would rather influence than impose—we would rather be respected for our knowledge, skill, expertise, and wisdom than for the strength of our weaponry. Schools as educational institutions are full of the symbols and rituals of these deeply held values: there is the demand of proof and logic in geometry; the concern for critical thinking in social studies; and the stress on coherence, unity, and emphasis in English. We are asked to assemble our information and to distinguish between fact and opinion. We are told of the dangers of propaganda, of the necessity of precision and objectivity in science. We do not like bullies; we jeer and fear them as mindless brutes, on a level with wild, uncivilized, uneducated animals. We are certainly taught to be courteous and respectful, which represents both an antidote and rebuke to violence and personal insensitivity. Schools, as educational institutions, celebrate brain not brawn, the mind not the body, reason not force, dialogue not violence, character, rule of law, and all that kind of thing. Yes? No? Well, hardly.

The slide from authority can be relatively benign ("Well, I think it *is* time for you to go to bed") or stern (e.g., the use of corporal punishment). Schools in their acculturation and socialization functions put great stress on obedience and deference to established power, which would seem to undermine their educational commitment to authority, as well as to the scholarly tradition of skepticism. Students are told generally of the value of critical thinking but quite directly that operationally it is neither proper nor wise to think critically of their school environment. Moreover, this rule applies to the school itself in that there is no particular pressure placed on teachers to be any more authoritative than, say, the home gardener, and maybe less. Teachers not only do *not* try to persuade students that homework is a sound idea, they themselves typically do *not* have solid evidence that it is. (Indeed, they are often unaware of the evidence that it is not.) Schools glibly adapt and utilize grading systems of a profoundly dubious nature without a murmur of apology or regret. Indeed, a powerful and effective part of the school curriculum is to do what the teacher and administrator tell students to do and to come to see this as inevitable, necessary, and routine. For those who do not, the school has its own arsenal of coercive weaponry—suspension, verbal abuse, corporal punishment, withholding of affection, denial of "privileges" (recess, athletics, bathroom), and above all else the dreaded lower grade, or "bad" reference.

Personal exchanges and decisions in schools tend very much to be rule and power bound rather than negotiated individually. The permeating assumption is that the student accepts school policies and practices and does what teacher says. Those few students who dare to ask for exceptions are barely tolerated; perhaps they may be seen patronizingly as "cute," but more often they are quashed ultimately not by persuasion and deference to principle but by the impatience of a force that has vastly superior firing power. Tanks are very effective against the slingshots of complainers, whiners, nitpickers.

How does one explain the extraordinary anomaly of an educational institution willing to surrender the very essence of its legitimacy by its ready resort to force and coercion? To do so undermines the very soul of an educational institution and renders its basic purpose highly problematic. However, the way in which the schools' reliance on concern is tolerated indicates not an institutional but a cultural confusion. The ease and regularity with which schools do this and the support they get from the culture for this behavior speak to the importance the culture attaches to control.

Our political preference, indeed our passion for control, makes our traditional commitment to democracy highly problematic. Our twin traditions of freedom and responsibility make the partnership of education (not necessarily schools) and democracy (not necessarily government) intimate, inevitable, inextricable, and symbiotic. The ideals of democracy include the belief that an informed public can in good faith create a society of liberty and justice for all. Such is not only a valid way of describing the nature of a true education; it is also an apt description of where a true education can thrive.

CONTROL/DEMOCRACY

Perhaps because of the awesome traumas of the twentieth century—world wars, holocaust, famine, economic depression, nuclear bombs, pollution, and the real possibility of even more horrors—we have extended our human impulse to control our destinies to obsessive dimensions, most graphically expressed in the totalitarian regimes of Hitler and Stalin. Certainly the ways in which we as a culture express those tendencies fall far short of the fanaticism, arbitrariness, and ruthlessness of the modern, Orwellian police states on the left and the right. However, even in America we all worry how our heavily bureaucratized, computerized culture—embedded in strong traditions of pragmatism, behaviorism, and technical and engineering brilliance—edges into the outskirts of a consciousness that values work, productivity, efficiency, and uniformity over play, flexibility, diversity, and freedom. When the stakes get higher and a crisis deepens, we are apt to become open to drastic solutions that focus sharply on the problem but are blind to other normally deeply held considerations—due process, rule of law, personal freedom, human rights. The recent example of the rather mild gasoline and fuel oil shortages in the United States indicates that it does not take much to set off a sense of panic and, with it, the cry for quick, tough, centralized controls—an example of what has been called our tendency toward friendly fascism.

The concern for control is also expressed in the microcosms of society—in the home, in the workplace, and in the schools. Schools have been captured by the concept of "accountability," which has been transformed from a notion that schools need to be responsive and responsible to community concerns to one in which numbers are used to demonstrate that schools have met their minimal requirement—a reductionism which has given higher priority to the need to control than to educational considerations. The need for control produces control mechanisms, and for the schools this has meant a proliferation of tests—a kind of quality control mechanism borrowed crudely and inappropriately from certain industrial settings. We control the curriculum, teachers, and staff by insisting on predefined minimal performances on specified tests. In this way schools continue their love affair with industrial and business metaphors: in this case it means metaphors like efficiency, cost-effectiveness, quality control, productivity. Another industrial concept that impinges strongly in educational institutions is the emphasis on management, particularly in the concepts of productivity, quotas, planning, and engineering. It is routine for schools to expect teachers and curriculum workers to operate within a framework of a cycle of activities determined and revised by a process of predetermined objectives and continuous testing. The so-called Tyler rationale, so resonant with our traditions of pragmatism, engineering, reductionism, and control, is so pervasive in the thinking of the educational profession that it qualifies as perhaps the most dramatic instance of cultural/professional hegemony in the field. It seems literally inconceivable to most educators to conceptualize education in any other way!

Obsession with control also gets expressed in school policy on "discipline," an interesting term which transfers an intellectual notion to a personal one in order to gain control over personal behavior. If schools do nothing else they deal with issues of personal control, and hence with political matters. Who can talk and under what conditions; when can we go to lunch and to the bathroom and under what conditions; who can use which language; who gets to decide what the rules are and who gets to interpret and enforce these rules—these are just some of the political matters that are a major part of everyday school life. The dominant and operating principle that shapes responses to these issues is one of school control; it is vital even in those times when students "win"; even then it demonstrates that it is the school that decides, the school that allows, lets, gives permission, waives, makes exceptions. It is students who petition, request, and plead. What is learned at every moment of contention and decision is that it is the school's policy to affirm the necessity for significant control and to vest that control in the school. Politics becomes equated with control, and the basic mechanism becomes mechanistic and paternal, a kind of bureaucratic monarchy, rule by fiat.

This political system sharply conflicts with our dedication to democratic principles which stress self-determination and a process for both sustaining autonomy and adjusting conflicts. Indeed, it has been said that the public schools are the only major public institution specifically charged with the responsibility for nourishing and sustaining democracy. John Dewey's work represents and synthesizes the work of political, educational, and social leaders to integrate democracy and education. Dewey conceptualized the school as the "laboratory" of democracy where students and teachers could wrestle with the challenges of the democratic experience, which led to the many experiments in the process of education in and for democracy. It is this tradition that underlies programs in student government, courses in civics, programs in citizenship education, and various projects in community awareness and involvement. There have been times in our history when the issues of "social studies and citizenship education" were an important part of public debate and controversy.

Alas, one of the casualties of the current concern for "excellence" is the school's responsibility to nourish and develop democracy. We have stopped worrying about voter apathy, and we seem much less concerned about how informed our students are about important social and political matters; we are apparently not as concerned as we once were about the Jeffersonian principle that democracy can thrive only with a well-informed and powerfully literate citizen. Our concern for efficiency, productivity, competition, and individual success seems to have eclipsed our commitment to pursuing our democratic heritage. Student governance has become an inert issue following the flurry of efforts by some students in the 1960s and 1970s to allow for serious student participation in school decision making. Courses and programs in citizenship education have less cogency than courses in computers, and worry about the responsibilities of citizenship has been overshadowed by worries about the necessity of raising test scores, or, as it is euphemistically called, "raising standards."

ETHNOCENTRISM/UNIVERSALISM

What we do see, however, is an increased concern for patriotism, a cry for the inculcation of love of, and loyalty to, our country. This shift in emphasis from the principles of our nationhood to the nation itself perhaps reflects a similar shift from control to domination. There surely is a need for control in any culture. Indeed culture is in part defined by order, and the problematics of control are what are at issue rather than control itself. As we individually and collectively become more insecure, anxious, and even paranoid, our boundaries on control tend to extend into and beyond the realm of domination. With the impulse to dominate comes the rationalization of our own superiority and specialness which helps legitimate blindness to the legitimate aspirations of others.

The increase in patriotism, more broadly defined as ethnocentrism, provides us with pride, esprit, and energy. The recent orgy of self-congratulations and self-indulgence that we experienced in the 1984 Olympics and the deep emotions stirred by the Iranian hostage situation are examples of the depths of feeling which can be touched when we decide to push our patriotic buttons. A perhaps more appealing instance of this fervor is the solidarity, discipline, and commitment shown in World War II. Yes, there was a great deal of profiteering, jingoism, and racism, and there was the reality that the war involved our battling for geopolitical advantage. Yet the nation was also inspired by a rhetoric of a people united to put an end to totalitarianism, genocide, and military expansion. It was a time when we appealed to universal and human rights to justify our actions and sacrifices, and even if we insist on being cynical, we would all have to agree that the government found it expedient to include universal, transnational nature considerations in its propaganda.

We have since come as a culture to accept the rhetoric of a universal humanity and of human rights that cut across national, cultural, class, and tribal lines. Moreover, we have also come to experience much more of the world as community because of mass media and jet-fueled transportation and to realize that nations are truly interdependent economically and politically. We have added to our vocabulary concepts like "the global village" and we sing songs with titles like "We Are the World."

Educators have responded to this emerging awareness with ideas and programs, such as global education and international education; and many schools have adopted requirements for some exposure to non-Western history. However compelling and sensible these ideas may be, they still are seen as marginal and peripheral, comparable perhaps to drug education. Not only do these efforts conflict with the movement of curriculum reductionism ("back to basics"), but they are out of sync with the current expression of our traditional isolationism and xenophobia. We rather glibly brand various political movements as "evil" or as "terrorist"; we try to repress our uneasiness about immigrants; we have significantly resisted bilingual education and have mounted campaigns to affirm English as the national language or at least as *the* language of instruction. Our pride in ourselves as a polyglot people turns into fear and rejection when we realize that we are on the verge of actually being a polyglot culture. Once again, we face serious conflict in profound values—here it is the clash between our genuine belief in a common humanity and a pride in our uniqueness. We want to value and affirm all cultures and peoples yet we find ourselves suspicious, envious, even resentful of others, including those who have accepted many of our own values, customs, and cultural forms (e.g., Japan).

The humiliation of the Vietnam war is instructive in this respect. First of all, the government, the military, and the nation seriously underestimated the skill, courage, audacity, resilience, and imagination of the Vietcong, a miscalculation that probably significantly contributed to the debacle. Moreover, our defeat led not to a recognition and acknowledgment, however grudging and tragic, of the brilliance of Vietcong military achievements but rather to a concern for our mistakes. Better to acknowledge our mistakes than their success. More broadly, the Vietnam experience has not seemed to have had the effect of raising our awareness and appreciation of either the capacities of other peoples or of our shared values and talents, not as people of different nations but as humans on the same planet.

HUMILITY/ARROGANCE

We entered that war with arrogance, but we did not leave it with humility. This arrogance takes many forms, one of which is an ethnocentrism or provincialism that emerges out of intense competition. Schools reflect this even in the presumably benign activity of school athletics. Pep rallies urge us emotionally and viscerally to express our "number one-ness" and to energize us to "kill" our arch rivals from crosstown. Cheerleaders not only exhort the team but also inflame the fans by chants with the familiar themes of how great "we" are, how terrible "they" are, and why therefore we are bound to stomp them into humiliating defeat.

There is another kind of arrogance, that of intellectual certainty. Sometimes this is smugness; sometimes it is blindness; and sometimes it is rigidity. Nowhere is intellectual arrogance more inappropriate than in an educational setting, since the basic canons of educational inquiry include an awareness of the complex and elusive nature of truth and the vital importance of openness to and awareness of emerging consciousness. Education involves inquiry, and inquiry requires care, caution, and humility in the face of the enormity of the task. And yet, schools teach us to get the "right" answers, to take true-or-false examinations, and to rely on encyclopedias. Ironically, the educational process confronts us with intellectual blind alleys, and with confused, contradictory, and discredited theories that are as much a part of the search for truth as are the triumphs of research. Although we may not actually remember a particular right answer, we have learned that there is a right answer. It is not so much that schools invest in particular theoretical formulations but rather that they do not anguish over the validity of conflicting ones. The extraordinary sameness of the school's curriculum is a powerful lesson; at the core of every school's curriculum are five subjects—English, social studies, science, a foreign language, and mathematics. In a nation of diversity and pluralism, with fifty states and with over twenty thousand separate school districts, we could reasonably expect some variation on what constitutes the core of a curriculum. The lack of truly significant variation is another strong example of cultural hegemony, of beliefs so strongly ingrained that they are beyond examination and criticism.

Certainly, as educators we know that the more we know, the less sure we become, and that there is a high correlation between an academic's intellectual strength and humility. We are not equating humility with modesty; to be humble is not to disregard one's achievements but to be awed and amazed at the intricacies and complexities of what is being studied. Instead of teaching students of the limitations of our research techniques and the extent of our ignorance, we have grossly distorted the state of intellectual life by utilizing a curriculum that has been accepted as true and valid. We need to not only teach what we claim to know but to speak to what we know we don't know. In *On Hearing Mahler's Ninth Symphony*, Lewis Thomas speaks to this issue:

> I suggest that the introductory courses in science, at all levels from grade school through college, be radically revised. Leave the fundamentals, the so-called basics, aside for a while, and concentrate the attention of all students on the things that are not known. You cannot possibly teach quantum mechanics without mathematics, to be sure, but you can describe the strangeness of the world opened up by quantum theory. Let it be known, early on, that there are deep mysteries, and profound paradoxes, revealed in their distant outlines, by the quantum. Let it be known that these can be approached more closely, and puzzled over, once the language of mathematics has been sufficiently mastered.
>
> Teach at the outset, before any of the fundamentals, the still imponderable puzzles of cosmology. Let it be known, as clearly as possible, by the youngest minds, that there are some things going on in the universe that lie beyond comprehension, and make it plain how little is known.
>
> Do not teach that biology is a useful and perhaps profitable science; that can come later. Teach instead that there are structures squirming inside all our cells, providing all the energy for living, that are essentially foreign creatures, brought in for symbiotic living a billion or so years ago, the lineal descendants of bacteria. Teach that we do not have the ghost of an idea how they got there, where they came from, or how they evolved to their present structure and function. The details of oxidative phosphorylation and photosynthesis can come later.
>
> Teach ecology early on. Let it be understood that the earth's life is a system of interliving, interdependent creatures, and that we do not understand at all how it works. The earth's environment, from the range of atmospheric gases to the chemical constituents of the sea, has been held in an almost unbelievably improbable state of regulated balance since life began, and the regulation of stability and balance is accomplished solely by the life itself, like the internal environment of an immense organism, and we do not know how that one works, even less what it means. Teach that. (1983:151–52)

This is a formulation in which humility is an asset and a strength rather than weakness or timidity. There is another sense in which we need to consider humility as an ally to our quest for a life of meaning. We need to be humble about our accomplishments and our specialness. We have a right to be proud of ourselves as a people who have struggled for justice and freedom, as a people who have enriched our lives by technical advances such as the telephone and the automobile, and as a people who have devised a technology that has improved our health with such products as penicillin and snowplows. As a people, however, we need to be humbled by the reality that we have enslaved and tortured other humans, that we have put our health and environment in peril by dint of human effort, and that we live in a world where huge numbers of people—tens of millions of them—live the hell of starvation, pestilence, and degradation. With all our genius, with all our brilliance, and yes, with all our education, we as a people face the real possibility of extinction by several scenarios such as war, starvation, and ecological catastrophe.

There is yet another facet to the importance of humility to the educational process. It is certainly part of our faith as Americans, as pragmatists, engineers, optimists, and responsible people searching for existential meaning, that we can and should intervene in nature to create a joyful and abundant society. However, we have reason to be humbled by those efforts. We have encountered viruses which adapt to overcome antibiotics and pesticides, and we have seen disastrous ecological effects at attempts to change the natural rhythms of the life cycle. As basic and profound as these humbling experiences are, none is more basic than the humbling that has accompanied the loss of a divine perspective. With the Enlightenment came the attempts to replace religious and spiritual frameworks with human ones. We have developed theories of natural law, elaborated a variety of orientations with humanism at the core, and have in the process created a number of paradigms of immense significance, vitality, and wisdom (e.g., Marxism, Freudian thought, and existentialism). However, as Richard Rubenstein's (1975) *The Cunning of History* so tragically demonstrates, the substitution of the state for God, and the absence of a law higher than man's, led, however inadvertently and unintendedly, to Auschwitz. Left to our devices, we have failed miserably to replace the myths of creation, meaning, and redemption that we have been so clever and brilliant in discrediting. We have become intensely aware of one of our most fiendishly clever inventions—namely, profound alienation. We first obliterated our path and now curse the fact that we are lost, although we still insist that we can create better, faster, newer paths. However, it is not only the paths that have been blurred; more importantly, in the frantic effort to develop new paths we have forgotten our destination.

Ironically, the only significant movement to involve religious concerns with the schools does not at all respond to the intellectual necessity for a posture of awe and reverence of the mysteries of life and of the universe. Rather, many politicians have seized upon school prayer as an issue in the arrogance that God and America have a special relationship and that the spiritual search is to be reified by ritualistic affirmation of a particular and narrow religion. This movement is another example of our anti-intellectual impulse. Since serious spiritual inquiry is as suspect and threatening as serious intellectual inquiry, we are deflected to the formulistic, distracting, and ultimately less threatening issue of prayer. Serious religious and intellectual inquiry cannot tolerate arrogance, nor can it co-exist with the smugness and satisfaction of status quoism. Humility ought not to lead to modesty and timidity, as we have said, but quite the opposite, for it is the recognition of how little we know and have accomplished that ought to lead us to protest, to stir, to excite, and to act. It is arrogance that leads to stillness and silence (and vice versa), and humility that leads to agitation and response.

The last aspect of humility I wish to discuss does merge into the area of timidity, indecision, and fear. There is the kind of humility, more aptly called loss of faith, that comes from those who are unable to find meaning and direction in life. We speak directly to the phenomenon of alienation—the term often applied to a series of feelings and attitudes involving a rejection of traditional creation and meaning myths (e.g., as exemplified in Western religions), a sense of life as empty, absurd, devoid of meaning, and an inability to identify with natural or social forces which produces feelings of anxiety, loneliness, and dread. Alienation also gets expressed in the fragmentation of lives which is reflected in the concepts of role, role differentiation, and role conflict. We divide our time and consciousness into various compartments: we have work time and leisure time; attitudes toward family which are different from attitudes toward colleagues, ideals that we can express in the living room but not in the workplace. Religion is to be private and, for that matter, so probably should politics; when we do express our religious sentiments it is to be done in a particular place at a particular time, and political opinions are most appropriately expressed on election day. We are bored (if not appalled) by those who try to bring political and moral issues into discussion of popular culture or the fine arts. The combination of the loss of faith, resulting from the principles and process of the Enlightenment, the fragmentation that emerges from industrialism and bureaucracy has many of us searching for coherence and meaning in a state of bewilderment and frustration. We surely do not seek and value this alienation; indeed, our literature and social criticism is full of descriptions of the destructive and paralyzing nature of a consciousness of alienation, anomie, and despair.

Schools, however, do more to nurture than to overcome alienation. They are a major source of the fragmentation and absurdity: "You just can't study what interests you"; "If you can't pass math you can't play basketball"; "Work hard now for your future"; "When you get into the real world . . ."; etc. The harsh separation of courses and subjects not only is of a dubious nature intellectually but tends to perpetuate the myth of hard and fast intellectual compartments. Having a separate physical education program actually accentuates the false dualism of mind and body; the separation of English and social studies serves the same process in a parallel way for "fact" and "fiction." The stress on pleasing teacher with "right answers" reifies and externalizes knowledge, which deprives students from articulating their own personal knowledge and their relationships with other knowledge. Urging students to work hard and do well in areas in which they have little or no interest or ability is a way of encouraging mindless, instrumental behavior.

ALIENATION/COMMITMENT

Perhaps it is more what schools do *not* do in this area which is more damaging and problematic than what they do. In its rigid and manic concerns with facilitating the individual pursuit of socioeconomic success and preserving the existing social and political frameworks, the schools come to see their curriculum and other practices as instrumental to those goals. Indeed, it is the techniques themselves that have come to be revered rather than that which has ultimate significance. Most teachers and administrators will deny that material success represents their conception of the Ultimately Significant, while at the same time it is likely they will strongly defend as realistic and reasonable helping students to adapt to and succeed in the current culture. However, such discussions usually end when the question is raised of what they do believe to be of ultimate significance or when the basic issue is posited as the necessity to integrate the ultimate with the educational process. My belief, however, is that the inability of such a conversation to go on does not mean that educators do not view these issues as important and relevant, but rather it represents conflict and confusion on the issues themselves. In fact, the major crisis for educators is the same as it is for the culture—namely, our inability to make lasting and profound moral commitments that can energize and legitimize our day-to-day lives. Educators mirror the pain and anguish that are consequences of alienation; they are aware of its corrosive and corrupting potentialities and are often sensitive to historical, intellectual, and ideological dimensions of this crisis. They are also very much aware of the dangers of the glib and facile "solutions" to the problem that come mostly from the far Right. Many educators are aware of the complexities involved in finding meaning (some of them are humble), and most are conscious of the political fallout that comes from making sharp shifts in the school program (many of them are timid).

The culture and its educators are faced with a very serious problem given their alternatives. They can go on as they have, and accept the reality that to do so is not only to fail to stem alienation but actually to deepen and widen it. The alternative of taking active steps to overcome despair and emptiness perforce involves the search for, and the affirmation of, an overarching moral and spiritual framework that provides a center of meaning for the culture. This alternative involves serious political, personal, and intellectual risks given the division of opinion, the diversity of subcultures and religious affiliations, and the volatility and seriousness of the issues. However, it is my conviction that we as educators must address these problems as part of our professional ethic, and that our response should be one of humility not of avoidance, of courage not of arrogance, and of commitment not of alienation. We simply cannot allow the educational process, which has at its deepest roots a concern for meaning, to become instead a mechanism for pursuing a way of life we already know is rich with the possibilities of despair, absurdity, and destruction. Educators must come to see themselves not as apologists for this way of life, nor technicians in its service, but as moral leaders who can with others continue humanity's struggle to create a vision of meaning and fulfillment.

DISPLACEMENT/COMPLACENCY

As I have indicated, such a responsibility involves great risks; although we must also remember that *not* accepting this responsibility is equally risky. A major problem in assuming this responsibility is that it clearly involves disrupting the smugness and disquieting the self-deception. In this problem we again meet paradoxical traditions and values in our culture, for although we value "peace and quiet," calmness, serenity, stability, and the status quo, we are also a culture of protest, dissent, and even revolution. We are, after all, a people who continue to be strongly influenced by the Puritans, who saw themselves in the line of the biblical prophets with the responsibility to storm against the transgressions of the culture. It is not only that our political tradition has revealed the necessity and value of disruption (recall Jefferson's comment that we needed to have a series of revolutions), but our personal experience and psychology are sensitive to the dangers of complacency and of standing pat. Our ambivalence about the importance of disruption is well described in Janet Gunn's (1984) paper on the works of Flannery O'Connor. In this paper, Gunn characterizes O'Connor as one who believes that before redemption must come the pain of displacement, the agony that is the inevitable consequence of confronting seriously and concretely the requirements of a redemptive life. These requirements include a jolting awareness of the "sin" or the gap between our highest aspirations and how we actually live. Gunn points out that the major figures in O'Connor's stories time and again are given the opportunity for redemption as a consequence of seriously disruptive events—a sudden death, a kidnapping, the intrusion of a new powerful person into a hitherto stable community/family.

Teachers also know of the educative power and significance of blowing up the ice on the lake of complacency and are also very conscious how peaceful and untroubled life on Lake Complacency can be. They also know that the surrounding community does not like to have its calm interrupted by explosions, however muffled and remote. Educators must come to recognize that the unexploded ice is a menace, that it can choke the life around it by chilling the hopes for a new and refreshed life.

FAITH/REASON

Making commitments not only involves disruption but also requires that we have sufficient confidence and investment in those commitments to sustain us in the difficult struggle to act on them. If we accept the vital importance of setting our work within a set of moral commitments, then we must remember why it is so difficult to make them. We must have compassion for each other and accept as part of our assumption that the matter of making such commitments is of great significance to each of us and that it is very likely that many of us have struggled mightily with this issue. Making moral commitments is not the same as deciding to get more exercise or resolving to read the newspaper more carefully. The difficulty in making such commitments stems from very deeply rooted phenomena, such as the Enlightenment (e.g., faith in rationality and science, revelation of corruption in religious and moral institutions); the cynical exploitation of religious and moral beliefs; the failure of religious and moral institutions to respond to moral crises in the society); and the elaboration of the hidden forces that shape our lives (e.g., as drawn out by Freud and Marx). It was first said by Nietzsche, and more recently by theologians, that God is dead. Michael Harrington (1983) has elaborated on that metaphor in *The Politics at God's Funeral*, in which he discusses man's effort to fill that void with humanly constructed rather than revealed cosmologies.

There are, of course, many who have experienced a revealed God, and they represent a group of increasing significance and power. There is an even larger group who are open and perhaps eager for revelation. We as a people yearn for powerful religious experiences and many of us are open to the power of the nonrational. Yet we are a stubbornly rational people and are committed to approaching truth by the path of science, logic, and rigorous thinking. In fact, our rational sophistication has developed to the point that many of us are persuaded scientifically and logically of the limitations of science and logic. We have been reminded of the necessity to make value and moral judgments that transcend scientific and technical criteria and have learned that much of science rests on a number of at least so far unverified (or even unverifiable) assumptions. It is our physicists who have become our modern mystics with their talk of mysterious forces in an expanding universe of "black holes" and "quarks" that probably began and will end not with a whimper but with a "big bang."

Schools take on the mantle of science and rationality even when they absurdly and crudely distort their essences. Their pretentiousness includes their claims to be intellectual, to value the rigorous demands of scholarship. It is clear that schools have botched this effort (e.g., a recent study estimates that less than 50 percent of Americans are more than marginally literate), but I want here to mention that there is another educational orientation that they have yet to botch because they have not seriously addressed it—namely, the issue of reasoning from a faith, of helping people to consider the major question that transcends science. We are not here opposing faith to reason but rather examining the foundation and underpinnings of reason, that which provides its roots and substance. Nor do we wish to glibly equate faith with creed or a belief structure; faith here is meant to be closer to the concept of trust than to belief.

William Fowler's *Stages of Faith* is an eloquent and valuable source for the description and analysis of this phenomenon. At one point he describes faith as "a person's way of showing himself or herself in relation to others against a background of shared meaning and purpose" (1981:4). In another section of the book he cites H. Richard Niebuhr's (1960) notion that faith emerges out of an initial concern for caring and trusting and "the search for an overarching integrating and grounding trust in a center of value and power sufficiently worthy to give our lives unity and meaning" (1981:5). Thus faith has more to do with in what and to whom do we commit our trust and our loyalty. Fowler quotes Wilfred Cantwell Smith (1963) on this distinction: "Faith, at once, deeper and more personal than religion, is the person's or group's way of responding to transcendent values and power as perceived and grasped through the forms of the cumulative tradition. Faith and religion, in this view, are reciprocal" (1981:9).

Fowler posits a concept of "faithing" as a mode of knowledge and argues that people differ not so much on the basis of having faith or not having faith, but in the nature and quality of their "faithing" process. "Faith is the forming of images of and relations to that which exacts qualitatively different initiatives in our lives than those that occur in strictly human relations" (1981:33). Smith's pointed question gives further insight to this notion: "What hope and what ground of hope animate you and give shape to the force field of your life and to how you move in it?" (quoted in Fowler 1981:14).

This is clearly an elusive concept, but I believe that most people have struggled with this phenomenon with or without a mediating conceptual language. However, it is not only that we want to have deep faith and thus find it very difficult to commit ourselves to some faithing process in authentic and satisfying ways, but we have difficulty in the language of faith. The schools have either abandoned or ridiculed other paths to truth than conventional (if not outdated) scientific models, but more significantly they have totally ignored the search for wisdom. We can tell a lot about a culture and its institutions by the quality of its hypocrisies. As we have stressed over and over again, it seems quite clear that the schools' major preoccupation is with perpetuating a system based on the individual, competitive struggle for material success. This goal, however, is masked in the rhetoric of concern for knowledge and truth, and hence the schools do not even pretend to seek higher truth, higher meaning, or wisdom. Indeed, the term "wise" has come to have a pejorative connotation as in schools which do not tolerate "wise guys."

We as a people have come to see that reason and knowledge can be used evilly even as we either deny the existence or are confused about the meaning of the concept of evil. We prefer wisdom and knowledge at a time when the concept of wisdom is discounted in educational institutions. There surely has been a knowledge and information explosion which, ironically enough, is presented as a problem. Sometimes the problem is defined as a technical one (e.g., access and dissemination); however, the essential problems are ones of interpretation, significance, and its implications. We search for context and yet our educational energies are directed to filling in the blanks. Schools present education less as an endeavor to create a vision of meaning than as a paint-by-numbers exercise.

This narrow approach to education surely undermines major tenets of serious scholarship such as care, precision, uncertainty, humility, awe, and passion. Scholars are often people who are very much in touch with their matter of faith, and it is that which accounts for the devotion and dedication of their work. Scholars typically do not equate scholarship with knowledge, facts, and data, but rather they pursue models, theories, and schemata that give order and meaning to otherwise random observations. What the schools have done is more of a perversion of scholarship in their stress on textbooks, right answers, minimum standard performance, and external controls.

If this distorted notion of education does not serve scholarship and the pursuit of truth, it does serve other, more pressing items on the school's agenda. Pseudoscience, narrowly defined academic goals, and predetermined answers are antithetical to serious educational inquiry, but they are excellent ways of facilitating the emphasis on grading and competition. They are effective control mechanisms and give a legitimate flavor to the hierarchical power structure in schools. Thus, schools are not terribly interested in faith or reason, truth or wisdom, but use them as part of the rhetoric of justifying the direction of enormous energy to the rather vulgar duty of helping people to make money and raise their status (thereby, no doubt, also helping to catch up with Taiwan and to thwart Soviet expansionism).

This, as the old saying goes, leaves the culture up the creek without a paddle. As we drift toward the currents of destruction, we search for stability and a new course. This predicament is not likely to be resolved entirely, as some suggest, by new technical or scientific breakthroughs, though they will help. The more fundamental and much more difficult task is that of setting the course, of having a clearer sense of direction that can give us the courage, the energy, and the hope to make the effort and sacrifices worthwhile.

What I have tried to present in this chapter can be described as an essay on cultural confusion, self-deception, and self-defeat. We have seen that we are confused and perplexed by the inherent dilemmas of making moral choices. It has been pointed out that the difficulty in moral decision making is actually less severe in choosing between right and wrong (it is clear that we *want* to choose right though aware that to do so may involve other negative consequences) than having to choose between and among rights. Moral confusion comes with the territory, and yet the schools have done precious little to help us to cope with the confusion. Indeed, we continue to exacerbate the confusion by our contradictory behavior—our insistence on wanting to behave righteously while not being able, willing, to do so.

SELF-DECEPTION/PROFESSIONAL RESPONSIBILITY

This is the point at which confusion and doubt intersect with self-deception or what Sartre calls "bad faith" (1956:67). Walter Brueggemann, a prominent contemporary American theologian, candidly reflects on his own personal experience of this intersection:

> As I reflect on ministry and especially my ministry, I know in the hidden places that the real restraints are not in my understanding or in receptivity of other people. Rather the restraints come from my own unsureness about this perception. I discover that I am as bourgeois and obdurate as any to whom I might minister. I like most others am unsure that the royal road is not the best and the royal community the one which governs the real "goodies." I, like most of the others, am unsure that the alternative community inclusive of the poor, hungry, and grieving is really the

wave of God's future. We are indeed "like people, like priests" (Hos. 4:9).
That very likely is the situation among many of us in ministry and there
is no unanguished way out of it. It does make clear to us that our ministry
will always be practiced through our conflicted selves. (1978:111–12)

This honest and courageous statement stands as a model for both
anticipating and dealing with the human inevitability of self-deception. The phenomenon of self-deception is an intriguing and elusive
one since it involves the paradox of our being aware of our own
duplicity (i.e., why knowingly we deceive ourselves). Herbert Fingarette
(1969) deals extensively and insightfully with this paradox in *Self-
Deception*. He suggests that a way out of this paradox lies in a full
understanding of three major concepts: "spelling out," "engagement,"
and "avowal." "Spelling-out" has to do with being explicit, thorough,
and forthcoming about one's beliefs and values (1969:39), while "engagement" refers to one's active participation in life (1969:40). "Avowal"
is the process of explicitly defining one's self in a purposeful and
responsive way (1969:70). Fingarette explains a self-deceiver as one
who "will be provoked into a kind of engagement which, in part or
in whole, the person cannot *avow* as *his* engagement, for to avow it
would apparently lead to such intensely disruptive, distressing consequences as to be unmanageably destructive to the person. The crux
of the matter here is the *unacceptability* of the engagement to the
person" (1969:87).

Note the significance of taking responsibility and the risks that are
involved, namely, to the point of considering them to be destructive.
It is this fear, according to Fingarette, which leads some to self-deception, to the refusal to spell out. "The policy of refusing to spell out
one's engagement is the most 'visible' feature of self-deception. Though
highly visible, it is a concomitant of a far more fundamental man-
oeuvre. The self-deceiver is one who is in some way engaged in the
world but who disavows the engagement, who will not acknowledge
it even to himself as his. That is, self-deception turns upon the personal
identity one accepts *rather than the beliefs one has*" (1969:66–67; Italics
added).

Self-deception not only involves denial, fear, avoidance, and fragmentation, but it is also ultimately self-defeating. When we deceive
ourselves and our community, we undermine our efforts to act upon
our deepest beliefs. We can, of course, be cynical and consider our
self-deception to be part of the sublimation process—we need to cover
our self-serving needs for control, domination, greed, and lust. It is
also possible to psychologize this problem, to see self-deception as
neurotic or pathological. One could also despair at the extraordinary
entanglements of life, shrug our collective shoulders, and press the
c'est la vie button. However, as Fingarette points out, the consequences
of self-deception are enormous:

Purity of heart is to will one thing and to will it absolutely—it is the self as the unity of the entire individual acknowledged as self; it is thus the finding of the eternal, of that which endures change and even within change; it is the condition of the truly ethical life, and ultimately of the truly saving religious life. Insofar as the person fails even to avow, or disavows his individual engagements, he is to that extent immersed in the particular and immediate, has abdicated the harmonious unity and synthesis of the ethical, and is in despair. It is in the nature of despair that it is double-mindedness. Whether we view the self-deceiver as (inwardly) evasive in a clever way towards himself, or whether we view him externally as nothing but engagement in the temporal, the particular, the immediate, there is a fundamental multipliness in his existence. In either case, he is seen as the victim, within time, of particularity, rather than as the eternal surveyor of time and multiplicity. There is thus in self-deception a genuine subversion of personal agency and, for this reason in turn, a subversion of moral capacity. (196:141)

THE RESPONSIBILITY OF EDUCATORS IN A TIME OF CULTURAL CRISIS

As educators we must have the courage to confront this human impulse and necessity for self-deception and have the wisdom to discern its destructiveness. We have special responsibilities to be sensitive to the psychological and moral pressures to deny or discount the harsh realities of our professional lives.

As educators we must also confront ourselves as both oppressor and oppressed. We must have the courage not only to examine the nature and impact of the culture but also to consider how we as individuals reflect the values and norms of the culture. As educators we often are the system, even as we are both its cause and effect. As the contemporary German theologian Dorothée Soelle puts it in referring to those in the ministry:

It is not enough to criticize property rights and the import duty imposed on manufactured goods from developed countries, so long as we, as "powerless" individuals, are not able to clarify how we are entangled in the general structures, that is, how we profit from the structures and how we conform to the introverted norms that we regard as self-evident— for example, the norms of achievement, consumerism, reasons of state— and pass them on to others, even when we reject them privately and verbally. A criticism of society which does not take account of this introversive mechanism, and which therefore does not detect and give expression to the capitalist or the concentration camp guard that is in each one of us, but instead creates enemies in hostile projections, I consider political propaganda, plain and simple, and not a political interpretation of the gospel. (1974:92)

This is by no means to say that education can "solve" these problems, nor that educators are the only or even the most important people in the process of dealing with the cultural crisis. I am saying that there is very definitely an educational aspect to the crisis and I am reiterating my faith that serious educational inquiry can in fact provide the necessary, if not sufficient, resources to re-create our world. I will also insist that educators must respond to these concerns within the canons of our professional ethics: we are educators not indoctrinators; we persuade, we do not force; we are primarily social and moral leaders, not partisan politicians; we examine political, religious, and moral issues, we do not promulgate political, religious, and moral dogma.

And yet, in this matter of professional ethics we once more confront the crux of our crisis: the difficulty of creating a vital, authentic and energizing vision of meaning in a context of significant diversity, pluralism, division, skepticism, dogmatism, and even nihilism. As educators we must simultaneously address these issues personally and communally as we profess to give our students insight into these questions. To avoid the issues is to further the confusion, heighten the self-deception, and contribute to our downfall.

The rest of this book represents one educator's effort to develop an educational response to the issues as I have so far described and defined them. In order to present specific educational suggestions and ideas, I have found it necessary to offer a broader theoretical framework which informs the notions of curriculum and instruction which are presented in the final chapter. This framework represents an effort to develop language and concepts that can provide a working consensus needed to facilitate creative and constructive responses, but not enough to foster uniformity and standardization. We must, therefore, begin with the fundamental issues of spiritual and moral values and necessarily confront this extremely sensitive, crucial, and volatile area. It is certainly a risky and dangerous zone filled with land mines, but since it is also populated by time bombs, avoiding the area is at least as dangerous.

4

A Religious and Moral Framework for American Education

The question ... for any theology is whether it makes men more capable of love, whether it encourages or obstructs the liberation of the individual and the community.

Dorothée Soelle, Political Theology

Men and women cannot decently live by demythologies alone.

Michael Harrington, The Politics at God's Funeral

Man's capacity for justice makes democracy possible; but man's inclination to injustice makes democracy necessary.

Reinhold Niebuhr

If God did not exist we would have to invent him.

Voltaire

If God did exist we would have to abolish Him.

Mikhail Bakunin

RELIGIOUS, MORAL, AND MYTHIC LANGUAGE

My description and analysis of current American culture has emphasized its interpenetration with our public schools. A great deal of this analysis has a religious and moral character to it, and in this chapter I will elaborate on the rationale and nature of our religious and moral interpretations. In addition, I will present and propose a set of religious and moral principles that I hope can serve to inform our educational policies and practices. It is my general position that education is at root a moral endeavor and that its present crisis is best seen as such in order to reflect not only on the educational process but on the larger culture as well.

Although this is not the place to attempt a definitive or even thorough explication of what is meant by the terms "moral" and "religious," it is quite appropriate to deal with the ways I am using these terms. In this work I am very much aware of the powerful and varied connotative meanings these words evoke and will try to be sensitive to their inherent complexities and subtleties. For purposes of clarifying my own meaning, however, I take *moral* to be a term that focuses on principles, rules, and ideas that are related to human relationships, to how we deal with each other and with the world. Moral can be used prescriptively (e.g., people *should* love each other) as well as descriptively (e.g., she treats him with little respect) In both cases the concern is for the attitudes, values, and behaviors that constitute one's way of being with (other people). Moral questions and issues are largely people-to-people ones, and are hence of a social and political nature, but they also extend to how we deal with all our neighbors (i.e., the animal kingdom, the environment, and nature). Moral theories and codes serve to regulate and legitimize proper ways of dealing with these human relationships.

I am using *religious* in reference to ideas, principles, and tenets that have to do with our relations with forces beyond the known world. Religious questions are concerned with our relations with the cosmos and with the unknown or unknowable. Religions serve to explain fundamental questions of origin, meaning, and ultimacy and to generate human responses to these formulations.

Religion and moral orientations differ in how these two realms relate to each other. Some religions (e.g., Judaism) seek to strongly integrate moral and ethical behavior with basic religious belief, while others (e.g., Hinduism) put far greater stress on metaphysical and spiritual concerns. There are, of course, moral theories which are not based on a particular set of religious beliefs—for example, the notions of natural philosophy and humanism rest on assumptions that speak to the human or natural determination of ethical behaviors and norms. It is also important to note that we are for the most part using these terms heuristically to facilitate communication. We also note the ubiquity of these concepts across time and space; indeed there are those who maintain that *the* essential human characteristic is humanity's interest in and capacity for creating religious and moral images, metaphors, and schemata.

However, their ubiquity in no way means consensus on either their meaning or their significance. It is obvious, for example, that there are formulations which reject religious inquiry as spurious and distracting ("religion is the opiate of the masses"), just as there are those who reject moral theories as magical thinking ("we need to go beyond freedom and dignity"). Indeed, as educators and citizens we must confront the possibility of moral and religious language becoming reified through the process of critical neglect and reductionism. We will be emphasizing such formulations as moral and religious *dimensions*, *aspects*, and *concerns*, and although we urge our colleagues to unashamedly celebrate certain religious and moral principles, we will (and so urge that other public educators) not capitalize on them, that is, we will not, and cannot, endorse or promote any particular religious tradition (Judaism, Christianity, Buddhism), never mind any particular denomination (e.g., Orthodox Judaism, Unitarianism, Shiite Moslem), but will seek to support and sustain key principles and formulations that cut across religions, sects, denominations, and ideologies.

We need also to point out the difference between "religion" as a theoretical construct and its institutional manifestations (i.e., religion is not synonymous with mosque, temple, church, synagogue). It is a difference that parallels the distinction between education and schooling, in that the institution of schools, although clearly connected to education, has an important number of organizational, political, fiscal, and cultural concerns which are at best only indirectly related to strictly educational concerns. There are people who feel strongly that schools do not provide "real" education, just as there are people who see the church, synagogue, mosque, or temple as the wrong place to find a truly religious experience. I do not in any way want to deal with a significant critique of institutionalized religion (although it will be very difficult to totally avoid this) but instead wish to focus on religious and moral ideas and images. I very much intend, however, to focus on a critique of institutional education, particularly in its congruity with "true" educational concerns. One can be passionate about the value of education and still (or because of that) be highly critical of the schools. In the same spirit, I ask that those who are highly critical of organized and institutional religion be open to the power and significance of religious ideas, metaphors, concepts, and insights.

Our culture includes in its plethora of significant ideas and orientations a number of formulations that can be and are named religious and moral. This is a fact of cultural life; for better or worse our human experience is, in part, defined by its effort to formulate ideas and practices of ultimate meaning involving cosmological and metaphysical concepts. These formulations generate further formulations, as well as controversy, hostility, counterformulations, and, equally significant, indifference. We need also to point out that twentieth-century America is a culture that not only has a variety of theoretical orientations toward religious and moral issues but is also a highly diverse, pluralistic, complex society with a great number of constituencies and interest groups in perpetual conflict over the protection of their position. We have disagreements and disputes, some friendly, some academic, but some others are much less friendly and much more real. Even the "academic" disagreements can, become volatile since they touch upon fundamental conceptions of who and how we are to be. No set of issues is as explosive, controversial, emotional, and threatening as moral and religious disputes. None is more vital.

Toward the Development of a Myth

The analysis in the first three chapters reveals contradictions and confusions over our basic values marked by self-deception and self-destructiveness. We argue that the cultural and educational crises are rooted in these and other moral ambiguities and confusions, and we further point that these moral difficulties emerge from our inability to deal with the even broader and deeper religious or metaphysical bases of moral, political, and social policies. We take the position that this can be conceptualized as our failure to develop an overarching mythos of meaning, purpose, and ultimacy that can guide us in the creation of a vision of the good, true, and beautiful life and in the work that this vision creates for us. It is our position, furthermore, that as educators we must actively participate in the process of creating that vision as part of our responsibility—a responsibility which coincides with our vital need for such a vision to provide directions for our professional activities.

As educators, however, our responsibilities, are not simply to promulgate visions but to inquire into them, not just to study them but to be critical and discerning of them—to be contributor, critic, and celebrator. Hence, we cannot in good educational conscience avoid the serious and volatile disputes on religious and moral matters because they are controversial, complex, and outrageously perplexing. Quite the contrary: *because* they are so important and *since* they beg for awareness, understanding, clarification, and insight, they are central to significant educational inquiry. Both the culture and educators are caught in a vicious circle of doubt, confusion, and skepticism that enters a realm of despair and frustration, which leads to destructiveness and nihilism, which in turn leads to hope and prayer for clear visions which are quickly subjected to criticism and doubt. So, as educators we have the dual responsibility to examine that circle *and* to be part of the process that can transform that static circle into a spiral of movement. The crux of the dilemma is to paradoxically have a vision prior to having one, to be able to break the circle without a sense of direction and without breaking faith with our intellectual and political heritage.

I believe, to change the metaphor, that we educators and academics have been playing a "stalemate" game, a game which stresses "defense" where the basic strategy is to keep others from "scoring" by harassment of a close and constant nature. Such games usually have their action mostly in the middle of the field and in a narrow range of action which consists of modest efforts at developing an offense, which immediately and aggressively are undermined and disorganized by a pressing defense galvanized primarily by an intense desire to keep the "offense" out of "scoring range." When it comes to contests of alternative educational orientations, or when there is an agon of moral/religious frameworks, we usually wind up with a scoreless tie. The academic community has done far better with its oppositional critical capacities than with its creative responsibilities.

This is not to say that we should in any way ease or soften our efforts to be critical, skeptical, wary, precise, and thoughtful. We must, however, complement these skills with the creative and imaginative arts that can provide us with richer, truer, more satisfying schema, models, visions, and paradigms. Criticisms are by themselves necessary but not sufficient conditions for the development of such visions, theories, and orientations. In fact, in some ways the quality of our critical capacities may have been "too" effective in the sense that they have undermined some of the foundations of our civilization. Our ability to provide equally powerful replacements for those foundations is heightened and perpetuated by a belief (tragically mistaken in my estimation) that it is impossible for us as a people to forge a consensus of religious and moral beliefs that is specific enough to be significantly energizing and meaningful. Our despair becomes full when we come to believe this pessimistic view, especially when the opposite is the fundamental requirement for any hope for survival and cultural prosperity. It is my strong belief that we have exaggerated the difficulty of creating that consensus and underestimated the powerful cultural forces that seek to pursue (as opposed to impose) moral and religious community. It is the purpose of this book to facilitate and further the creation of such a search for consensus by indicating important areas of potential convergence. I do not believe, however, that this process will at all be facilitated by failing to note the enormity of the difficulties and perplexities in such an undertaking. I call on colleagues to be open to *both* our differences and similarities, to convergence and divergence, to criticism and creation.

For me, the most promising aspect of this effort is the general, if implicit, agreement across religious orientations, classes, and ideologies that it is vital and valuable to have some kind of model of ultimate meaning—some way of conceptualizing a response to those critical questions of where did we come from, who are we, and where are we going. It is perhaps gratuitous to point out that there are enormous differences among these conceptualizations, but it is imperative to note that we very much want to, and in fact do, respond to a felt need to provide *some* narrative explanation. Some prefer to call these conceptualized narratives our creation, meaning, and destiny myths, which are stories designed to help us connect our lives in the everyday world to a cosmology. Myths provide us with stories of creation, meaning, and fate populated by personifications, metaphors, and parables, although they are also taken literally by some. Myths provide bridges between the Other and us—between the Absent and the present, between mystery and what is known, between heaven and earth, religion and morality, religion and politics, and so on. Another way of formulating our cultural and educational crisis is to say that we no longer have myths and seem incapable of creating, sustaining, and energizing them. Furthermore, it can be said that although we differ on what constitutes a legitimate source of myth and which myths are acceptable, we must recognize that there is a great deal of agreement on the value and need to have such myths. By myth we obviously do not mean ideas that are demonstrably false or wrong but rather imaginative constructions of the meaning of universe and our place in it. We can and should continue to debate the complexities of the concept of religion and myth, and we can and should continue to study the amazing range of mythic and religious images and beliefs. We can and should, at the same time, recognize the strength and persistence of this ancient, continuous, and ongoing impulse to create meaning systems that give order and direction to our lives. We must not deny that reality by obfuscating arguments about the nature of myths, religions, and moral theories, and neither must we be seduced by soothing and reassuring myths that lull us into uncritical docility.

The richness of our culture means in effect that we are rich in our mythic traditions, or, put another way, that many metaphysical, religious, and moral traditions have found expression in our lives. We are a polyglot nation which speaks several sublanguages and blends a number of unique histories. Cutting across the score of ethnicities, peoples, cultures, and traditions, one can sense a number of transcendent values which amount to elements of a broadly held common heritage—a heritage of common, if not universal, pride and aspiration. This heritage has both commonality and divergence, and, indeed, part of our heritage includes a commitment to such a tension. We can broadly categorize this heritage into three parts: political, moral, and intellectual. We will deal with the notion of a religious heritage after describing what I consider to be aspects of our belief systems which, comparatively speaking, have a greater degree of community.

Political Heritage

Our political heritage clearly involves a deep and enduring commitment to democratic principles. As a nation we identify ourselves primarily as a democratic society, as reflected in our major celebrations and in our most cherished images. There is a common rhetoric of the American Revolution being waged on behalf of democratic principles as enunciated in the Declaration of Independence and their epiphany expressed in the Constitution of the United States of America. The powerful and enduring mythical figures of our political pantheon (e.g., Washington, Jefferson, Madison, Jackson, and Lincoln) are presented as heroic defenders and nourishers of democracy. Robert Bellah (1975) and others have singled out Abraham Lincoln (especially in his Gettysburg Address) as perhaps the one best able to conceptualize the image of America, the land of Democracy, in mythic and religious language. It has often been pointed out that America was perhaps the first nation to be deliberately founded on a set of principles—principles which are primarily democratic.

The democratic heritage celebrates a number of political principles—preservation of civil rights and, above all else, the principle of government requiring the consent of the governed. Here we can see most clearly the close relationship between the political and moral, since democratic principles rest primarily on a major moral principle: the dignity and autonomy of the individual.

Moral Heritage

Our moral heritage, in addition to a commitment to the sanctity of the individual, includes an intense concern for justice, equality, forgiveness, mercy, and, most important, an aspiration for a community infused with love. We are a culture that celebrates and reveres such expressions of moral principles as the Ten Commandments, the Sermon on the Mount, the Declaration of Independence, the Rights of Man, and the United Nations Declaration of Human Rights. We revere the historical Moses, Jesus, and Buddha, the lives of Gandhi, Schweitzer, and Martin Luther King, insofar as they represent the forces of love, equality, justice, compassion, and redemption. Our recent responses to African famine and oppression reflect how deeply these moral commitments lie within us and the degree to which we seek outlets for our urge to reach out to the troubled and vulnerable.

Intellectual Heritage

The intellectual heritage that we cherish finds its roots in the Greek passion for the free pursuit of truth. We value freedom of inquiry and expression, we revere creativity and originality, and we urge ourselves to be open and tolerant in the force of conflicting and differing ideas.

We also revere careful, precise, and thorough scholarship; esteem a strong critical capacity; and cherish those who express themselves eloquently. We admire clarity as well as the provocative and the evocative. We recognize that the paths to truth are many, that they sometimes crisscross, and that we need to both challenge these paths as well as affirm them. Our culture values knowledge and the pursuit of knowledge, and indeed part of our myth (or faith) is that knowledge or truth or science or whatever it is called can help make us free. Many have come to regard the myth of science (read: knowledge) as the worthy successor to the myth of an omniscient God—that is, it is science that can unlock the mysteries of the universe, as well as science and knowledge that can provide us with a life of abundance, peace, and joy.

Here we can see the outlines of how these heritages merge into each other and evoke the outlines of a grand consensus myth. We are a culture that has as part of its heritage a commitment to the development of a life of justice, freedom, and equality which can be built and sustained through love and compassion, utilizing human potential unlocked by the free and rigorous pursuit of truth. Each of these heritages depends on the others—our intellectual heritage provides inspiration for our political system, and our political heritage requires an informed and free citizenry.

Let us once again reiterate that we do not intend to gloss over serious differences and conflicts within this broad heritage. We certainly have deeply significant differences in our conceptions of key concepts such as democracy, justice, and equality. We also have enormously important differences of opinion on how best to relate these principles to specific policies and practices. Many would say persuasively that if there is a consensus that constitutes our heritage, it is so broad and at such an abstract level that the only true measure of consensus is that which can obtain in the context of practice. We must not in any way minimize or paper over these vital and important differences, and we must also be reminded of the important areas of commonality that are the convergent sources of our divergences. Perhaps most importantly of all, it is critical to test whether there is real consensus on the broad outlines of our heritage and to challenge our commitments to the heritage. It would be, for example, a bracing no-lose situation if people were to have continuous debates and contests on the best possible ways of enhancing justice, *provided* it was clear that justice was the goal and not the surrogate. One way that can be used to determine the nature and strength of these basic commitments is to probe even more deeply; to seek out the nature of one's basic orientation to meaning, to human nature, and to humanity's origins and destinies. We can gain enormous insight into our political, moral, and social views by examining our metaphysical assumptions, our religious outlook, or perhaps the nature of our myths. For this reason we must now turn to the matter of our religious, mythic heritage.

Religious Heritage

Our history is one in which the terms *religion* and *church* have from time to time (including the present) become intertwined. We say officially that we are a nation "under God," that we trust in God; yet, we constitutionally have mandated separation of church and state. We are a culture with significant religious traditions, but our society is for the most part officially secular. The reasons for this lie in our tangled historical roots, which we will briefly discuss in the knowledge that this will, at best, be a cursory glance at a complicated and highly textured set of issues and events.

From the earliest times our Puritan ancestors made no separation between church and state, and as Sacvan Bercovitch (1978) makes clear, they saw the colonization and development of the new world as an opportunity to further the Puritan revolution in a wilderness that was a nascent Eden. The Puritans were the first, but by no means the last, to see America as having a special place in the divine consciousness. As Bercovitch documents, the nation of America as the new Jerusalem, of America as being specially graced by God, of America as having a divine destiny and a special responsibility to speak (and act) for the Almighty, is a particularly enduring myth that continues to permeate our beliefs and practices. Thus, we have as part of our religious heritage a tradition that speaks sometimes arrogantly about a sacred America, blessed and graced by God with special responsibilities and resources to do God's work, at least as some Christians saw and see it.

At the same time we have a religious heritage that strongly values religious freedom and diversity. Although the story that people came to America in the sixteenth and seventeenth centuries because it tolerated religious diversity is largely wrong (people came to practice their own religions, not to tolerate others), the early significant intolerance gave way to political realities. Given the number of different sects, each pursuing its own ways, the culture developed a *modus vivendi* that emphasized toleration and a live-and-let-live spirit rather than one of outright hostility and repression. The American Revolution came at the height of the Enlightenment, a cluster of viewpoints which included a harsh critique of established religions as oppressive, corrupt, and stultifying. Given the fears of both a strong central government and an established central church, it is not surprising that the famous wall of separation was built into the First Amendment of the Constitution. It is important to note that the First Amendment built the wall around the *federal* government, and the policy of established churches in individual states persisted until 1832.

Our history is also marked by significant religious intolerance and bigotry, most dramatically exemplified in anti-Catholic, antisemitic, antiblack movements such as the Ku Klux Klan. We have had our share of violence rooted in religious differences. Furthermore, there continues to be deep suspiciousness of certain religious groups as organized religions become identified more strongly with volatile political issues (e.g., civil rights, abortion, and nuclear testing). Historically, then, we can safely say that our religious heritage includes, in addition to significant reverence and piety, a history of theocracy, religious intolerance, disestablishmentarianism, and religious pluralism.

Many recent analyses of religion in America have focused on sociological dimensions of the role of religion in American life. These analyses speak to the essentially middle-class nature of organized religion which serves to legitimate and sustain mainstream American culture. Bellah (1975) has written about the American civil religion as an amalgam of certain national and patriotic rituals and symbols with religious symbols, such as expressed in the holidays of Thanksgiving and Memorial Day. Herberg (1960) and Cuddihy (1978) write of a consolidation process in which it has become acceptable and expected that an American very likely will be either a Protestant, Catholic, or Jew, provided that religious views are expressed as private and personal, thus avoiding contentious cultural conflict and struggle. In these formulations religious ideals and symbols are seen as being co-opted by the secular society and serving as an important means of cultural acculturation, stabilization, and integration. Peter Berger goes further and sees the role of the church in America as part of the process of cultural denial and blindness. He puts it this way: "The churches play a key role in the elaborate social-psychological process by which unpleasant realities are suppressed.... But religion also reinforces in a general way, quite apart from ideological distortions, the notion that the world one lives in is essentially and ultimately all right. For lack of a better term, we could say that religion ratifies the 'okay world' " (1961:120–21).

The complicated and contradictory nature of our religious heritage (only suggested and hinted at in this very brief glance) is part of the reason why so many people despair at forging an overarching framework of meaning for our culture. Religious differences are real and they are deep—a situation aggravated by the reality that there are forces that consider themselves strongly nonreligious, if not actually antireligious. In spite of these realities I believe that we can significantly narrow the gap of beliefs among these groups. An important dimension to this possibility lies in the conceptual distinction between the sacred and the profane. We here return to a key assumption— namely, that most of the culture supports the idea and value of having metaphysics and myths that provide meaning to our existence.

The Sacred and the Profane

Further evidence of this has been proposed by anthropologists and historians of religions who point to the persistence across time and space with which cultures insist on defining what is sacred and what is profane. Theorists as different as Mircea Eliade and Emile Durkheim have insisted that all cultures develop myths and religions to express their conception of what is ultimate, of what is beyond the boundaries of acceptable behavior, of a line between what is permissible and what is not—between what is "clean" and sacred and what is profane and "dirty". Robert Nisbet has not only noted Durkheim's interest in religion but the more widespread interest among post-Enlightenment figures in religious thought.

> In many ways this is the single most impressive aspect of 19th century interest in religion. its roots in the rationalist or utilitarian-minded who, despite personal indifference or hostility, were able to see religion's profound relation to the structure of human society and to the deepest regions of human consciousness. More than anything else, I think, it is this ethnological, historical, sociological and psychological envisagement of religion that separates the nineteenth from the eighteenth century. (1974:157)

In addressing the centrality of the sacred/profane concept in Durkheim's work, Nisbet cites the work of a nineteenth-century scholar of classical civilization, Fustel de Coulanges: "The heart of religion, Fustel emphasized, is not belief or faith or external authority, but the idea of the sacred; in its first form, the sacred fire. The sacred fire in each family hearth was, in the beginning, the very identity of the family [quoting Fustel]. . . . 'It was a religious precept that this fire must always remain pure; which meant literally, that no filthy object ought to be cast upon it, and figuratively, that no blameworthy deed ought to be committed in its presence' " (Fustel, as quoted in Nisbet, p. 162). Nisbet then goes on to discuss how Durkheim came to elaborate this direction as the crux of religions across time and space, as expressed in Durkheim's definition of religion: "A religion is a unified system of beliefs and practices relative to sacred things that is to say, things set apart and forbidden—beliefs and practices which united into one single moral community called a Church, all those who adhered to them" (quoted in Nisbet 1974:164).

Durkheim, the resolutely agnostic and superrationalist social scientist, sees the role of religion as crucial, not as a supernatural force but rather as a vital social element in the fulfillment of cultural aspirations. Nisbet summarizes Durkheim's strong interest in religion as having four aspects.

> First religion is necessary to society, not merely in an abstract sense, but as a vital mechanism of integration of human beings and as a realm of unifying symbols.... Second, religion is a key element and a basic context of social change.... Third, religion's.... most fundamental and enduring elements are social.... The greatest power of religion lies not in what it teaches man about the after-life or about cosmology, but in what its symbols and rituals, cults and churches and sects of membership in society, the feeling of belonging to what Edmund Burke had called the partnership of the dead, the living, and the unborn.... Fourth, there is an unbreakable relation between religion and the origins of human language and thought. (1974:164-65)

Durkheim (as indicated by Nisbet) thus avoids the language of revelation and the controversies over the existence of a supernatural. Instead, he sees religious expression as an inevitable and necessary aspect of developing a society. Religion serves functions, has roles, and reflects the society's expression of what has meaning—what the society can, and wishes to, aspire to and what it can accomplish.

Religionists clearly have a far different perspective and are much more likely to speak of society and culture as secondary concerns. From the perspective of a cosmology of universal creation, meaning, and destiny, religious considerations precede and dominate all others and provide the moral and analytical language of human behavior. Mircea Eliade sums up this perspective in this way,

> Whatever the historical context in which he is placed, homo religious always believes that there is an absolute reality, the sacred, which transcends this world but manifests itself in this world, thereby sanctifying it making it real. He further believes that life has a sacred origin and that human existence realizes all of its potentialities in proportion as it is religious—that is, participates in reality. The gods created man and the world, the culture heroes completed the Creation, and the history of all these divine and semidivine works is preserved in the myths. By reactualizing social history, by imitating the divine behavior, man puts and keeps himself close to the gods—that is, in the real and the significant. (1959:202)

This sharp difference, of course, represents an eternal argument in the sense that it has been going on for a very long time with every reason (if not hope) that it will continue in the furthest future we can envision. However, here again we must note an important area of consensus, namely that religion—as for example conceptualized by Durkheim as distinguishing between sacred and profane—is a major part of human thought and experience, that it plays a very important role, and that it could play a very important *positive* role. I am concerned, as an educator in twentieth-century America, to find ways in which our schools can be energized with images and language that have force and meaning. I am not speaking here as a theologian but as an educator examining the possibility that theological language might have for this effort. I share with Michael Harrington a hope that in spite of history, religious ideals can inform and sustain the work of making these ideals manifest and real.

> *I like religious people, feel a sense of awe on the communion of the universal, but without a religious interpretation of the origin of that communion.... The serious atheistic humanist and the serious religious humanist are, I suspect, talking about the same reality. That these languages differ is not a minor detail to be forgotten by reducing antagonistic philosophies to a vague emotion. Such a promiscuous ecumenism is, of course, empty of content. But that common emotion does offer a common point of political departure. (1983:200)*

Harrington goes on to quote Jacques Maritain to support his position on the need for "a coming together on 'common practical notions,' not in the affirmation of the same conception of the world, man, and knowledge but on the affirmation of the same sort of convictions requiring actions. This involves 'a sort of common residue, a sort of unwritten common law, at the point of practical convergence of extremely difficult theoretical ideologies and spiritual traditions'" (1983:203).

ELEMENTS OF AN EMERGING MYTH

> *Religion is the greatest utopia, in other words the greatest "metaphysic" that has appeared in history because it is the most grandiose attempt to reconcile in mythological form the real contradictions of historical life: indeed it states that men must have the same "nature", that man in general exists, as he was created by God, and consequently the brother of other men, equal to other men, free among other men, and like other men, and that he can see himself in God, "the autoconsciousness" of humanity; but it also states that this is not of this world, but will happen in another (utopian) world.*
> *Antonio Gramsci (as quoted in Henri Desroche 1979: 24)*

As educators we can participate or not participate in that important, perplexing, immensely exciting series of debates and arguments on the existence of God, the origins of the universe, the comparative validity of different religions, and so on. Educators may or may not decide that it is appropriate to engage their students in these inquiries. However, all educators can recognize the value and necessity of how our culture has distinguished between the sacred and the profane.

At the very least, all educators should be aware (and reflect that awareness in their practice) of how "religion," "metaphysics," or "conceptions of the sacred" significantly influence our culture. More than that, educators should become more sensitive to the possibility of consensus on the *desirability* of both becoming more aware of shared values and working on increasing and deepening them. Educational communities must meditate on the question of what it means to be sacred and how an education might facilitate the quest for what is holy. This book can be seen as an attempt to sacralize the educational process, to imbue it with a spirit of what is of ultimate significance and meaning. We are not talking here about religious education (as in Sunday school), nor about acculturation, but rather about the sacred dimensions and properties of education, of seeing the educational process not in instrumental terms (it gives us more power, status, etc.) but as endowed with those qualities we feel are sacred. I want to begin by stressing that many existing educational ideas can be seen as sacred and, indeed, seeing them in this way can illumine and heighten their significance. I have particularly in mind the centrality of careful, rational, critical, searching, and rigorous thought to the educational endeavor.

The Socratic Tradition

The tradition of intellectual criticism as central to education can be traced to Socrates, as revealed in the continuing reverence we have for what has come to be called the Socratic method. The Socratic method puts great emphasis on clarity and on the thorough examination of propositions and statements, on skepticism, and on logical analysis. Socrates presented himself as a humble person who insisted that the more he studied and learned, the less he knew. He also felt it extremely important to test out the adequacy not only of his own beliefs but those of his fellow citizens. We see in Plato's accounts of these encounters the relentless, persistent, and brilliant displays of unsettling questions and probes that often led people to a state of intellectual bewilderment and devastation (and rage). It is very important to note that this was not simply an intellectual exercise or a way of twitting and teasing, but that this process was of profound importance to Socrates. Socrates strongly believed that virtue could be taught, that the proper function of education is to teach virtue, and, moreover, that the appropriate pedagogy for such an endeavor is one of critical examination of conventional thinking. He also was careful to affirm his own religious affiliation and saw his role as necessary in order to fulfill the wishes of the gods. Thus, Socrates integrated his pedagogy into an educational orientation as it emerged from a social and sacred vision. Critical thinking was not seen primarily as an esthetic or economic concern but also having political and religious significance. We are apt to think of the Socratic method as a metaphor for detached, logical, probingly critical thought, but we must remember its religious and political context: Socrates was devoutly religious and a strong supporter of democracy Athenian-style; he felt even at his execution time that his educational efforts were necessary to sustain those beliefs and institutions. The fact that he was charged with a capital offense (subversion) only accentuates the seriousness with which Athenians viewed educational orientations.

We reaffirm the unquestionable importance of open, thorough, and careful inquiry as the cornerstone of the educational process. I cannot believe that there is any significant number of educators who would challenge the importance of clear and critical thinking to any educational theory. We perhaps can add to this area of consensus that critical thinking can be seen as sacred or, at least, as compatible with the sacred. There is, of course, the religious notion that expression of capacities such as critical thinking reflects divine grace, or perhaps it reflects higher human aspirations. There is, however, a broader way of expressing the sacred nature of critical thinking, one that can perhaps allow for a greater degree of consensus. What I have in mind is the notion, as Robert J. Ackermann (1985) has expressed it, of "religion as criticism" (Italics added). Ackermann's position is that religion has played an important role in providing critical criteria for judging the moral adequacy of a culture, in participating in the active change process of protest, organization, and in offering a set of alternatives. Indeed, he goes on to assert that only those religions which engage in social and cultural criticism can retain their legitimacy and vitality.

> Religions have arisen as legitimate protests against societies and ways of life, providing in the process the overpowering foundations for laying down one's life to improve the lot of humanity. . . . Religion is a perennial source of social critique, but religion . . . always retain[s] the potential of developing pungent social critique, no matter how accommodating a form they have assumed in particular institutional contexts. If religion is to provide the possibility of social critique, it can never be reduced to a set of mechanically understood dogmata, for in that form it would necessarily lose touch with changing social reality. . . . Critique does not exhaust religion, but religion that cannot critique is already dead. . . . The main thread of religion may be one of potential opposition or criticism of a surrounding society by the development of a picture of life as how it should be lived. . . . What is being suggested is that the core of religion is potentially critical rather than functional or accommodating. (Ackermann 1985:ix:24)

What we see here is criticism as informed by, and in the interest of, a theory of a life of meaning; it is not a conception of "critical thinking" as a "skill" apart from meaning—not a series of mathematical procedures devoid of human context. Socrates was not teaching "critical thinking" or "cognitive development"; he would not be interested in coaching the debate team—he was rather a religious and political leader who took his convictions so much to heart that he was willing to give his life on behalf of an educational process he thought would enrich and sustain those beliefs. In this sense, I suggest that another possible source of a religious or mythic consensus lies in the significance and value of informed and principled criticism—rigorous, precise, thorough criticism directed at and emerging from a vision of a life of purpose and meaning. In this sense, critical reflection can be seen as sacred.

The Prophetic Tradition

The most powerful source for Western culture of this integration of religion and criticism is surely the stirring and intense messages of the biblical prophets. These amazing men not only spoke to their times but set the foundations of a tradition that continues to flourish, inspire, excite, and energize. It is a tradition that consciously and passionately combines deep devotion to sacred ideals with a determination to speak out vividly and loudly on the profane—that is, a tradition that insists on crying out against discrepancies between what we value and what we actually do. The prophets did not specialize in predicting the future, for they were not endowed with extraordinary powers of clairvoyance. Rather, they were keenly aware of what were understood to be divine imperatives and very much aware of human responses to them. Their prophecy lay in their deep understanding of the severe consequences that were in store for a people who where flaunting and rejecting their own highest aspirations. Prophets were passionate social critics who applied sacred criteria to human conduct and, when they found violations of these criteria they cried out in anguish and outrage.

The most eloquent and insightful scholar of the prophets is Abraham Joshua Heschel (1962), and it is his work which I rely on most in my analysis. His definitive two-volume work titled simply *The Prophets* is a work of soaring power and haunting beauty written with extraordinary elegance and eloquence. I see in his interpretation of the biblical prophets intriguing possibilities for an educational framework which combines a sense of the sacred and a sensitively to political and cultural realities with a strong reliance on the development of a critical consciousness. Heschel presents the prophets as social critics who castigate and judge their society, utilizing the society's own highest goals and deepest values. Prophets re-mind—that is, they demand that we return to a mindedness that we have affirmed as our vision. They also urge, prod, dare, and encourage us to change our ways and continue the struggle to create that vision; they moan and curse, but not with despair alone: their outrage moves us to act and change rather than to be defeated and resigned.

The prophetic voice speaks most directly to issues of justice and righteousness; it is a voice that not only roars in protest at oppression, inequity, poverty, and hunger but cries out in pain and compassion. It is a voice that haunts us because it echoes our own inner voice which speaks to our impulse to nourish and care for others. This partly explains why the prophetic voice often produces the anger and resentment which follow our recognition of our failure to sufficiently exercise responsibility (sometimes called guilt). The prophet was religious in the sense that he was imbued with a sacred set of beliefs on origins and meaning; a social leader in the sense that he was keenly aware and interested in historical and current social, economic, and political events; and an educator in that he directed his energies toward increasing public awareness and insight into the ultimate significance of these events. Heschel puts it this way:

> The prophet seldom tells a story, but casts events. He rarely sings, but castigates. He does more than translate reality into a poetic key. He is a preacher whose purpose is not self-expression or the "purgation of emotion" but communication. His images must not shine, they must burn. The prophet is intent on intensifying responsibility, is impatient of excuse, contemptuous of pretense and self-pity. His tone, rarely sweet or caressing, is frequently consoling and disburdening: his words are often slashing, even horrid-designed to shock rather than to edify.... [The Prophet is concerned with] wrenching one's conscience from the state of suspended animation. (1962:7)

It is vitally important not to overstate the case for the value of this particular tradition to the development of an educational framework. The biblical prophets must be considered in the context of a particular history of a particular people in particular times. As educators we are not comfortable with the role of "preachers," nor do we wish to "shock" more than "edify." However, what we can value here is the prophets' passion and commitment to persisting values—justice, compassion, and concern for the oppressed; the strong authority (as opposed to power) that their criticism provides; their courage in expressing their convictions so loudly; and the energy and hope that they inspire. It is important to remember that the prophetic voice is one that speaks not only to criticism; it is also a voice of transformation. "Almost every prophet brings consolation, promise, and hope of reconciliation along with censure and castigation. He begins with a *message of doom*; he concludes with a *message of hope*.... [H]is essential task is to declare the word of God to the here and now; to disclose the future in order to illumine what is involved in the present" (Heschel 1962:12). Nor do we have to accept the prophets' own belief as to the source of their inspiration, mission, and powers (the Bible indicates that prophets were devout and pious Jews who had direct communication with their God). We can recognize how essential aspects of this tradition have been reflected in other times and places.

The prophetic voice has been expressed in a variety of settings either as explicitly recognized or as echoed in other traditions. Surely our history includes oppressive and excessively pietistic expressions of this tradition (e.g., the Puritan revolution). Yet, there is a corresponding theological tradition that seeks to resist religious arrogance and dogmatism. For example, in describing aspects of the work of Paul Tillich, Alvin Porteous makes this point: "The Protestant principle . . . contains the divine and human protest against any absolute claims for a relative reality even if this claim is made by a Protestant church. . . . It is the guardian against the attempts of the finite and conditioned to usurp the place of the unconditional in thinking and acting. It is the prophetic judgment against religious pride, ecclesiastical arrogance, and secular self-sufficiency and their destructive consequences" (1966:129).

When I urge educators to consider and utilize religious language and metaphors in their work, it is clearly meant to be, and must necessarily be, on a selective basis. More to the point, my view is that our work as educators can be significantly enriched by the prophetic voice that speaks not only critically but compassionately, one that also speaks of love, mercy, and forgiveness. Our history and that of our brothers and sisters in other lands and times are marked and blessed by remarkable leaders who have from time to time given full expression to that voice.

Two such examples are represented in the persona and movements led by Mohandas K. Gandhi and Martin Luther King. These men emerged from very different religious traditions, but both led political movements directed at human liberation and shared a common vision of the relationship between the sacred and the temporal. They were both able to articulate the growing chasm between modern technological and materialistic society and the quest for justice. Gandhi in India and King in the United States represented the continuity of a standard of criticism first generated by the prophets and applied it to the specifics of their particular context. This criticism has been characterized by Heschel as follows:

> *Modern thought tends to extenuate personal responsibility. Understanding the complexities of human nature, the interrelationships of individual and society, of consciousness and the subconscious, we find it difficult to isolate the deed from those circumstances in which it was done. But new insight may obscure essential vision, and man's conscience grows*

scales: excuses, pretence, self-pity. . . . Above all, the prophets remind us of the moral state of a people: Few are guilty, but all are responsible. If we admit that the individual is in some measure conditioned or affected by the spirit of society, an individual's crime discloses society's corruption. (1962:14,16)

Gandhi and King had the courage to call attention to social corruption and to both the importance of the individual's responsibility in contributing to that corruption as well as the process of correction and reform. Both saw the struggle for social justice as divinely willed and focused on universal themes—love, justice, kindness for all. These were holy men who fought political battles passionately and intensely; they rejected the fragmented and alienated modern consciousness in which religious and moral concerns are considered to be private and personal. Their basic approach mirrored much of the prophetic tradition: a direct, clear, ringing denunciation of the evil of the society based on higher principles; a call for direct actions against the existing power structure, utilizing techniques (nonviolence, endurance, petition, fasting, sit-ins) consistent with these high principles; and deep faith in ultimate victory. Gandhi and King represent those who dare to openly challenge the inertia and decay of a corrupt society and who have the audacity to try to hold their society to its commitments. Such people do not sharply separate the secular and the holy, or theory and practice; rather they see them in dialectical relationship. Prophets like Gandhi and King are *very practical* people for they are not merely idealists but idealists who insist on the practice of these ideals. They provide a practical answer to those who are skeptical if not contemptuous of the value of abstract ideals. King and Gandhi made us pay moral and spiritual attention to our practices and policies and gave us an opportunity to imbue them with sacred qualities.

A more general model of the prophetic tradition has been delineated by Walter Brueggemann's (1978) *The Prophetic Imagination*, where he posits two broad cultural modes, one of which he labels "the prophetic consciousness" and the other "the royal consciousness." Although his background is in biblical scholarship, his analysis is directed to the parallels between biblical images and ongoing history. In his description of what he calls the "royal consciousness," he uses several examples including the regimes of the Pharaohs, the Solomonic era, and modern American culture. Brueggemann characterizes the consciousness of such cultures as having a sense of "static triumphalism," cultures smugly mired in a self-congratulatory inertness. To support and sustain this royal culture, God is co-opted to provide legitimation and protection. It is a society of affluence for a few and of oppression and exploitation for the many. The royal consciousness becomes a dominant culture when "now and in every time, [it] is grossly uncritical, cannot tolerate serious and fundamental criticism, and will go to great lengths to stop it" (1978:14). Although it is a politically strong culture, its pietistic self-righteousness has to be propped up by military might, a conscripted God, and heavy insulation from criticism. However, this is "a wearied culture, nearly unable to be seriously energized to new promises from God" (1978:14). The royal consciousness is too proud and smug to change, yet at the same time is unable to conceive that change is possible even if necessary.

In sharp contrast to this cultural mode is what Brueggemann calls the "prophetic consciousness," in which the major emphasis is justice and compassion in a community where basic equality is the goal. In this consciousness, humanity is free to accept its responsibility to create a life of meaning for all and has a cosmology in which God is also free from entanglements with the establishment. This consciousness is energized by its devotion to its principles and its openness to transcendence, (i.e., to the possibilities of a re-created world).

The quintessential prophetic image for Brueggemann is reflected in the story of Moses and his leadership of the Hebrews. The youthful Moses seems to have accepted along with both the Egyptians and the Hebrews, the "static triumphalism" of Pharaoh's rule as immovably entrenched. The great gift (grace) of Moses was that somehow (through what Brueggemann calls divine amazement) Moses came to be able to imagine what had hitherto been thought of as "impossible"—a vision of liberation. Here we note the second major theme of our framework—not only is criticism vital to prophecy, but so is imagination. Moses has an inspired, highly imaginative conception: he literally creates through his imaginative powers a "new world." The image is shaped by both moral criticism and moral imagination; he "sees" the horrors of captivity and oppression and "foresees" the possibility of liberation. As a prophet his mission becomes one of raising awareness (very much like the process that Freire [1970, 1973] describes as *conscientization*) of a people who are in despair and unable to consider that the world might be otherwise. Moses tries to persuade Pharaoh peacefully to free the Hebrew slaves in what becomes a battle between sacred sources. However, Moses has to contend not only with a rigid and powerful ruler but also with a fearful and skeptical Hebrew community numbed by years of oppression into accepting their situation as tolerable by dint of its seeming permanence. Moreover, Moses is torn by self-doubts and his sense of inadequacy to the task. What Brueggemann stresses is the extremely important role of an audacious imagination inspired by very deeply felt forces (called God in the Bible) to somehow transcend these fears, doubts, and resistances.

This vision is not limited to a conception of escape and liberation, but, most importantly of all, this prophetic imagination is concerned with an alternative society, one with sacred dimensions. Moses is not only a dreamer who shares his dreams but a leader who urges his people to dare to make the dream a reality. He arouses, he energizes, he leads, and, moreover, he participates in the long and arduous process of creating a new community, one centered in divinely inspired commitment to a way of life grounded in the pursuit of justice.

To Brueggemann, the major contribution of Moses and other great prophets is their ability to transform cultures by "holding together criticism and energizing" (1978:14). Prophets show us our deficiencies, failures, and sins, but they offer us hope and possibility by the force of their authority, passion, and commitment. Their authority is powerful to the extent that we accept the sacred quality of their concerns, the beauty of their imagined transformation, and the acuity of their criticisms. Prophets offer conceptions of life that are true, good, and beautiful, and fresh insights into what is involved in creating that life. Brueggemann's book is probably written for an audience interested primarily in religion, but it can easily be seen as having a powerful message for educators. He describes a concept of "prophetic ministry," which I believe could just as well serve as a description of what might be called a "prophetic education." This mission (goal, concern, dimension) "is to nurture, nourish, and evoke a consciousness and perception *alternative* to the dominant culture" (1978:13). This "ministry" (education) involves the dimensions we have described—sharp criticism, dazzling imagination, a sacred perspective, commitment to justice and compassion, hope, energy, and involvement. Freedom does not come, according to the prophets, from adaptation and acceptance, nor does freedom emerge out of numbness and callousness to injustice. Freedom for the prophets emerges from caring, and lies in hope, possibility, and commitment.

Liberation Theology

The reality and vitality of this tradition is vividly seen and felt in the enormous struggles of Latin America, as expressed in the writings and activities of what has been called liberation theology. This theology emerges out of a struggle to overcome centuries of poverty and oppression rooted in colonialism and exploitation; it also reflects simultaneously how organized religion in this regime has served both as problem and response. Liberation theology is certainly controversial, and though it has deep and widespread support from Catholic clergy and laypeople, it is often in sharp conflict with the part of the traditional Catholic Church which, if not in league with the existing power structure, is not inclined to resist it. It is a theology which is very much rooted in the prophetic tradition and, hence, views Jesus as a prophet and the Gospels as an instrument for the deliverance of the poor and the oppressed. Jesus' humanity is stressed, at least as much as his divinity, in his compassion and concern for the poor and in the loving and tender way he relates to them. Jesus in this perspective is critical of a society that is more concerned with the accumulation of wealth and the exercise of power than with the suffering of the needy. To the liberation theologist, the first priority for the Church is to feed the hungry and house those without shelter. From this perspective the spreading of the gospel is therefore most appropriately accomplished by acts of caring for the oppressed.

Like other prophetic traditions, this movement is one in which ideals and practice are intertwined; its basic approach, though not violent, is literally to construct alternative communities. Their concern in building these communities is less with ontology than with history, less with theory and more with praxis. Harvey Cox (1984) sees the phenomenon of what are called the Christian base communities as a manifestation of new theological thinking emerging from the "margins and fringes of society" (the poor, the Third World, women). As these communities are built and developed by small groups of peasants, clergy, and volunteers, they discuss the connections of their practices to biblical thought and vice versa. This process of praxis, the integration of theory and practice for purpose of change and liberation, is rooted in Marxist thought, and it is this tendency of liberation theology to attempt to blend Marxist analysis with Christian theology that helps to explain the strenuous resistance to this movement. This resistance highlights the risks involved in the prophetic tradition since it involves fundamental criticism, demands for change, and active efforts to make changes. It is a tragic yet revealing measure of the powerful threat that prophetic movements generate to note not only the serious ongoing efforts to silence the leadership of the liberation theology movement but also the violent fate of other great prophets like Socrates, Jesus, Gandhi, and Martin Luther King.

Though it is clear that we are not a Third World people, it is equally clear that we face the same critical issues—illiteracy, poverty, oppression, hunger, discrimination—albeit in different degrees and forms. We must confront the realities of our abundance and richness as well as the reality that in spite of our wealth (some would say because of it), our nation includes millions who are below or at a near subsistence level. Our politicians love to proclaim that "one hungry, poor, unemployed person is too many"; if one such person is intolerable, what concept can characterize the reality of over thirty million people in the U.S.A.? Liberation theologists demand that we confront this outrageous and obscene reality with our profession to be a nation rooted in the Judeo-Christian ethic of justice and love.

Liberation theology, in addition to its more particular Latin American roots, emerges of course, from traditions common to American culture, most particularly the tradition of Christianity. It is a historical and sociological reality that we are a nation with very strong ties to Christian ideals, doctrines, and institutions. Christians constitute more than 90 percent of the religiously observant in America, and despite serious denominational and sectarian divisions, they are united in part in their reverence for the teachings of Jesus. Among those who do not consider themselves to be Christians, and those who are "nonreligious," there is also a very high percentage of people who are stirred and inspired by the historical personage and teachings of Jesus as prophet and social critic. One of the great casualties of religious wars and quarrels has been our ability to examine the power and significance of his teachings apart from their theological interpretations. I do not mean to diminish in any way the significance of the disputes regarding the divinity of Jesus, not only to Christianity but to other religions as well. These are indeed serious matters, and they clearly will continue to be central to the development of religious thought. However, I believe that it is possible and desirable to incorporate some important aspects of his teachings into our cultural and educational myths.

Liberation theologists suggest ways in which this might be done in their reemphasis on love, compassion, justice, and mercy and in their profound concern for the poor. These are values that are certainly part of the American experience and we should be able to affirm them without embarrassment even if they are part of the credo of particular religious institutions. The liberation movements in Latin America also remind us that prompt and serious action is required in the face of desperation. Liberation theology pictures Jesus as a daringly active leader who challenged the power elite by undermining their moral and religious authority, and in true prophetic traditions, by raising the consciousness of the poor and oppressed and presenting extraordinary images for the possibility of hope and redemption.

Our situation in America is both similar and different. As is very well known, we have incredible wealth, but what is less well recognized is our astonishing poverty and deprivation, particularly when seen in the context of our wealth. America ranks ninth among 105 nations in a measure of illiteracy, tenth in longevity, seventeenth in infant mortality, and first in military expenditures. But even if some of these statistics, like most statistics, may be misleading, or even if at some time America should rank first in all positive realms, there are other unbelievably harsh realities that confront us. Two hundred million people in the world are hungry, millions do not have decent nutrition or drinking water, millions of children die every year before the age of ten, millions do not have adequate housing or education. The message of Jesus and other major religious and moral leaders in different ages and places is that we are *one* people, *one* world, that we *are* our brothers' and sisters' keepers. For Americans (or any other group) to live prosperously and contently while hundreds of millions struggle for minimal existence is absurd and unacceptable. If we consider the very real possibility that our prosperity is at the expense of human misery, then the situation is obscene and outrageous. Such a state of being does more than oppress and violate the basic human rights and needs of those in misery; the obscenity of poverty dehumanizes and abases the impulse of the prosperous to love, to show compassion, and to do justice. We need an education that has this concern at its center and, at the same time, resonates with the particulars of our own culture, history, traditions, and symbols. I believe that much of the language and many of the images of the Socratic dialogues, of the prophetic tradition, and of liberation theology are of inestimable value in developing such a framework. There are of course other contemporary and energizing movements of a clearly American stamp which rise to provide moral and religious insight into our lives. A particularly intriguing and potentially very valuable movement is called creation theology, whose prime spokesman and theorist is the American Dominican priest Matthew Fox.

Creation Theology

The creation theology movement appears to be a synthesis of several current strands of contemporary American thought. These strands include "new age" thinking, which has come mainly to mean an openness to spiritual experiences and to a reservoir of untapped human potential. New age thinkers tend to be optimistic about the future because of their faith in beneficent cosmic forces and in the human capacity to be in touch with those forces. These thinkers decidedly do not oppose science and religion and indeed point to the frontiers of scientific research as confirmation of their intuitive notions about the nature of the universe. They tend to urge us to supplement the recognized powers of rationality and analysis with the equally valuable powers inherent in intuitive and nonrational processes. Such thinkers see the current research in the functions of brain hemispheres as the basic metaphor for their epistemology in that so-called right-brained and left-brained functions are both valuable, that both need to be developed, and that the most important function is the one which integrates them. New age thinkers tend, however, to be less explicit on the need for change in social and political institutions which presumably are more likely to change as the underlying human consciousness changes—a kind of trickle-up theory.

The creation theology movement, however, is much more explicit in its political, moral, and economic agenda. There is major and deep concern for social justice as revealed in their serious criticism of capitalism and colonialism. Fox (1979) continually refers to the economic theories of E. F. Schumacher as being very influential in the formulation of creation theology. There is an explicit recognition that social and economic matters are integral aspects of religious thought and an explicit plea for smaller, more humane, more just communities in which equality, dignity, and compassion are the major informing principles. Creation theology also differs from many new age writings in its emphasis on collective and responsible action designed to transform and not just ameliorate. Another central tenet of creation theory is its passionate ecological concern in which the issues of reverence for nature, environmental pollution, and materialism are integrated with our current political and economic policies.

Indeed, creation theology represents itself in the terms of creating, constructing, building or, more accurately, re-creating and re-constructing. It is a movement that blends new-age cosmology with contemporary political theory rooted in important theological traditions and in the explicit rejection of certain religious ideas. It is a theology which rejects emphases on sin and guilt, and instead celebrates joy, creation, and responsibility. The title of Fox's (1983) broad statement on creative theology is *Original Blessing*, which he uses in opposition to the concept of original sin. Fox makes a thoroughgoing critique of conventional Christian theology and practices and offers a significant reformulation in which much more emphasis is placed on human sensuality, joy, and compassion, and much more faith (which he says is really trust) is placed in the human capacity to be worthy of our responsibilities as co-creators of the world. It is a theology that rests on the prophetic traditions, the teachings of Jesus, and on those who connect mystical with human concerns, particularly the writings of two medieval mystics, Meister Eckhart and Hildegard of Bingen.

We have already described in chapter two Fox's (1979) distinction between compassion and sentimentalism, as his strong emphasis on compassion is central to a vision of community, justice, and joy. In *A Spirituality Called Compassion* he rejects a number of traditional religious symbols, particularly one which he calls the image of Jacob's ladder. This image of verticality, of a struggle to achieve success rung by rung, of human hierarchy, evokes an ideal of people removed from human concerns and compassion and instead urges us to move closer to a contemplative consciousness of the cosmos. It is an image that furthers the dualism of history and religion, of God and humanity, and of heaven and earth. Fox suggests as an alternative to this image a metaphor he calls "laughing Sarah's dancing circle." The "laughing

Sarah" is an allusion to the biblical Sarah who laughs joyously when it is revealed that at the age of 102 she will soon give birth; it represents the possibility of divine miracle and its response of human joy and delight. The image of the circle stresses the horizontal quality of the life in contrast to the verticality of Jacob's ladder, and the metaphor of dance reflects human creativity reacting to the demands of time and space. It is a kind of folk dance in which people are both individual and part of a group, and in which individual variations and differences can easily be accommodated to the basic choreography. Such a dance allows not only for individual creativity but for the opportunity to help those who stumble and for the nimble to relate meaningfully with the awkward. It is an image of joy, creativity, community, and responsibility, a human dance energized by a divine presence, which erases the dualistic qualities of the Jacob's ladder image. For Fox, to "dance" in this manner is the "original blessing" which is the opportunity to act on our capacity to create with God a world of joy, love, and justice. The general direction of the dance is clear but it cannot be complete without human will, creativity, and energy.

Another major Christian image that is reexamined by Fox (1979) is the cross, typically used to represent the suffering and martyrdom of Jesus. Fox contends that the enormous reliance on this image has served to emphasize the pain rather than the joy in the life of Jesus, and that it focuses attention on death rather than life. He suggests that Christians instead elaborate the great potential inherent in the image of the burial cave of Jesus. This image can serve to heighten the consciousness of the regenerative and renewing aspects of the story, moving the forces from crucifixion to resurrection, from death to life, from despair to possibility. Fox sees the possibility of the re-creation of life, of the reality of hope and transformation—even at the most tragic and despairing moment—as vital dimensions to the spreading of the gospel of renewal and hope.

Fox elaborates the image of the cave by contrasting its curved and circular properties to the severe and sharp lines of the cross, and bemoans the fact that the imagery of a cross turned on its side allows the image to be switched to that of a sword. The cross evokes the linearity of Jacob's ladder, while the cave evokes for Fox the gentleness and wholeness of the circle. The imagery of the burial cave reminds Fox of the shape of the womb and evokes feminine metaphors of birthing, nurturing, and compassion. Indeed, Fox points out the common derivation in Hebrew of the words for womb and compassion. In addition, the imagery of curve and circle facilitate metaphors of a renewing and continuous spiral of a dialectical relationship between the historical and divine responsibilities that humanity faces. Fox sees life as constant movement upwards, but as a movement in which people participate joyfully and in concert with each other.

The focus of this movement is creation in a sacred mode—people inspired and energized by a sacred impulse to make a world of joy and justice. The key source of the concept is the biblical phrase "God created man in His own image," with the interpretation that man/woman is here described as imaging and echoing God the Creator. In this creation myth, man/woman is asked to assume responsibility as God's partner in the further creative and constructive processes needed to make the vision real. The original blessing, then, is the opportunity to create and re-create, and sin becomes the inability, refusal, or rejection of the invitation to continue the re-creative process. Creation is directed at life and is that which nourishes and deepens the joy of life, and, hence, it is a blessing, while sin is destructive in that it is antilife when it blocks the possibility of joy, abundance, and justice. Creation theology celebrates creativity as that which connects God with humanity and people with people. It is a theology that has reenergized and renewed the symbolic relationship between criticism and imagination. The image of a world requiring re-creation allows us to be critical of a world that does not reflect that image, and it is this loving criticism that impels us to revise and reform the world.

This is a paradigm that has obvious implications for an attempt to fashion a consensual mythos of belief and meaning. It is also a formulation that has quite particular implications for a corresponding educational paradigm, particularly in the vital importance of the creative process and esthetics. The formulation puts esthetics and artistic concerns in a place of particular importance in that it encourages us to pursue a life of aesthetic fullness, a life of heightened, if not ecstatic, beauty and joy. Fox (1979) sees sensuality, ecstasy, and pleasure not as "sins" but as the fruits of the creative processes that we have been inspired to elaborate and develop. Rather, it is sinful not to participate in these blessings and to interfere with the imagination that makes them possible. Art becomes the process of integrating the true, the good, and the beautiful, which means an esthetics of wholeness in which we are free to revel in the creations that represent this wholeness.

The concept of art, creativity, and imagination is, however, not limited to the fine or applied or performing arts, not limited to what is narrowly defined by the academy and the commercial world as music, painting, drama, dance, etc. All aspects of life have their esthetic dimensions and are to be seen as humanly constructed, as works of art. By seeing civilization, culture, and social institutions as human constructions and as art not only enables us to more clearly recognize our own brilliance and failures in the adequacy of these constructions but heightens the awesomeness of our challenges and responsibilities. It also provides us with the opportunity to examine the creations from an esthetic perspective.

In creation theology, we have noted, there is an esthetic of wholeness and relationship, harmony, joy, justice, and love, an esthetic which can be applied to our institutions. When we look at our criminal justice system, for example, how does it measure up to this esthetic standard? Would we describe public housing as beautiful in the way it facilitates dignity, community, and peace? These critical dimensions, of course, have been applied to schools, and this has helped us to understand their shortcomings as well as those of the larger culture. These critical insights also help us in guiding the direction and nature of our re-creative and reconstructive efforts. The esthetic of creation theology is one which I believe resonates with much of mainstream American thinking and beliefs. It is an esthetic which at the very least is not alien to us and provides no particular barrier to the development of teaching strategies which can sustain and nourish such sensibilities. This formulation provides an esthetic that goes beyond mere taste and allows us to be freed of the elitist notion that sees art as the province of the talented and the discriminating few rather than as an inevitable human response to life's demands.

Critical to this emphasis on creativity is a faith in the creative process itself when seen in its constructive sense as part of the sacred responsibility to create a world of love, justice, and joy. It also puts stress on "work," on the active, ongoing engagement in the creative work necessary to meet those responsibilities. Fox captures this notion by urging us to consider concepts like peace, faith, and justice not as nouns but as verbs, since the process requires not only awareness and expression but commitment and action. "Peace . . . is something that needs to be won, fought for, and in fact is never fully achieved. Like justice, it is a verb and not a noun" (1979:78).

Two more quotations can serve to summarize the essential role of creativity in the pursuit of sacred meaning. Quoting Jose Arguelles, Fox distinguishes spiritual creativity from other art forms:

> [Arguelles] insists that art as spirituality is always distinct from enter-
> tainment. Art for him is "the means by which all matter may be regen-
> erated as spirit." Art is transformation of spirit that touches the very
> purpose of life which "is its transformation." The true art, he insists, "is
> the art of transformation" and to this transformation, both the artist and
> the scientist must die and be reborn. It is this death and dying and
> suffering that true art involves and that so distinguishes it from enter-
> tainment or titillation. William Blake also insisted on the universality of

creativity. Not to be an artist is to betray one's own nature.... Creativity unlike entertainment, makes demands. (1979:110)

Finally, "Creativity *is* a way of living, a spirituality, just as compassion is. It is a way that all persons travel in responding to life and we call it 'the art of survival.' Everyone who survives, we might say, has proven what an artist he or she is. But of course there are qualitative differences in the way some persons choose to survive. The fullest of the arts of survival would be the creative art of compassionate living" (1979: 111).

THE PROBLEMATICS OF MYTHOS IN AMERICA

This marks an appropriate place in which to review our analysis and to indicate the inherent difficulties and dangers of what we are proposing. We have argued that the educational crisis is rooted in the moral and spiritual crisis of the culture as reflected in the value confusions and contradictions discussed in chapter three. This analysis shows that certain social and cultural demands have frustrated and distracted us from our impulses to our basic commitments of love, justice, equality, community, and joy. Our culture's insistence on competition, individual success, and privatism is reflected in a school program which puts cultural considerations of achievement, order, control, and hierarchy over educational values of free inquiry, the development of a critical and creative consciousness, and the struggle for meaning. I argue that this cluster of confusions and contradictions, while certainly not new, has deepened and, in conjunction with other current cultural and international crises, has produced a condition that seriously impels us to confront the possibility of a new world or of no world.

This book focuses on educational processes but takes the position that the intimate relationship between education and culture requires educators to be sensitive to major fundamental cultural concerns. I have shown how critical moral and religious issues and ideas interpenetrate the larger culture and, hence, our educational institutions. Furthermore, this means that as educators we have the opportunity and responsibility to participate in the dialogue of meaning in order to ensure that education is directed toward that pursuit. It is my position that we educators must reaffirm our faith and humility in the significance of the educational process to facilitate that struggle. We are well aware of the enormous social and cultural constraints under which we work and that the difficulties are at their peak when the concerns are identified to be of a moral and religious nature. The challenge is formidable: (1) We must find ways to avoid paralytic and wishy-washy responses to the conflicting, strident, and self-righteous demands of narrow interest groups; (2) at the same time we need to be responsive to the legitimate concerns of the constituents of our pluralistic, multicultural nation; (3) we need not have to choose between the rhetoric of (1) and (2); but can strive to reexamine our traditions and seek language and images that give us common direction and purpose.

In these three points we see three different formulations of the educator's political vulnerability, and it is my belief that it would be best to respond to the complexity and difficulty of the problem by engaging in a project of re-creating an overarching mythos that can energize the culture, and with it the schools. It is vital that we confront the difficult and thorny dilemmas that emerge from any effort to find common ground, and equally vital that we face the consequence of not finding or even searching for our commonality. I have tried in this chapter to sketch out some possibilities for the fashioning of a vision that might provide for more rather than less focus of concerted energy, imagination, and hope.

This process is based on the assumption that virtually all of us can accept the importance and desirability of making a basic polar distinction between what some would call natural and unnatural, sacred and profane, good and bad, etc. This extremely important and basic agreement between believers and nonbelievers, between atheists and agnostics, between theologians and sociologists, represents an apparent agreement that people do make such distinctions, that it is vital to do so for a valid civilization, and also that there are enormous differences among us as to how to constitute and define the basic polar distinction.

We also posit a basic belief that we as people not only yearn for and create systems of meaning but also in spite of that continue cruelly to violate our own standards and measures of meaning. As educators, we need to accept these assumptions as the starting point for our efforts, since we must also assume that people have the interest and capacity to become aware of these violations so as to develop responses that can overcome them.

The first set of problems then immediately becomes clear, namely the reality that there are those who would challenge the basic notion that we can or should make affirmations and are eager to act on them. Connected to this problem is the inherent difficulty that emerges from the willingness to accept and act on any assumption or any framework—that is, the reality that assumptions and conceptual frameworks can conceal as well as reveal. I cannot deny nor will I try to overcome this difficulty because it is one inherent in our present existence and underscores the dilemma, risk, and inevitability of making choices.

However, I will point out two countervailing notions that can to some degree mitigate, even though they cannot obviate, this serious difficulty. The first is that we also affirm the importance of a posture of humility and a critical consciousness as tools to guard against rigidity and dogmatism. Wariness, awareness, and humility are necessary in our present state of consciousness, but not to the point of stalemated paralysis. The similar dictum that we be "whole-hearted and half-sure" is echoed by Sharon Welch's plea (1985) for "absolute conviction and infinite suspicion." Both can serve as guides to dealing with the paradox of the need for both commitment and criticism.

Thus, our second counterresponse to the difficulties inherent in having clear assumptions is to point to the risks and consequences involved with "objectivity," "detachment," "neutrality" (i.e., the inability or reluctance to affirm any set of assumptions). There is of course a problem with the set of assumptions that holds that we cannot, or should not, make any assumptions except those which are incontrovertibly true (of which so far there do not seem to be very many useful ones). The difficulty with a policy of extreme caution and skepticism is that it can promote sterility, relativism, solipsism, if not nihilism. As has been pointed out, there is a difference between being open-minded and being empty-minded. It is therefore a matter of choosing among risks, for there is no question that our current problems are rooted in both wishy-washiness and dogmatism; we can suffer from too much as well as from too little skepticism, and there can be a penalty for those having strong commitments as well as for those having none.

We believe, however, that there is less risk in committing to a set of values and principles that inherently demand and insist on a rewarding life for all people. We must, however, recognize that such statements reflect another set of problematics which involve the dangers of sentimentalism and glibness. As educators we struggle with the problem of passion—that is, we know that living (hence education) necessarily involves intense feelings and literally requires heroism, deep devotion, and dedication in order to transcend our limitations. At the same time we are rightfully wary of how emotions can be manipulated, and we see that coolness and detachment are also required dimensions of the educational process.

It is easy enough to regard my analysis of our religious/sacred traditions as sentimental pieties that gloss over harsh realities and complex ideas. Much, if not all, of that analysis has not been "proved," nor can it said that the validity of these ideas has been presented with overwhelmingly persuasive logic. They represent, at their core, assertions and prescriptions; not only is their "validity" problematic but there is enormous debate over whether and how such prepositions are or can be validated. To a large extent we are confronted here with issues of language, and with theories of knowledge and truth.

Are we, for example, required to use the same language for our mythos that we use to describe our legal system? Do we have to "prove" our metaphysical assumptions in ways that parallel our assumptions about the requirements of valid nutrition? If there are different appropriate languages, how do we move among them without obfuscation, manipulation, and deception? Can we develop an esthetic of language that inspires us and points to transcendence but nevertheless disciplines and flexes our mind?

I offer these questions without expecting answers that can quiet these concerns since I do not believe they are questions which can or should be stilled. Nor do I believe that they should prevent us from taking on the risk of affirmation or of passion as well. We need to guard against sloganeering, glibness, and the manipulation of powerful images and intense feelings. We also need to guard against the consequences of strangling our aspirations and ideals by choking our voice of passion with the cold hand of detachment. Again, great horrors have been perpetrated because of intense passions, and many of them have been allowed to happen because of indifference and dispassionate analysis. Slogans can distort; aphorisms can also illuminate; truth can be felt as well as falsehood; logic has led to the Peace Corps *and* to the Holocaust, there is an esthetic dimension to the Taj Mahal *and* the guillotine.

Nonetheless, we must be aware of these problems in the same spirit of humility, awareness, skepticism, and criticism that we have described in the response to the problems of affirmation. We must build into our mythos the faith that our basic principles are strong enough to withstand and, indeed, require, significant criticism and are sufficiently flexible to allow for a continuous process of discovery and transformation. As American educators we must assume our critical responsibility with special care, given particular tendencies in our history to become arrogantly pietistic.

In his *The American Jeremiad* Sacvan Bercovitch (1978) has elaborated on how very early in our history certain cultural themes developed and have continued strongly to influence our national ethos. More particularly, he carefully and thoroughly describes certain Puritan traditions, images, and ideals which were in the beginning explicitly recognized as the guidelines of the new colonies and which subsequently came to quietly but strongly permeate American culture. This book not only provides wonderful insight into our origins but also points to the dangers of excessive piety, self-righteousness, and religious arrogance that represent further and deeper the problematic nature of a consensual mythos.

As we have already noted in the first part of this chapter, Bercovitch points out that the Puritans who came to colonize America were part of the great Puritan revolution in England that resulted in the execution of Charles I and the establishment of the English Commonwealth ruled by Oliver Cromwell. This revolution was deeply rooted in very intense religious concerns focused on the need to purify and cleanse the country of cultural decadence and "popery." This revolution was itself overthrown and the monarchy restored at about the time significant colonization in the new world was beginning. Those Puritans who came to America had the same zeal and passion as their European counterparts about the utter need to change the direction of society. Bercovitch, however, points to an important difference, one that was to continue to characterize America. Whereas in Europe the failures and disappointments to achieve reform had encouraged an existing sense of European pessimism and a tragic sense of life, the American experience was quite different. Clearly, the colonists had a very different task than overthrowing a well-established culture and power structure with a very long history, replete with its traditions, heroes, images, rituals, and conventions. They did not see themselves as conquerors and invaders, intent on dispossessing the legitimate incumbent whom they arrogantly and ignorantly called "Indian," but as discoverers and developers of a "new world." By using this metaphor they brushed aside the reality that this was a very old world, new only to European consciousness. Furthermore, this metaphor could easily be converted into a new garden of Eden and, hence, opened up the possibility of a new Jerusalem.

The American Puritans then, according to Bercovitch's analysis, tended to be much more optimistic about the future and their capacity to shape the boundaries of this new promised land. They indeed saw the discovery of this new world as an indication of divine providence, and with that grace came a definite divine imperative to do God's work on earth. From the very beginning, then, came the thread in the American myth that God and America have a special relationship, that America has a special responsibility in humanity's destiny, that, in a word, God has in fact blessed America. We can also see the origins of the optimism, if not glee, that comes with the opportunity to start freshly with a clean slate; and even when the slate has been written on, it can be disregarded because it is in a strange language. We see not only the disregard of history but the passion for social engineering with all its elitist arrogance. What we cannot accuse the Puritans of is timidity, humility, or tentativeness, for it was certainly not their purpose to promote diversity or pluralism. Eventually they had to accept the political realities of other competing groups, but the Puritans believed that their beliefs and values were the right ones and that the leadership had a strong moral obligation to "help" others to see the right—that is, to impose their culture on all.

This self-righteousness was supported by an intense commitment to a religious perspective, and hence they were able to justify what we call dogmatism and arrogance as the responsibilities of acting on the word of God. The Puritans saw themselves as the new chosen people entrusted for perhaps the last time to redeem the Fall with a new pure, or at least much purer, world. Bercovitch maintains that these tendencies continue throughout our history even though they have lost their purely Puritan rhetoric and flavor. He sees these themes strongly repeated in major figures of nineteenth-century American literature such as Melville, Emerson, and Whitman. We can surely see their persistence in contemporary American foreign policy. We have leaders who tell the world that it is America's manifest destiny to control the New World, that it is America's responsibility to make the world safe for democracy, and that the Soviet Union is an "evil empire" and America is God's greatest gift to humanity. When a character in John Patrick's play *Teahouse of the August Moon* promises to bring democracy to an occupied territory, even if he has to kill everybody in the process, we laugh in the recognition, irony, and sorrow of our strange blend of naivete, good intentions, and blind arrogance.

Our history itself represents the dangers of arrogance, self-righteousness, self-deception, and the corruption that ensues when power and piety are integrated. We must be aware that we have abused our power and are likely to continue to abuse that power, in the name of divine intentions and/or moral imperatives. We must be on guard for the incipient tendency, grounded in our history, to be ruthlessly intolerant and maddeningly superior in the rigidity and smugness of our self-appointed task as God's hammer.

We will not, however, serve this responsibility by retreating into amorality and vulgar pragmatism, nor by a futile retreat into a sterile noncommitted posture. That is not only facile but counterproductive to the struggle for a life of equality and justice. It is a far more difficult task to more honestly confront the very real problems by struggling with the necessity of shaping a consciousness where serious moral convictions can co-exist with skepticism and openness. The avowal of skepticism without moral commitment, at best, amounts to incompleteness and evasion and, at worst, to irresponsibility and cowardice. As much as we deplore our history of arrogance and self-serving moralizing, we must not in the wake of this revulsion fail to affirm those generous impulses to do justice that are also part of the American tradition. A failure to affirm that which is truly noble in our efforts is to surrender to the forces of destructiveness and evil. A failure to affirm the evil and destructive forces in our culture does the same.

The final chapters represent an attempt to respond to these challenges as professional educators. As educators we cannot be expected to fully solve our problems by ourselves, but it is our responsibility to help others to become aware of the problems, to provide conceptual schema to probe and understand them, and to share and nourish the intellectual, psychological, artistic, and experiential resources that are the sources for responding to the problem. The schools are part of the culture's resources needed to pose the problems and questions as well as to generate energized and wise ways of dealing with them. Schools are not only a way of dealing with cultural concerns; they are a culture in that they are places where life is not only studied but lived. Hence, schools need also to be places where education deals with its own opportunities to be loci of joy, justice, and love, places where people can be affirmed and the pleasures of reflection, growth, and challenge can be experienced.

I will in the remainder of this book sketch out a number of curricular and instructional implications of our analysis of the educational crisis and of the suggested element of a consensual mythos and their problematics. These chapters represent an effort not so much to posit a new pedagogy but rather to reorganize and reorient the wealth and treasure of the wisdom that is reflected in many educational writers and practitioners. My basic notion on re-forming education is not essentially "technical." I believe that the problems are less in our ability and capacity to do what we sense is right and more in our willingness to do so. I have enormous respect for the ingenuity, imagination, and artistry that our gifted teachers continue to demonstrate. There is in the lore of accumulated practical genius a vast repertoire of marvelous techniques and approaches. Our task is to inform these techniques with principles that are intellectually and morally sound.

5
Education in a Prophetic Voice

The two dominant attitudes of prophetic faith are gratitude and contrition: Gratitude for creation and contrition before judgment; or in other words, confidence that life is good in spite of its evil and that it is evil in spite of good. In such faith both sentimentality and despair are avoided.
   Reinhold Niebuhr, An Interpretation of Christian Ethics

A basic theme of this book is the intimate interconnection between culture and education, and in this chapter we will focus more sharply on the implications of the proceeding moral and religious analysis for educational practice. The remainder of the book is an attempt to lay out the meaning of our interpretation for the profession, for curriculum and instruction, and for broad educational policy. In this chapter we will deal primarily with issues concerning the profession itself, with particular focus on the possibilities inherent in the profession for significant cultural and educational leadership. Our basic position is that the profession must confront its possibilities, as well as its structural limitations, and that its redemption can emerge from a frank and courageous recognition of its responsibilities and capabilities. Therefore, we begin our specific analysis of educational practice with a consideration of the single most vital professional element, the profession itself.

THE EDUCATION PROFESSION

When we talk of an educational program we cannot limit ourselves to discussion of materials, techniques, course of study, etc., for as we well know one's educational experiences are shaped by a host of other phenomena. We have already spoken at length on how cultural, social, and moral views permeate the schools and classrooms in powerful ways, but the hidden curriculum includes not only the values and attitudes but the quality of school life, its atmosphere and tone, and the nature of human relationships. The quality of school life is, in turn, significantly influenced by the nature and background of the staff, the conditions under which they work, their values, and their professional beliefs. Clearly, what students learn is strongly related to the school's constitutive structural elements and the sum total of human experiences in that school. Although it is a cliché to say that teachers and administrators are part of the "curriculum," it is cliché because it is said so frequently and not because we pay a great deal of attention to its significance. We need, therefore, to address more sharply the nature of the profession itself, as a major constitutive and structural element of educational experience.

We are, alas, a very weak profession, captured in part by our difficulty in admitting to our condition. I believe, however, that we are not weak by chance and that our weaknesses reflect the culture's basic ambivalence about the power and value of education as discussed in chapter one. What is maddening is that although we have been constituted to be weak, we are nonetheless brutally criticized by the culture for the consequences of our weakness. We are criticized for not being intellectually strong, yet the culture tends to channel its best and brightest students to other professions, such as law, medicine, and the sciences. We are berated for our sloppy theorizing and numbing jargon, yet scholars in older, well-established fields tend to ignore the serious study of education or insist on substituting their naivete about educational matters for informed dialogue. Teachers are asked to perform at very high-level tasks of profound importance and yet are given resources that are absurd and insulting. Moreover, because school budgets tend to be prominent and distinguishable, they are often subjected to minute and haggling examination, which puts the educational community in the posture of beggars who ought to be content with their customary dole.

We have also been unable to stem the forces that seriously work to make our profession reluctant to take initiative and assume leadership, and this is because in part our resources and destinies are largely controlled by people who want to keep down the budget, the complaints, the demands, and the quality of thinking. There are, of course, exceptions, such as the case of teacher organizations and unions pressing very aggressively for somewhat better working conditions and pay. However, it is often the case that in these situations, even when the professional groups ask for quite modest changes, there is at best cool community support and often community hostility. We are also a docile and passive profession for another basic and more troubling reason, one that we are reluctant to discuss publicly. I believe that we must confront our own inadequacies as a profession; we must deal with the reality that our members include a great many who are not very gifted intellectually, many who are timid or narrow about exercising leadership, and many who see teaching as a job requiring fairly modest technical skills and lots of hard work. Yes, there are lots of incompetents in other professions, and yes, the culture does do a lot to keep brighter, abler, more energetic people out of our profession. It is also true that the well-known defensiveness of the profession is partly a function of the cruelty and ignorance that permeates much of the public criticism of the schools.

However, we do not do ourselves or the culture any favor by refusing to acknowledge serious deficiencies in the basic structure of the system (which includes our competence) and the culture's very significant responsibility for those deficiencies (including ours). We are more feeble than we need be because we have allowed, if not encouraged, the culture to set the terms and boundaries of the debate and discussion of educational issues. Educators are typically put in a reactive posture and usually find themselves co-opted to work within a parameter of policies that many educators find fundamentally false. In this way educators become technical staff engaged to administer and execute policies set by those who are likely to have serious reservations about providing serious education for all. This has worked to let the profession off the hook of exercising its own responsibility to participate in, and enrich the process of, providing broad cultural leadership. The profession finds itself in a vicious circle—it is looked upon with disdain or perhaps indifference because it lacks the intellectual clout of genuine authority, and yet those in power see a confident, authoritative, and persuasive profession as a serious threat to existing arrangements. Our profession is further weakened by our own brand of specialization, divisiveness, and fragmentation. There are walls among and between teachers and administrators, among and between schools and universities. There is a myriad of worlds within worlds (gifted and talented; elementary; such organizational rubrics as science, middle school), a wide range of educational ideologies ranging from those that are "child-centered" to those totally loyal to institutional concerns. As professionals, we are divided and conquered.

Stanley Aronowitz and Henry Giroux (1985) have provided a concise and powerful analysis of the growing erosion of teacher autonomy and what they call the "proletarianization of teacher work." It is their position that there are steady pressures to reduce the significance of the teachers by increasing administrative controls, using such techniques as competency testing, the development of "teacher-proof"

materials, and by emphasizing an increasingly technical and instrumental orientation toward instruction.

> *Teachers are not simply being proleterianized; the changing nature of*
> *their roles and functions signifies the disappearance of a form of intel-*
> *lectual labor central to the nature of critical pedagogy itself. Moreover,*
> *the tendency to reduce teachers to either high-level clerks implementing*
> *the orders of others within the school bureaucracy or to specialized*
> *technicians is part of a much larger problem within western societies, a*
> *problem marked by the increasing division of intellectual and social labor*
> *and the increasing trend toward the oppressive management and admin-*
> *istration of everyday life. (1985:24)*

In their brilliant essay on intellectualism and teaching, Aronowitz
and Giroux distinguish among various forms of intellectual activities
and maintain a firm view that the requirements of serious and sensitive
teaching include the capacity for serious intellectual inquiry. Their
commitment, however, is clearly to a kind of teacher they label as a
"transformative intellectual," a concept that seems ideally fitted to the
teacher as prophet.

> *Central to the category of transformative intellectuals is the task of mak-*
> *ing the pedagogical more political and the political more pedagogical.*
> *In the first instance, this means inserting education directly into the*
> *political sphere by arguing that schooling represents both a struggle for*
> *meaning and a struggle over power relations. Thus schooling becomes*
> *a central terrain where power and politics operate out of a dialectical*
> *relationship between individuals and groups, who function within specific*
> *historical conditions and structural constraints as well as within cultural*
> *forms and ideologies that are the basis for contradictions and struggles.*
> *Within this view of schooling, critical reflections and action become part*
> *of a fundamental social project to help students develop a deep and*
> *abiding faith in the struggle to overcome injustice and to change them-*
> *selves. (1985:36)*

It does not seem to be in the interest of those currently in power
to encourage and empower the education profession to seek that
intellectual and moral authority. On the other hand, there are educators who believe strongly that it is very much in the interest of those
who struggle for a culture of love, joy, and justice to demand that our
profession develop such a vision. These educators also believe that
members of our profession have a basic right to pursue their calling
(vocation) with integrity and pride and to seek to fulfill their responsibilities to participate in the struggle to achieve those conditions. All
educators must come to define their autonomy in relationship to these
broader struggles rather than as a minor component of an existing
bureaucratic apparatus. Individual members of the profession have
the opportunity and indeed the imperative to search for their own

meaning within the context of their work as calling rather than as job. Therefore, they need not see their professional interests as necessarily coinciding with those of school boards, college admission offices, personnel offices, state departments of education, nor even those of school administrators. Professional autonomy in this sense is not to be confused with the self-serving, self-protective ethic of so-called professionalism, which translates into a consciousness of being quiet, polite, and deferential (e.g., "we mustn't wash our dirty linen in public" and "don't make waves"). It is nothing short of tragic that the concept of professionalism has become so distorted that it can connote narrow protectionism rather than dedication to high principles. We should as a profession profess our high ideals rather than being fearful to confess our shortcomings.

We must accept the responsibilities of being the kind of a profession which involves independence and autonomy, and in order to merit that independence and autonomy we must be competent; we must have a sound basis for our authority, and we must have a set of principles and ideas that can inform our professional ethic. As long as we see ourselves as employees or staff or technicians, we will not be a profession that leads but a camp that follows the parade. But we need more than power to lead; we need moral, intellectual, and professional authority that influences rather than imposes. As a profession we need to develop our own overarching professional mythos—a shared set of images and ideals that can guide and inform all our various specializations and concentrations. We suggest that the prophetic tradition provide direction for such a mythos.

EDUCATION AND PROPHECY

Both the culture and individual educators need a profession with a critical capacity and the courage and expertise to provide insights into cultural problems and suggest reasonable responses to them. There are many people and institutions charged with the responsibility of noting and detecting our achievements and shortcomings and of suggesting ways of dealing with them. We urge that the education profession be one of those institutions which accepts that responsibility. In this way, educators would be working within the prophetic tradition that seeks to remind us of our highest aspirations, of our failures to meet them, and of the consequences of our responses to these situations. In order to act in this tradition, educators need to be well-equipped with intellectual powers, expertise, psychological strength, moral courage, strong convictions, and inner strength that derive from a sense of responding seriously to profoundly important issues. Again, it is not in the interest of the existing power structure to stress the extraordinary power and importance of teaching, but it is to our common interest that we all be mindful of the magnificence and nobility of those who seriously teach.

The educator as prophet does more than re-mind, re-answer, and re-invigorate—the prophet-educator conducts re-search and joins students in continually developing skills and knowledge that enhance the possibility of justice, community, and joy. His concern is with the search for meaning through the process of criticism, imagination, and creativity. Such a role (as Socrates found out) is in fact seriously threatening to those fearful of displacing the status quo. Most importantly, the educator as prophet seeks to orient the educational process toward a vision of ultimate meaning. The prophetic model, hence, does not allow the individual educator to go in individual or happenstance direction, for the great prophets like Socrates, Moses, Jesus, Gandhi, and King have performed their critical and creative functions within a broad but particular conception of the meaning and significance of human creation and destiny. Educators who accept the concept of their profession as having a prophetic function must then affirm a set of sacred and moral principles—a mythos, a set of metaphysical or religious assumptions—or commit themselves to that which has ultimate meaning to them. As human beings we need to consciously participate in the process of both forming and being informed by these principles, and as educators we need to help our students to learn how to participate in that process. We have indicated what at least some of these principles might be, and note that educators not only have a responsibility to be reflective, thoughtful, and critical about these principles but also have a responsibility to reflect on their own basic assumptions, however implicit, tacit, or preconscious they may be. A profession without a mythic dimension that provides a vision of ideals and goals is not capable of providing serious cultural leadership and instead serves as a tool that is manipulated by those who have such a vision in place.

Educators are culturally well positioned to have a sense of how the culture is responding to its highest ideals and, consequently, ought to be able to respond to its opportunities for providing social criticism. Traditionally, however, the profession has not seen itself as a institution with such responsibilities and has tended to acquiesce to the dominant culture's self-definition of what the major problems and needs are. The profession needs to establish as its central concerns those policies that correspond to the culture's highest ideals and not those that distort them or deceive us. Although it is reasonable to make some link between cultural success and failure with educational success and failure, it is crucial that the profession be free to focus on what actually constitutes success and failure. For example, schools are criticized, perhaps appropriately, when S.A.T. scores go down, but perhaps they should also be criticized when there is a war or when charitable donations drop. Educators must point out serious social and moral problems of our culture as part of their responsibility to be self-critical and as a way of setting a professional agenda for action. When brilliant economists and other social scientists say they can't control the economy, they are, at least partly, saying something about the inadequacy of their knowledge, of the limitations of their research, of their lack of imagination (i.e., of their education). Such problems should not logically lead us to intensify the very schooling that produced these difficulties but rather to seriously reconsider some of its basic assumptions.

As educators we must confront ourselves and the public with the harsh reality of the basic ignorance and intellectual failures of those who by conventional standards have had the very best education. The fact that the best and the brightest have done very well in some areas and very poorly in others should not fill us with defensiveness or shame but with humility and determination.

Our failures surely speak at least partly to the limits of our knowledge, or perhaps the political constraints on inquiry, as well as to the failure of the educational system to provide enough opportunities for greater insight and imagination. Educators must reflect on how they have contributed to major structural failures like persistent unemployment and poverty rather than focus on their inability to lower the dropout rate or keep schooling costs down. Educators must confront our moral failure by seriously considering the relationship between the realities of hunger, poverty, and misery and the nature of existing educational programs. The culture that produces and allows any such oppression or degradation fails, and all its institutions must share in the responsibility for that failure. The profession must begin with the perspective of hunger, war, poverty, or starvation as its starting point, rather than from the perspective of problems of textbook selection, teacher certification requirements, or discipline policies. If there is no serious connection between education and hunger, injustice, alienation, poverty, and war, then we are wasting our time, deluding each other, and breaking faith. I believe, however, that there are strong connections and it is these connections which give educators purpose and enable us to see ourselves as having prophetic responsibilities.

In order for educators to accept and meet their responsibilities as social critics and leaders, they obviously will need to have sufficient resources. One of the most telling indications of the weakness and timidity of our profession is its acceptance of the basic framework of the conditions under which teachers in elementary and secondary schools are expected to work. Even though there is a consensus that teachers are grossly overworked and underpaid, efforts directed at change are almost always ameliorative rather than transformative in character. In fact, it takes enormous efforts simply to maintain work-load and pay standards at their currently absurd levels, lest they become worse, as they have in many communities. As has been said, we see in this situation evidence of the dominant culture's fear of a strong educational program and its respect for the potential impact of schools populated by stimulating and imaginative teachers who have been given sufficient resources and a reasonable work load. We must also, however, closely examine the reality that the profession has not made a serious concerted effort to convince the American public that its allocations to the schools are not merely inadequate but shocking, insane, and destructive. There is, for example, the extraordinary variance in salaries and working conditions between those who teach in grades K-12 and those who teach at the university level, private and public. Salaries in universities are two or three times what they are in the lower grades, opportunities for advancement and development are infinitely greater, and the differences in teacher load are astounding (i.e., typically twelve hours vs. thirty hours). Moreover, the differences in autonomy, respect, and status are such that it is extremely difficult to consider teachers in both institutions as being in the same profession. The profession itself has contributed to the glib and irrational belief that these differences are "natural" and perhaps even desirable. Do we really want to take the position that teaching at the elementary or high school is less important or less taxing than university teaching? Are we prepared to defend a position that says that those who do not teach at the university do not need or want to do scholarly research? More to the point, why has the profession failed to address seriously not only this particular lunacy but broader question of what a proper, high-quality environment for serious teaching and learning would really entail?

One explanation is that, sadly enough, many members of the profession have come to accept the existing framework as reasonable, perhaps needing adjustment from time to time, and have failed to reflect seriously on its inadequacies. A related explanation speaks more clearly to the basic fear in our profession, a fear which produces our prodigious docility and passivity. What one hears regularly from many professionals in response to the pitiful working conditions for teachers is the belief that "we" should not seriously rock the boat lest "they" react in anger and retribution. This is the employer-employee, master-slave mentality in which we are reminded of our place and our powerlessness, urged to count our blessings, and warned about the consequences of protest. We are a profession which has, to a very large degree, internalized the oppressors' consciousness.

Let us contrast this posture of appeasement and passivity with that of the biblical prophets. Of course we cannot in any way return to those times, but we can hope that their example will help illuminate our present condition. First of all, there was, according to some scholars, a recognized role and function for prophets in ancient Israel. Prophesy as the process of reminding, criticizing, and warning was considered to be a necessary role in that society; and while prophets were not always given official status, they were accepted and valued as legitimate, if sometimes difficult or troublesome, members of the quasi-formal leadership. They were often consulted by the priests and kings and sometimes, nevertheless, imprisoned for their views and their agitations. However, there seems to be strong evidence that the *prophetic function* was considered necessary even though the acceptance of individual prophets varied enormously. Buber describes their functions not as magical but as functional:

> The Israelite prophet utters his words, directing them into an actual and definite situation. Hardly ever does he foretell a plainly certain future. YHVH does not deliver into his hand a completed book of fate with all future events written in it, calling upon him to open it in the presence of his hearers. It was something of this kind the "false prophets" pretended, as when they stood up against Michaiah (v. 11ff) and prophesied to the king, "Go up and prosper!" Their main "falsity" lay not in the fact that they prophesy salvation, but that what they prophesy is not dependent on question and alternative. This attitude is closer to the divination of the heathen than to true Israelite prophecy. The true prophet does not announce an immutable decree. He speaks into the power of decision lying in the moment, and in such a way that his message of disaster just touches this power. (1960:103)

The power structure no doubt paid attention to the prophets for a variety of reasons. First, like anyone else, they were particularly interested in a prophet's capacity to foretell the future, even though prophets were definitely not in the same category as sorcerers and magicians. The prophetic capacity of predicting the future is more akin to the aspirations of contemporary social science or punditry—that is, it emerges from a keen understanding of how underlying forces are affecting events. Second, prophets probably both reflected and influenced community attitudes and, hence, their views had important political meaning. Third, and not necessarily least of all, prophets claimed to have privileged communication with God, or at the very least to have special sensitivity to know God's will. The power structure for whatever combination of reasons, would certainly want to connect their decisions and policies to what were accepted as sacred imperatives. The priests on the other hand were too closely identified with the power structure and were probably more interested in dealing with issues of ritual and observance than with political issues. The culture apparently felt it was well served by the existence of a group whose independence, special sensitivities, and intense concerns could serve the function of actually preserving the culture by pointing out the necessity of appropriate change. Prophets were neither wholly inside nor wholly outside the system but clearly committed to the system's long-range well-being, and, therefore, their criticisms and cries of outrage could not be dismissed (although they sometimes were) as work of cranks or subversives. This is certainly not to make a historical claim that prophecy was without its serious problems and resistances in ancient Israel, but only to point to a model of a culture's attempt to institutionalize a way of maintaining its commitments to its conceptions of the sacred through continuous criticism and affirmation.

Buber, in talking of the role of prophets in ancient Israel, speaks of the reluctance of that nation to have "kings" in the modern sense. Israel held onto the idea that the spirit of God should serve as sufficient governance, but eventually the Israelites came reluctantly to accept first "judges" and later "kings." Buber believes that the inevitable tensions created by monarchy contributed to the importance of prophecy.

> *The dynastic continuity implies a continuity of responsibility to fulfill the divine commission. . . . The fundamental and practical opposition of the kings to this constitutional obligation resulted in the mission of the prophets. . . . Against the tendency of the kings (frequently supported it seems by the priests with their sole concern for the autonomy of the social domain) to sublimate the commission into a divine right without any obligation, a divine right granting the kings to stand in accordance with ancient customs, as sons of the deity invested with full powers (cf. Ps. 2,7)—against this tendency the prophets set up the theopolitical realism which does not admit any "religious" subtlety. Over and against YHVH's vicegerent on the royal throne, acting unrighteously and therefore unlawful, but powerful, there stands the bearer of YHVH's word, without any power, but certain of his mission, reproving and claiming, reproving and claiming in vain. (1960:152–53)*

Clearly our culture is inevitably very different from that tiny society that struggled and flourished four thousand years ago. However, as cultures surely differ, they also have a great number of challenges in common—particularly those involved with the struggles for survival and fulfillment. Our culture does not formally recognize the prophetic function, although many individuals and institutions seek to perform it, and we are certainly not suggesting any formal institutionalization of it by creating something like the Department of Prophecy. Ideally, all our institutions and every individual could incorporate those dimensions within their work, and indeed, the nourishment of those impulses should be considered as a prime goal of the educational process. In order to encourage "prophecy," educators themselves need to be "prophets" and speak in the prophetic voice that celebrates joy, love, justice, and abundance and cries out in anguish in the presence of oppression and misery. Educators share this prophetic responsibility with others in the culture, but they have special and critical roles in applying the prophetic perspective to professional issues, concerns, and standards. The educator as prophet needs to be particularly concerned about the degree to which the culture and the profession are keeping their sacred commitments. Prophetic educators must facilitate the dialogue on what these sacred commitments are, how they are to be interpreted in the light of particular situations, and what constitutes appropriate responses to them. In this way we can respond to this challenge from Walter Brueggemann: "The educational task of the community is to nurture some to prophetic speech. But for many others, it is to nurture an awareness that we must permit and welcome and evoke that prophetic tongue among us. Otherwise we will be diminished into the prose world of the king and, finally, without hope. Where there is no tongue for new truth, we are consigned to the coldness of the old truth" (1982:54).

Prophetic educators focus not only on the culture and the profession but on their more specialized practice. Educators have parallel responsibilities to be guided in their practice by their vision of the ultimate/sacred/holy and their responsibilities to be critical of shortcomings as well as to be responsive to them. Such educators must regard themselves and their students as holy and sacred, not as tools and mechanisms, hence as ends not means; they must be committed to the development of institutions of learning in which all those involved (teachers, administrators, staff, students) are full citizens, each of whom has the inherent right of personal and social fulfillment, each of whom has inherent and full dignity, and each of whom has the inherent right to grow, learn, and create as much as he/she possibly can. Thus, schools can be transformed from warehouses and training sites into centers of inquiry and growth where participants share their different abilities and talents in the pursuit of the common goal of creating a culture of deepest meaning. Such a conception of the profession will, I believe, serve the culture and educators well, for although it certainly puts the profession into a service role, it does not put it in the service of pursuing the profane, but rather the sacred. Paradoxically, such a role limits the profession, yet liberates it from servility and collaboration in unworthy tasks to a role of participating in the creation of freedom and justice.

Educators as prophets must therefore be mindful that their specialization plays a crucial moral and social role; they must be mindful of the professional and personal requirements necessary to meet these responsibilities. They must act simultaneously as citizens, professionals, technicians, and leaders. If educators are indeed to be prophets, it is obviously critical that they be aware of a vision that informs and guides their practice. It is to the delineation of this vision that we must now turn.

CREDO AND HISTORY:
THE DIALECTIC OF EDUCATIONAL GROUND

We are at the point of articulating our basic orientation toward educational practice, one grounded in the dialectical relationship between a commitment to a broad vision of what is sacred and an understanding of the significance of this particular moment in history. As prophet educator in the tradition of Moses and Jesus, we must be in touch with our highest aspirations; as educator-prophets in the tradition of Socrates, Marx, and Freud, we must be aware of the problems involved in our understanding of this vision, and as educator-prophets in the tradition of Martin Luther King and Paulo Freire, we must be alert to its significance in the light of contemporary events. Education is a dynamic, ever-changing process that must be able to respond to the shifts and twists of this dialectic process, and hence I believe it both appropriate and imperative to attempt a basic statement on an educational framework that ought to guide our work for the next generation.

The historical grounds for this statement have already been discussed in prior sections of this book, but it is perhaps useful to summarize them in the form of several propositions:

1. We live in a moment of utmost precariousness, a time unlike other times, when particular cultures, nations, and groups are at risk, but when the entire civilization and planet confront the possibility of extinction.

2. We live in a time of massive injustice, ranging in severity from serious and devastating to unimaginably horrible. We confront staggering conditions of starvation, unemployment, poverty, misery, exploitation, and oppression.

3. We live in a time of estrangement and apartheid, ranging from moral and spiritual alienation, narcissism and personalism, to the legitimized structures of racial, economic, and social separation. Paul Tillich helps us to understand the relationship between this alienation and our concern for the sacred, an alienation he calls estrangement.

Estrangement as sin has a threefold character. It is the wilful turning away from the divine ground of our being (unbelief), combined with the elevation of our own selves to the center of all things, thus usurping the place of God (hubris). *It expresses itself also in "concupiscence"—the lustful striving not only for sexual conquest, but for knowledge and power as well—in other words "the unlimited desire to draw the whole of reality into one's self." (Quoted in Porteous 1966:113–14)*

4. We live in a time of particularly dangerous self-deception and arrogance derived from our reluctance to accept the extent of our ignorance. Peter Berger has written on how organized religion (and by extension the schools) can contribute to moral numbness. In *The Precarious Vision* he has this to say:

> *To reject the comforts and security of religious submission is to have the courage to admit the precariousness of existence and to face the silence of the universe. This certainly does not mean that one must resign oneself to meaninglessness or that one must give up the quest for meaning. It does mean the surrender of illusionary meanings and false reassurances. This also involves a relentless intellectual honesty which abhors bad faith and seeks always to be conscious to the fullest possible clarity. Such intellectual honesty forces the admission that there are many questions, even vital questions, of which we are ignorant. (1961:151)*

5. We live in a time of increasing despair, a time when more and more people perceive themselves as victims and as powerless even in the face of the realization that "powerlessness corrupts and absolute powerlessness corrupts absolutely." More and more we have edged into a paranoic state where the "system," however irrational and unwise, becomes ever stronger, more remote, and less responsive. José Miranda characterizes this view and its effect on, or commitment to, social justice and community:

> *The system forces the man to surrender himself, with all his existential weight, to assuming his economic future and to regarding the problems of others as completely foreign to himself. It forces him to surrender himself to the spirit of calculation, to the ideology which says that a man's value depends on his cleverness in situating himself within the system. And he must do this because of the system itself, independently of indoctrination by propaganda or education or ideology; he must do this necessarily, to be someone, to be able to survive, in order not to be crushed by the social machinery. (1974:8–9)*

6. We also live in a time of hope that emerges from increased consciousness and sensitivity, as well as from the achievements and potentials of our creative, artistic, scientific, and intellectual genius. We are experiencing enormously exciting and profound changes in our knowledge, theories, and paradigms in our arts, sciences, crafts, and professions. We continue to demonstrate our creative capacities to re-create the world with the increasing demands for justice, joy, and meaning for all as we widen the realm of possibility.

Given these possibilities as educators and citizens we *must* regard this moment as a time of utmost crisis and, therefore, must respond to these priorities with all our energy and imagination. We cannot disregard the horrors of misery, starvation, poverty for millions of people, nor the possibility of nuclear destruction of billions of people. Not to act or not to respond fully are acts of enormous consequence. As educator-prophets we can be guided by Heschel's precept that "it is an act of evil to accept the state of evil as either inevitable or final. Others may be satisfied with improvement, the prophets insist upon redemption" (1962: 181). Nor can we disregard the immense human capacity and interest in continuing the struggle for a world of love and joy. We must confront our enormous capacities for both good *and* evil: what we have broken we surely can fix, what we have yet to create we can surely construct.

AN EDUCATIONAL CREDO: A STATEMENT OF GOALS

As educators we have the specific responsibility of forging a broad educational belief system ever mindful of the problems of any such effort as well as the problems involved in not making such an attempt. The following represent an effort, therefore, to sketch out broad educational goals which reflect our cultural mythos and which, together with the just completed historical perspective, can help generate the somewhat more specific educational objectives described in the next chapter. The credo represents very basic values and assumptions that are in a sense "non-negotiable," even though we are simultaneously convinced of their "truth" and nervous about their problems. In recognition of the twin dangers of being either dogmatic or uncommitted, we affirm that the goals of current educational practices ought to include:

1. *The examination and contemplation of the awe, wonder, and mystery of the universe.* As educators we have the responsibility to examine the world and universe we live in and to share our reactions authentically and rationally and have a concomitant responsibility to be aware of and share with our students the process of observation and examination used by different scholars and observers. When we do so, we *always* find at least one common result—namely, enormously different observations, reactions, and explanations across and within time and place. Not only is there an immensely different assortment of cosmic explanations, but there is diversity even within very narrow fields of explanation. We find not only differences of opinion but also agreement that every field is extraordinarily complicated.

We can and should confront this reality as a reflection of our comparative youth as a species in a universe which numbers its birthdays in the billions of years. Thus, we are appropriately humble as any novice would be, maintaining however the confidence that over time we have come to know more and more, and perhaps at an accelerating rate. However paradoxically, our knowledge explosion has also led to a deeper sense of the mystery of the most fundamental process of origin and destiny. The areas of the unknown may have been narrowed, but their mystery has been heightened. When we look at the incredible biological process within the human body, or the physical process that forms mountains and continents, or when we contemplate the immensity of space, we are struck with the sheer wonder of it all—we are left (almost) speechless, in awe. Whatever cosmic explanations we use, it is inevitably and inherently breathtaking and incredible in scope. It is just as mind-blowing to posit a God who created the universe as it is to posit a universe created without a God. This awe and wonder need not and should not be sentimentalized, nor should it be a matter of indifference. It is intellectually honest to recognize the mystery and to examine ways in which to reduce the needlessly mysterious—that is, to do the research and the teaching designed to reduce ignorance. It is intellectually necessary to be honest not only about what we do know but about what we do not know. This is not humility for the sake of religious ritual, but necessary for the pursuit of truth, knowledge, and meaning.

Educators perforce provide a basic context for their program of studies, and as part of this context we need to establish the reality of the immense mystery that is the surround of our existence of awesome complexity. This context is critical in that it locates us not only as an interested observer of the mystery but as an aspect of the mystery as well. Thus, we have to establish from the beginning our ontological dimension (i.e., that we are a people engaged in a process of defining our being). Moreover, this context helps to establish that such a process is an ongoing one, fraught with uncertainty and, hence, one that requires serious knowledge, reflection, and research. Furthermore, it is a context that posits that such a process will require that we be ever mindful of the profundity of the task and the modest nature of our progress. In this way we also catch a glimmer of our responsibilities—we are required to respond to our condition, for if humans are to survive they must respond.

2. *The cultivation and nourishment of the processes of meaning making*. With the experience of awe and mystery comes the recognition that though we as a species are required to take initiative for survival purposes (e.g., we have to build shelter and search for food), we are also a people intent on creating systems of thought that explain our

past and guide our present and future. When educators examine these various thought systems, they confront the same kind of diversity and complexity of cosmic explanations. In a parallel way, educators must also deal with the context of meaning within which educational activities are to be presented. The educational goal is not so much to teach a particular meaning systems but rather to teach for the process of responding to that challenge. Educators must remind themselves and their students that any civilization or any culture is a human construction, and it is a human responsibility to create and re-create culture; thus, it is intellectually unsound to encourage the notion that cultural institutions, values, and beliefs are given. We are to a very significant degree, though certainly not entirely responsible for the creation of our lives—we create our culture and our culture creates us. We live in dialectical relationship with the mystery, with nature, and with the culture. Therefore, in recognition of our important though limited role in the vast drama of existence, it is incumbent that we respond to our creative responsibilities.

Educators must help us all to see the nature of this creative process by sharpening our creative capacities and by exposing us to a variety of cultural creations. We need to create not only a culture that enables us to live but one that needs to know that such a possibility exists and that there are others who have responded to that opportunity. The educational process is based on a very basic notion that the world makes sense and that we are involved in both determining and creating that sense. From almost the very beginning of their lives, people try to understand and control their world, and educational institutions must elaborate and nourish these impulses. This is not say that educators should in any way encourage solipsism and self-indulgence. Rather they should stress the collectively human basis of our culture, regarding subjectivity and imagination not so much as channeled into self-expression but as necessary to the impulse to create a life of moral significance.

3. *The cultivation and nourishment of the concept of the oneness of nature and humanity, with the concurrent responsibility to strive for harmony, peace, and justice.* Here we very definitely enter a realm of affirmation — that is, the acceptance of basic cosmological and moral principles. In this statement we accept as an assumptive belief that there is an ultimate sense in which we are essentially connected with each other, with nature, and with the universe. We posit, therefore, that our goals should include the development of a consciousness in which peace, harmony, and justice are integral. We assume that in a universe of harmony and meaning each individual human is inherently of worth and that the dignity of all elements of the universe is

significantly interrelated. Harmony, therefore, by definition demands justice and peace—dignity is indivisible. As public educators we have special responsibilities to remind ourselves of this truth and to find ways in which to make this truth real. Since we have already assumed that we have a responsibility to help create a world of meaning, we can set in motion this process by affirming these very basic meta-physical assumptions—namely, that we add to our educational context the notion that we are directed toward the struggle for harmony among the cosmic elements. We are happy to reaffirm and, as educators, to act upon these universal truths—that *all* people are created with equal worth and dignity and that it is our responsibility to sustain and nourish that initial position through our lifetimes. We would urge educators to provide the intellectual and emotional resources needed to take on the struggle that is involved in maintaining this commitment.

We must also be mindful of our place in the universe and our relationship to nature, particularly in our responsibilities to preserve and enrich our environment. We must confront without hyperbole how we as species have threatened not only certain social institutions but the very existence of the planet as a living organism. Our struggle is to participate in the cosmic impulse for an ecology of natural, human, and universal joy, love and justice, or, as we sometimes call it, harmony. Indeed, we see major and exciting possibilities emerging in this area in the emergence of the extraordinary consciousness-raising efforts represented in both the women's and ecological movements. Both of these broad movements have at their center a fundamental concern for intimacy and harmony, based on the recognition of our interdependence and our vision of wholeness.

By accepting these principles, we as educators need to model and instruct in ways so that we can actually participate in this struggle. We need not only to be encouraged and supported in our impulse to love, to do justice, and to be one with our humanity and nature, but we also need to learn that we must work continuously, creatively, and intensely to act on these impulses. Educators must become aware of and share the techniques of the theory *and* practice of meaning making, and the making of a world. Educators must, however, also be candid about the complexities, paradoxes, and contradictions of human existence. We can celebrate harmony as a goal, but we must also recognize the enormous difficulties and serious resistance to the struggle for universal justice and peace.

As educators we must honestly and candidly share our knowledge of the plurality of modes of consciousness and of cultural variation. We must also note that our traditions, including educational ones, put stress on sharp divisions, as seen in the dualisms of mind and body, the individual and the group, and in the nurture vs. nature controversy. Given the mystery we have discussed, and by the same token given our assumption about the ultimate universal harmony, we can sustain our faith in the face of these dualisms by affirming the concept of the dialectic. We cannot avoid the danger of dualistic thinking by denying the power of one of the dyads (e.g., by denying that our lives have a significant degree of determinism to them, or that the body has a reality of its own).

4. *The cultivation, nourishment, and development of a cultural mythos that builds on a faith in the human capacity to participate in the creation of a world of justice, compassion, caring, love, and joy.* Educators here again are in a posture of affirmation, not only of these moral principles but of their "sacred" quality. As public educators in an American context, we cannot and should not paint ourselves into an ideological corner by identifying ourselves totally with one of a number of sects, denominations, or movements with a religious or quasi-religious orientation. As educators we can and should confront ourselves and our students with the serious and important questions and issues that are inherent in these matters and offer us insight and tools of analysis to increase our understanding. However, as I have tried to demonstrate, teaching for understanding is not enough, for we must also teach for meaning.

Educators can and should include in their broad context of practice the broad areas of moral consensus that we have discussed in the previous chapter. Educators can and should also offer to their students the opportunity and responsibility to wrestle with the moral and religious dilemmas and paradoxes that permeate our culture. We can as educators offer and act on our wisdom that we are well advised to accept a sacred/profane distinction of some kind, leaving open of course the question of whether such a conception represents revelation or sociology. We can as educators and humans also in very good faith insist that we accept and act on the moral principles of love, justice, compassion, and joy for all. As educators we must also stress the enormous difficulties inherent in the ways in which these terms are defined, experienced, and implemented.

5. *The cultivation, nourishment, and development of the ideals of community, compassion, and interdependence within the traditions of democratic principles.* As educators we should not in the least be embarrassed by embracing and nourishing our democratic heritage, which is a political response to the moral requirements of equality and individual dignity as well as the social realities of interdependence. Democratic theory is a pragmatic response to a culture's desire to deal with the everyday requirements of living within the moral

contexts of two profound but potentially contradictory values: equality and freedom. Democracy both affirms a moral position and offers concrete procedures and principles to allow us to work on the challenges of this contradiction. We as a people have faith that we can at least approach a society where every person can do as they like provided that it does not, paradoxically, interfere with what others may want to do. Our heritage calls for individual autonomy *and* concern for others; it speaks to individual freedom *and* social justice, to independence *and* compassion.

As educators and humans we should celebrate this tradition, and as educators we should be mindful of the problems, difficulties, and complexities that arise and will continue as a consequence of this moral orientation. There is surely no contradiction in affirming the broad principles and intentions of democracy and in being mindful of their problems. It is in fact the very spirit of democracy that allows, indeed encourages, continuous critical reflection and free inquiry by free people. Let us, however, not interpret this to mean a community without boundaries; flexible and supportive as we may be, the cultural/ sacred mythos we have been sketching does not allow for oppression, injustice, and inequality. We must also be ever mindful of considering the meaning of democratic institution in the particular context of the social and political realities of specific historical moments. Indeed, democratic procedures must be examined in the light of their impact on moral and spiritual aspirations, even in the faith that they are of one piece.

6. *The cultivation, nourishment, and development of attitudes of outrage and responsibility in the face of injustice and oppression.* As educators we must in our celebration of democracy also be mindful of the extraordinary importance of individual participation in the life of the community. Democracy demands a great deal from each person and rests on the faith that an informed public will be alert to its failures and responsive to the need to overcome those failures. If we are to take the major and broad elements of our mythos seriously, then we will see that oppression, injustice, and indignity are collective concerns, even though they may be focused on individuals or groups. Educators must also recognize that passion is an inevitable part of human experience and that it needs to be seen in its constructive as well as its destructive sense. We will not do our cause of justice and love any service by being merely civil in the face of oppression (i.e., being polite and decorous are totally inappropriate in the context of misery). At the same time, we must recognize that passion by itself is no guarantee of the presence of deep moral principles.

Outrage at oppression is, however, an intelligent and rational response to a situation where our highest values are being violated. We must be wary when we pass off certain violations as minor or modest—as in an acceptable level of unemployment or casualties. Oppression and misery are horrid and unacceptable for one person, and when that horror extends to large numbers of people, the horror becomes more horrible. However, we cannot use the logic of reversing this process in such a way that horror for a few became less horrible than horror for many for otherwise we will become tolerant of some horror. As Heschel says,

> *Modern thought tends to extenuate personal responsibility. Understanding the complexity of human nature, the interrelationship of individual and society, of consciousness and the subconscious, we find it difficult to isolate the deed from those circumstances in which it was done. But new insights may obscure essential vision, and man's conscience grow scales: excuses, pretense, self-pity. Guilt may disappear: no crime is absolute, no sin devoid of apology. Within the limits of the human mind, relativity is true and merciful. Yet the mind's scope embraces but a fragment of society, a few instants of history; it thinks of what has happened, it is unable to imagine what might have happened. . . . Above all, the prophets remind us of the moral state of a people: Few are guilty, but all are responsible. If we admit that the individual is in some measure conditioned or affected by the spirit of society, an individual's crime discloses society's corruption. In a community not indifferent to suffering, uncompromisingly impatient with cruelty and falsehood, continually concerned for God and every man, crime would be infrequent rather than common. (1962:14, 16)*

THE ISSUE OF INDOCTRINATION

We have to this point been discussing educational goals that are mostly those involving assumptions, beliefs, and values. The values and attitudes represented in these goals are derived from the dimensions of broad cultural consensus that might serve as a statement of our sense of the sacred, of our mythos, and of our platform of beliefs. We offer no apologies for being explicit about the place of values and beliefs in education, since we operate under the assumption that education cannot and should not be "value-free." Indeed, concern for fairness and openness represents values, and educators need to affirm them. Another way of expressing these values is to raise a concern about indoctrination, manipulation, and the imposition of teacher values upon students.

As educators we must recognize and confront this dilemma and be mindful of the difficulties and risks involved in teaching. There is no way of avoiding this risk, but attempts to avoid it are bound to distract and deceive us and, hence, will likely exacerbate the problem. Educators can be more authentic by sharing the problem with each other, the public, and their students. We also should be mindful that there are both gray areas and black-and-white ones in this realm. We can easily point to conditions which we can call manipulative and oppressive—situations in which coercion is used as a teaching technique (either crudely, as in punishment and grading, or more subtly, as in the denial of affection), or situations in which undue pressures are used (such as ridicule and ostracism).

The single most effective way to reduce the inherent political advantage of teachers is to reduce as much as possible, and as soon as possible, crucial politically significant gaps between teacher and student. These gaps include differences in the amount and nature of knowledge; modes of analysis; critical and creative capacities; poise, confidence, personal strength, and stability. Educators must maintain their legitimate authority but give away all their coercive power as soon as possible, and in this way they, as well as students, can be free to *study* the problems rather than to use them as part of a struggle for power and domination. Ironically enough, teachers are also oppressed by the presence of the fear of indoctrination and manipulation, since many sensitive and caring teachers bend over backwards to avoid even the appearance of taking advantage of their political position. A casualty of this process can be students losing out on the fully passionate consciousness of a teacher's commitments. Teachers and students need to be free of the fears of dominating and of being dominated in order to facilitate free common inquiry. For this reason alone, the primitive practice of "grading" students should be abolished. Grading degrades and dehumanizes in its inherent process of creating hierarchies. It is also anti-intellectual in its irrational and arbitrary character, and it is a serious barrier to the true educational process of inquiry, sharing, and dialogue.

The more specific educational goals to be discussed in the next chapter can be seen as not only vital to the overall purpose of education, as indicated, but also as part of the way we can help students and teachers avoid the possibilities of indoctrination and manipulation. They can be seen as intellectual equalizers, capacities that are enabling and empowering and that help us to be liberated from the oppressions of ignorance, incompetence, and powerlessness, and at the same time free us to make our moral commitments a reality.

6

A Curriculum for Social Justice and Compassion

While compassion implies passion, pathos and deep caring arising from the bowel and guts, it also implies an intellectual life. Ideals come from ideas after all and are important. Just as there can be no justice without ideas and an intellectual life, so there can be no compassion without an intellectual life, for compassion involves the whole person in quest for justice and a mind with ideas in an obviously significant portion of any of us. . . . To develop compassion, then, means to develop an ever keener awareness of the interdependence of all living things. But to develop such an awareness implies deep study, not only of books, of course, but of nature itself. It implies study as a spiritual discipline, as a means of entering more and more fully into the truth of the universe in which we live. It implies a rejoicing on the part of spiritual people at the facts of our universe that science can and has uncovered, and therefore an authentic kind of ecumenical dialogue between science and spirituality.

Compassion, being so closely allied with justice-making, requires a critical consciousness, one that resists all kinds of keptness, including that of kept academia and kept intellectuals. It implies a going out in search of authentic problems and workable solutions, born of deeper and deeper questions.

Matthew Fox, Original Blessing

This chapter focuses more sharply on the nature of educational experiences specially directed at the development of a culture of social justice and compassion. It is a framework that emerges from the discussion of priorities, given the nature of our moral and religious framework and present historical conditions.

I am using the term "educational" in this section in a somewhat narrower sense to refer to instructional or teaching strategies—that is, to school practices involving the what and how of teaching. However, there is no effort here at all to equate education with schooling even in the organizational sense, since other institutions such as the family, the press, the church, the synagogue, the media, and the work place have important and substantial educative roles to play. Indeed, it is important that institutions that are constituted as primarily educative in character (e.g., schools, universities, nursery schools) be aware of each other's role and contribution. I am not inclined in this book to deal in any detail with special roles and functions for particular institutions except to say that whatever is done should be in harmony with a society's most emancipatory and visionary goals. More specifically, schools do have a particular responsibility to respond to a very wide spectrum of educational goals, or at the very least the profession needs to stimulate public debate on the issues of what constitutes reasonable public expectations of an educational system.

Presently the public as we have already indicated has a great number of such expectations, what range from general acculturation to socialization; from job training to the development of hobbies; and from the three Rs to sex education. This list seems to grow as the public expresses its frustration and self-deception by adding to the schools' agenda and, paradoxically enough, simultaneously reducing the allocation of resources to the schools. The issue of what is or is not appropriate to be taught in schools is essentially moot as long as the schools' capacity to teach anything well to all students continues to be problematic. When the public asks us as educators to deal with a particular concern (e.g., global education, education for peace, "after-school" programs), our professional response must include consideration of intellectual, professional, and moral dimensions, as well as the nature of the resources required to meet the new or reconceptualized challenge.

The essential point here is that whatever the schools and the public determine to be appropriate for the schools' educational responsibilities must be addressed in such a way as to express our mythic goals, our sacred aspirations, and our moral commitments. If the schools are to be considered as preparation for work, they must do so by simultaneously being concerned with a society and an economy that is committed toward justice and dignity for all. If the schools are asked to develop a sports and athletics program, they should be required to do so in the context of the public's commitment to joy, dignity, and fairness for all. When the schools confront the inevitability of their acculturative role, they must also confront the public's expectation for serious criticism and imagination. The school that feels it appropriate to celebrate our nation should also see that such celebration would logically include an affirmation of those moral principles that affirm both the quality of human life and the importance of human freedom. Surely the schools should provide opportunities for those who have a deep commitment to research and scholarship, and an important dimension of those opportunities is guidance on the importance of the moral and spiritual boundaries of research and of the complexities of the underlying epistemological question regarding the nature of truth.

In this chapter I will present a number of critical/educational themes and dimensions directed toward the creation of a just, loving, and joyous community. The next section will present some ideas on how these themes can be and have been expressed within traditional, conventional, or experimental structures. I operate under the assumption that such themes can be presented in a great variety of ways and in the context of a large number of "disciplines" or "content areas." For that reason it is critical that we are clear that these themes of emphasis permeate the entire spectrum of educational activities— hidden, overt, planned, implicit, or otherwise.

At this point I wish to reiterate a crucial theme of this book, that *the school ought to be seen as an opportunity for the growth and learning of all who dwell in a particular educational institution.* Schools are places of learning where people grow through an enhancement of their own capacities and human possibilities. Clearly, teachers will generally know more and have richer experiences than students who in turn will be able to learn a great deal from them. Moreover, educators as professionals need to arouse and sustain their own curiosity and humility over intellectual and professional questions. No set of intellectual and professional questions is as important to address, more perplexing to answer, and more anguishing to confront than those dealing with the purpose and goals of education. Indeed, one continuing, very likely permanent, dimension of professional responsibility includes the serious reexamination of one's responses to these questions. Some of the questions have taken a classic form—What knowledge is of most worth?—but the essential question has been asked in a variety of ways: What is the purpose of education? What is the value of education? What is the nature of knowledge? What can and must I know? What should be left to chance? Whatever the formulation, it is critical that educators pose it for themselves and for the culture as well. It is vital that the question, if it is to be posed at all, not be presented with most of the answers already provided, as in such questions as What are the purposes of teaching history? or What are the goals of elementary education?—both of which are asked within existing premises (i.e., history is to be taught and there are to be institutions of elementary education). When these are asked as open questions, we are almost sure to find ourselves confronting basic questions of human origin, meaning, and destiny. Focused questions, (e.g., What are the goals of a fourth-grade reading program?) are more likely to keep our concerns technical and ameliorative rather than basic and transformative.

Professional educators tend to adopt a "goal-setting" framework in addressing these concerns, very much in a "problem-solving" manner. First of all, goals should not be "set" as in concrete or stone, rather they should be presented and posed in such a manner that they invite continuous examination, reflection, and criticism. Such goals are historical and social constructions and, as such, need to be critically examined as part of our ongoing conversation, goals that need to be made and remade and not merely found and carried out! Second, educational goals are to be seen not as finite problems that have a definite solution, similar to an engineer's responsibility to figure out a way to build a bridge given a particular terrain, climate, budget, etc., but as inherently elusive since they should represent what we believe to be the essences of the true, the good, and the beautiful. Hence, the perplexities of discussing educational goals are parallel to the perplexities of discussing the meaning of life, and thus must be done in a context of awe, mystery, and humility. What we present now are a set of educational goals intended to be more directly concerned with our framework of a discourse directed at justice and compassion.

THE IMPULSE FOR EMPOWERMENT AND TRANSFORMATION

Within the context of assuming responsibilities of co-creation and the moral principles of equality, freedom, justice, and community, we see the significance of the insight of the concept of liberation/empowerment/praxis. If we are to accept our commitments seriously, educators have a special concern for helping us to be liberated *from* the various conditions that oppress us, particularly those of ignorance and illiteracy. Freire (1970, 1973) has shown us that ignorance and illiteracy are more than embarrassing and troublesome in that they are necessary ingredients of poverty, hunger, misery, and oppression. He has shown us the powerful relationship between power and knowledge, how people hold on to their domination in part because the oppressed do not have the critical intellectual skills to overcome the powerful forces of acculturation which lead the weak to internalize the ideology of the strong. "Knowledge is power" is a well-known motto, but it is a bit misleading because it is clear that some knowledge is much more powerful than others. Educators have as part of their task to be sensitive to this relationship and to pass on to their students that knowledge and those skills that tend to empower *all* rather than a few.

However, to be liberated from oppression is a necessary but not sufficient condition for meeting our commitments. Croatto (1981) and Walzer (1985) remind us that the Exodus story has two major points. First, the escape from Egypt represents one dimension of liberation— an escape from oppressive political, religious, and economic conditions, and the energy to escape emerges from a divinely inspired criticism of the very foundations of the oppressed society. Second, the work of finding the "promised land" involves the task of dialectically relating the sacred imperatives with the actual building of a worldly community. It is not until the Israelites are at least partially free from their bondage that they are ready to be in touch with the sacred. As harrowing and dangerous as their saga of escape is, the trials and tribulations that the Israelites face as they embark on building their new life are even greater. The story of the trek to the "land of milk and honey" is one of rejection of the sacred imperatives, rebellions, counterrevolution, confusion, doubt, despair, disarray. Walzer's re- telling of the saga involves a depiction of Moses' leadership swings, which ultimately leave Moses taking on the role, not of general or king, but of teacher. In this sense Moses came to see that he could best lead his people to the promised land by teaching them the skills required to make a just world, a notion reechoed by John Dewey four millennia later in his concept of education as the process by which we can engage and make a world.

INTELLECTUAL PROCESSES AND FORMS

We need to know about the process of learning, the nature of knowl- edge, and the ways in which we seek and present truth. Students will need to study what has been called the structures of disciplines, not so much so that they might themselves become members of the dis- ciplines or admirers of them but rather to gain insight into how we come to know and how we come to accept knowledge. We often pride ourselves as a society dedicated to reason, research, and science, and one that sees at the very least a very strong relationship between knowledge and truth, and yet we do very little about learning epis- temological issues, research paradigms, and learning theories.

It is basic to one's education for liberation to have clear understand- ing of our system for symbol making—to understand language pro- cesses, modes of inquiry, theories of evidence, theories of truth, etc. We need to understand truly what is meant by such concepts as art, science, institution, proof, truth, verifiable, disciplines, logic, theory, paradigm, and the like. We need to know about knowing, think about thinking, and reflect on the meaning of meaning. I am not necessarily talking about a course in philosophy, but I am talking about the im- portance of gaining insight into major philosophical issues (i.e., issues often labeled as epistemological, axiological, and ontological). I am not necessarily talking about a course in the history of science or in intellectual history, but I do believe it is important that we know about the different ways we have to think and of their problems. We need in addition to be mindful of nonanalytic modes of knowledge—the artistic, intuitive, body knowledge, kinesthetic, dance, etc. Learning about learning can help us learn not only more about teaching but about the learning process itself. Learning about knowledge can also give us more understanding of the boundaries of knowledge and of our frameworks of knowledge.

A SENSE OF HISTORICITY

The importance of cultivating historicity is not at all to be equated with teaching courses in history, since the significance of the relationship between the past, present, and future extends much further than the discipline of history. We are a nation that is very much present—if not future—oriented, and our pragmatic and anti-intellectual impulses tend to prompt an ahistoric consciousness. We tend to be impatient about the past because we naively believe that we can create our world unimpeded by considerations of what has already been. Our optimism, energy, and sense of agency compel us to act first and maybe later reflect on the significance of what we have done.

A critical consciousness of history actually can be more liberating, for it enables us to remember that there are origins and beginnings to the present and that their origins are rooted in human events. We come to know therefore that our problems and opportunities have been "created," that they emerge from human interventions, human ideas, human responses, and human aspirations. This can help us escape the sense of inevitability with its tendency to reify the culture, thereby putting a bogus legitimation on the status quo which itself leads to inertia and despair. History reminds us that life means change and response and that not changing is an important response.

We must remember that history is more than major political and economic events. We need to be aware that child-rearing theories have histories, that the definition of work has a history, as do conceptions of math, history, music, art, and pedagogy. In other words, language and social practices are historical constructions and need to be treated as such. Knowing the changes that have occurred in our society may be very interesting to some, but it is likely to be enlightening to most. Not only do we have a buffer to a sense of inevitability and despair, but we have a built-in pressure for response and creativity. A strong sense of the past gives us the reality that we will inevitably create tomorrow's past, the present, and that our response represents not only a comment on the future but on the past. When we know our past, we can maintain continuity by whatever we do, since even drastic change would represent a thoughtful and conscious concern with both past and future.

A sense of history reminds us of our commitments as well as the ways in which we have responded to them. It also urges us to be connected with the humanity that we will never personally know, our brothers and sisters who lived before us and those not yet born. We are all connected by history, and our sense of harmony derives from a sense of a common history of struggle. History is the repository of the human struggle for meaning and represents the connection between memory and response. Forgetting is also a historical phenomenon and must be seen, if not as purposeful, at least as extremely significant. What we forget in part determines our destiny. The responsibility for humanity to participate in its destiny is central to a conception of an education directed toward a loving, compassionate, and just world.

THE DEVELOPMENT OF SOCIAL SKILLS

As I have said, it is theoretically possible to separate skills from substance, but it is a proposition that ought not to be emphasized for reasons already given. We present here a discussion of skills, not at all to reflect a separation, but rather to simplify the task of indicating the significance and interconnection of certain skills to the rest of the educational themes under discussion in this chapter. We are also aware that the distinction between knowledge and skills is problematic (like all distinctions), but again we wish only to draw attention to that vital aspect of education that involves experience and action. I believe that the relationship between theory and practice is truly dialectical; that they can be synergistic when thought of simultaneously, and possibly sterile when considered separately. Furthermore, I believe that we need to learn experientially, as well as analytically, and that an education directed toward the fulfillment of our sacred/myth commitments by definition includes serious concern for action.

Much of our culture teaches us not the skills of community building but rather of individual competition. We know that democratic communities do not simply happen and that their growth is certainly not inevitable. Democratic communities need constant nurturance and attention to remain dynamic and responsive. This means more than learning *about*; it also means learning *to do*; it involves not just an understanding of the structure and how it works but how it works in *particular and concrete* situations. This also involves the skills of communication, of understanding one's social self in addition to one's personal self; of learning how to work with others and how to increase the probability that political and bureaucratic process and machinery be responsive to our highest aspirations. Much of the knowledge that translates into power is the knowledge of practice. There are a relatively small number of people who have power simply because they know how to be competent, how to operate social machinery, which political buttons to push, and which not to push. This is not particularly esoteric knowledge; it is simply not widely accessible (Newmann:1975). Educators have a responsibility to determine those skills of practice that are critical to the defence and growth of our political and moral commitments. It would be tragic if our failure to live up to these commitments was based not on our rejection of these ideals but on our incompetence to make them happen.

I want to extend this list of educational themes with a discussion of other goals which actually permeate all the others and have already been stressed implicitly and explicitly along the way, namely, the importance of knowledge and of a critical and creative consciousness. Again in the service of clarity and emphasis, they shall be presented separately with the very clear assumption that these concerns are inextricably bound to all other educational goals. I present them last not because they are least, for I am not presenting a linear model. There is no need to frustrate ourselves with a chicken/egg paradox. The development of critical and imaginative capacities is absolutely critical to an educational program of liberation, justice, and love— they represent both conditions for, and results of, such a program.

THE ASSIMILATION OF CRITICAL KNOWLEDGE

This is a rather elaborate way of saying that education means, at least in part, that we "know" some information. When educators confront this issue of what we have to know, they of course confront inevitably the whole range of questions concerning purpose, direction, and destiny. In this section we will limit ourselves to the more limited and popular conception of "knowledge" that is remembered or at least retained in a relatively unblurry manner. A real difficulty here, of course, is the issue of what it means to have knowledge, for even in common-sense terms we forget a lot of what we have learned very rapidly. John Holt reminded us of some of the absurdity of defining education as the accumulation of knowledge when he remarked that the real difference between "smart and dumb" students is that the smart student forgets the answers *after* the exam.

There are several justifications for the importance of "having knowledge." One is that certain knowledge is required for various job and work-related competencies. There is no need to belabor this point since it is obviously true, but such a criterion is by definition to be applied differentially—that is, those interested in knowing what is basic to a job or profession should (and no doubt will need no urging to) learn that knowledge. If premed students need to know about inorganic chemistry to gain entrance into medical school and to become physicians, well then of course they should learn inorganic chemistry. The real issue is not what is required for individuals with specific and particular needs and interests, but rather which knowledge should be held in common in order to promote both individual autonomy and a just society.

There are several arguments for learning a common body of knowledge. My position is that we need not debate the metaquestion of whether there is such a body of knowledge, but rather we need to deal with the problem functionally as it relates to the larger framework we have been discussing. This would certainly allow for the possibility of maintaining that there is certain knowledge that everyone should have, but the issue would emerge from a consideration of the appropriateness of the knowledge to our framework, rather than vice versa.

For example, we have stressed the importance of developing a sense of community and universality. An argument can be made that community can be enhanced by (and indeed defined as) the possession of a common culture (i.e., a common body of knowledge). Let us then act on that hypothesis and examine the question of what common knowledge is most critical for that function. Similarly, we should be free to make a case that public solidarity can be nourished when we are all able to make allusions to paradigmatic stories, myths, dramas, literature. This is basically an issue of practice since it means figuring out which literary and intellectual pieces are most likely to enrich and bind us in ways that resonate with our myths and visions. Naturally professionals are certain to differ in their response, but what is important is that they struggle with the problem.

It is also critical that we at all times be sensitive to our concern for joy and individual fulfillment. There can be no question that we should allow opportunities for people who are genuinely interested in the pursuit of knowledge for its own sake (i.e., for esthetic reasons). This is in the realm of specialized and individualized education, and it is important to affirm and provide for those who want to know simply because they want to know.

We have our own "list," however, of what everyone should know, some of which has already been indicated. I believe that we all should have solid awareness of the substance of critical and seminal statements about our moral commitments—e.g., the Sermon on the Mount, the Ten Commandments, the Declaration of Independence, the Gettysburg Address. I obviously believe that all people should be able to read, write, and figure, but I shall deal with these "skills" later on in this chapter. It is certainly valuable for everyone to know at least broadly the major geopolitical features of our world and have a broad historical perspective on major worldwide political, ideological, and social events and trends. As indicated before, I believe everyone should know about basic modes of thought (mathematical, analytical, philosophical, esthetic, empirical) and about the properties of major disciplines. It is also valuable that everyone have a serious understanding of the properties of language, as I indicated above, and it is likely that this can be enhanced by learning at least one other language. Also, I am comfortable with teaching students knowledge which the culture believes gives one cachet; if we expect people to know the capital of the states, then perhaps we should teach it, as long as we remind ourselves and our students that this represents acculturation more than it does education.

However, the essential point is that we not start with a body of knowledge and then try to rationalize its importance. It is, on the other hand, legitimate to consider that the persistence of certain knowledge in the society may indicate an importance that needs to be discovered and articulated. What we need to say is that the educational vision that we have drawn very definitely includes the necessity for knowledge in the narrow sense. We have affirmed the value of knowledge for its own sake *for those who have that interest*; otherwise, when educators make a case for knowing this or that they will need to be persuasive that the possession of this particular information is functional to the vision. While knowledge is an end in itself for only some people, it is functional for all people. Knowledge must not be reified, nor must we become idolatrous of it. We must respect the process of creating knowledge and the enormous importance to us of what knowledge we decide to accept as true. We must also be aware of our relationship to knowledge—how we create it, how it shapes us, and what it means to us. To go beyond that, however, and try to make specific bits of knowledge or information sacred is to move into reification and idolatry. Nonetheless, let it be understood that we as educators must not only be prophets, idealists, and creators, but we must be knowledgeable ones, people who can make knowledge holy by connecting it to sacred imperatives.

CRITICAL CONSCIOUSNESS AND COMPETENCE

The issue of the vivid relationship between a critical capacity and education has been mentioned several times. Criticisms here refer to two general capacities, that of rigor and that of judgment. When I speak of rigor, it is within the Socratic tradition, which begins with the commitment to precise, rigorous thinking and a simultaneous skepticism and humility about our capacity to do so. In order to resist flaccidity and self-deception, one has to be alert to the likelihood that any statement or proposition is incomplete or misleading. Rigorous criticism is an antidote to such thinking, since it attempts to test thoroughly the validity of propositions, statements, policies, and pronouncements by carefully examining their logic, assumptions, evidence, and coherence. The skepticism and modesty rest not only on a degree of suspicion and a dash of cynicism but more broadly on a sophisticated understanding of the perplexities, subtleties, and elusiveness inherent in the pursuit of truth.

Criticism as judgment refers to the application of moral and esthetic criteria to propositions, policies, events, and other phenomena. Socrates, as we have said, adopted his critical posture as a mode of helping to do what the gods wished. The prophets criticized their society on the basis of the standards established by what was enunciated at Mt. Sinai. Criticism in this sense attempts to size up the quality of relationships between a set of prior standards and some specific and concrete phenomenon. When, for example, we read a movie review, we want more than a statement of whether it is good or not—we want to know the basis of the judgment, we want to know about the movie's believability, about its capacity to inspire, its point of view, its entertainment qualities, etc. To criticize means, among other things, to react, to respond, and to make relationships, and, hence, criticism can be seen as opposed to acceptance and passivity. Moreover, its intellectual center is one of relationships—that is, the capacity to see the connection between principles, ideas, criteria, standards, and individual events.

Criticism also involves us in combining rigor with judgment, in attempting to integrate careful thinking with our moral and esthetic principles. This is another way of characterizing a major essence of our educational vision in which we utilize our intellectual skills to create and make manifest that vision. In this way we can possibly avoid the horrors that come from intellectual skills being used for destructive purposes and the application of principles with more sentimentality than reason. Thus, in affirming the vital role of criticism, we underscore the major responsibility for educators to help us to be aware of our need to have caution as well as convictions, to celebrate as well as complain, and to value that which connects head to heart.

Paulo Freire (1970, 1973) is perhaps the most eloquent and compelling educator to write on the centrality of this capacity. He, in effect, defines literacy not as the ability to read and write but as the ability to read and write *critically*. His notion of *conscientization* represents a pedagogy designed to liberate people from the oppression of illiteracy, (i.e., an uncritical consciousness). To Freire, *conscientizao* represents "learning to perceive social, political, and economic contradictions, and to take action against the oppressive elements of reality" (1970:74). To be uncritical is to be unaware of the human character of our culture, to see the world's condition as "natural" or inevitable and one's particular condition as a function of uncontrollable forces. To be uncritical one has to be ignorant of historical processes and of the nature and significance of knowledge. One can remain uncritical by maintaining a primitive language and by refusing to learn how to analyze language and to analyze with language. Moreover, Freire cautions us on the immense significance of *not* trying to provide this capacity: "Any situation in which some men prevent others from engaging in the process of inquiry is one of violence. The means used are not important: to alienate people from their own decision-making is to change them into objects" (1970:74).

Critical thus takes on another connotation besides rigor and judgment—namely, it becomes crucial to freedom, autonomy, and justice. It is critical that people be critical in order that they can continue to be critical. To Freire, the development of critical literacy represents hope in that it provides a way in which humanity can freely and peacefully struggle for their freedom. Indeed, in this sense people have a responsibility to be critical once they decide on a life of meaning, for they must then discern the degree to which their lives are in concert with that sense of meaning. Human dignity entails responsibility, and responsibility entails being critical.

Maxine Greene (1978) puts emphasis on the critical consciousness that makes us aware of our presence in the world and of the existential reality that requires us to act upon it. She stresses the importance of "questioning the every-dayness" of our lives and of becoming ever more aware of how we might be free to contemplate the possibility that "life might be otherwise." In a similar vein, Richard Shaull has this to say in his introduction to Freire's *Pedagogy of the Oppressed*:

> There is no such thing as a neutral *educational process. Education either functions as an instrument which is used to facilitate the integration of the younger generation into the logic of the present system and bring about conformity to it, or it becomes "the practice of freedom," the means by which men and women deal critically and creatively with reality and discover how to participate in the transformation of their world. The development of an educational methodology that facilitates this process will inevitably lead to tension and conflict within our society. But it could also contribute to the formation of a new man and mark the beginning of a new era in Western history. (1970:15)*

Not only do we need to nourish critical consciousness, we need also to develop particular critical skills. The fundamental skills of reading and writing should be taught not as disembodied mechanics and certainly not in isolation from "content." If we insist on reifying reading and writing, let us at least qualify those terms, let us say *critical* reading and *critical* writing. We need to teach people what critical thinking is, and about the ways in which to critique research, scientific findings, policy statements, and artistic creations. We need to know about various sets of rules of evidence, about the nature of rhetoric, and how to sort out the tangle of assumptions, beliefs, values, and assertions (i.e., the way we dialogue). We must always remember however, to be critical of our criticism, to be wary of our impulse to avoid the disciplines of either intellectual rigor or moral boundaries. We must also be careful lest our criticism result in stalemate or moral paralysis, since our basic goal is to connect criticism with creation.

IMAGINATION AND CREATIVITY

We are here *not* talking of a conventional orientation toward art and creativity which essentially involves their reification. In our mainstream educational policies and practices, art and creativity have been consigned to fairly specialized areas, for the most part valued but given a special status that actually limits their significance as a consequence of their fragmentation. Art is typically characterized as a "subject" with its own space, teachers, materials, and traditions. Creativity has come more and more to mean a specialized talent to be original, fresh, and unique. Moreover, both characteristics are often associated with an unusual talent that some people have and others do not. The effect of this is to minimize the possibility of an education in which creativity and art could permeate the entire curriculum and to perpetuate the myth that only a few of us are "gifted" as artists.

Gibson Winter (1985) has written on how our culture's dominant "root metaphor" is changing from one of "machine" to one of "art." His position is that our consciousness is gradually changing from one that tends to see the world mechanically, as in a Newtonian system of regularity, order, precision, and predictability. The emerging consciousness is one in which we are putting more emphasis on human response, on subjectivity, and the dialectic between phenomenon and perception. Hence, we are less likely to view the world as a gigantic clock whose inner works have been set and whose operations are exact and orderly. We are more likely to see how much of our understanding of the world is mediated by our language, beliefs, values, and way of being. We are more likely, then, to become sensitive to the extraordinary importance of human constructions; to the process and product of human imagination. We have become more and more conscious of how our perception and images of the world affect our experience of the world. This point of view has been heightened by the understanding of the advertising industry in particular, and the commercial world in general, as they are clearly aware of the power of images and the potential for creating not only new products but, even more significant, the need for them. The film and television industries have created mythical cultures of America which do more than mirror America, they actually become our mirror. For those of us who are not clear on who we are, what we are supposed to say or do in particular situations, we can always look at an illuminated screen of people actually responding to these same situations. These artificially created reactions to real situations provide a model for the way things are—reality imitating art.

Creativity is not an exotic and mysterious quality but rather an inevitable and inherent aspect of human experience. All people constantly create: we create meaning; we create our responses to nature and culture; we create culture. It is our images that we use to make sense out of the world, and it is our imagination that enables us to give moral and religious significance to life. It is through play and imagination that we encounter our world and give shape to it. The capacity to play, to imagine, and to fantasize allows us to create visions and frees us to transcend the forgotten boundaries that we once ourselves established. We have created our world, and as good artists we should be able to be critical of our work since artists know that they must continue to create or, more accurately, re-create. Thinking of creation and re-creation as play provides us the freedom to escape hegemonic thinking—that is, to go beyond what seems fixed and irreplaceable.

PLAY AND IMAGINATION

Stanley Aronowitz and Henry Giroux elaborate on their notion of the critical part that intellectual discourse plays in transformative education with a strong and eloquent plea for the importance of play.

> We learn as much by assimilating the world to the dictates of the sphere we call "imaginary" (which cannot always be adjusted to practical tasks) as we do in the so-called socialization process, one that is increasing technologically directed. By imaginary we mean the proclivities toward creating an alternative world, not representing that which is. The imaginary is the foundation of play; it is the way we make a new world as well as achieve self-hood. Play can be understood as the interaction of two imaginaries, especially among children where the activity itself is directed toward creating not only the social self but also a self that "goes beyond" the given of existing social structures. The relationship between education as socialization, which is directed toward suppressing the imaginary, and learning as a means by which the imaginary takes control of the ego is inevitable in any society that wishes to insure the adaptation of its young to prevailing norms. The point of technological direction is to make the imaginary into an instrument of the prevailing order. (1985:18–19)

Educators as prophets will surely then critically examine the creative process and products as a basis for indicating an agenda for further imaginative works. We cannot be fully satisfied with our creations thus far; surely we cannot accept an esthetics of oppression, misery, and war. As critics, educators will discern which creations are indeed beautiful and which are ugly, and help their students to learn these modes of discernment. Our analysis in this book reflects an orientation in which we see a history of heroic efforts and brilliant creations (ideas, principles, theories, etc.); yet as magnificent as these efforts are, they have fallen short of our own hopes. Do we need to gather any more evidence for this? How many more wars, genocides, famines, depressions, plagues, epidemics, suicides do we need to convince us that we require radically new thinking, new visions, new paradigms if we are to survive, never mind prevail?

If we are to have faith in imagination, we must first be able to imagine what Maxine Greene has called the ability to "possibilize" that like Moses, and Gandhi, we can have hope rather than despair. There is extraordinary evidence of our limitless potential for creative and imaginative brilliance. Time and again our history gives us examples of intellectual breakthroughs, startling intuitive leaps, and dazzling poetic insight that have literally lead to significant changes in consciousness.

The women's movement is but one example of a major social phenomenon with profound consequences that has been largely enabled by the power of imagination, by a change in consciousness. There was a time when thoughtful and good people could not imagine a woman as a truck driver, airline pilot, or surgeon. Now such images come to many more people much more easily, and indeed for most of us they no longer constitute imagined reality. The changes in laws and policies are reflections of this re-creation of our image of women. Similar changes in consciousness have occurred in our own generation in our images of blacks, children, and homosexuals. The political and social activism associated with these movements is energized by imagination, and their success depends on the ability of others to re-create their long-standing images. Change by definition involves re-creation, and creation requires the full use of all imaginative capacities—play, intuition, analysis, conceptualization, and the body, mind, and spirit.

We also have ample and exciting evidence of an enormous flowering of creative and imaginative genius in our own times. Not only are more people involved in the arts than ever before, but there is more concern and interest in participating directly as composers, artists, and performers than as audience. Moreover, we see in virtually every academic discipline and profession very serious discussions about the necessity for making significant changes in basic assumptions about the nature of each field. For example, even the highly rigid and straight field of "educational research" is caught up in a major debate over the adequacy of its conventional, empirical, quantitative experimental research paradigm. Indeed, the concept of paradigm shift has become a virtual cliche. This may create difficulty for those interested in style, but nonetheless we are surely in a different place when we consider references to shifts in paradigms as routine and commonplace. Parents and teachers continue to be amazed at the increasing sophistication and creativity of young people, even as they may deplore their lack of traditional knowledge or skill. Each generation brings with it even more interest and sensitivity to the infinite possibilities of the imagination, whether it be reflected in science fiction, computer usage, musical groups, or new art forms.

Educators, therefore, need to provide more opportunities to develop the imaginative and playful potentials of their students more deeply and more widely. We must see art not as a separate activity. We must avoid associating creativity with the esoteric, and regard the imagination not as weird but necessary. We must allow our students and ourselves to be in touch with and affirm our own creative processes. Furthermore, we ought to find ways to foster these processes since they afford the possibility of possibility; they can enrich our lives personally and communally, for they can provide us with esthetic and moral delight. Our present and our future are reflections of our imagination, and our destiny will be determined by the creative capacities that are now being formed. Our belief is that the task of educators is to encourage and guide students to an imagination that goes far beyond ours, to help them to develop a consciousness that we are unable, because of the limitations of our education, to conceive. We must, as educators, continue our faith that we can continue to imagine that others will imagine what we cannot.

What we have presented is very likely a partial and initial statement of an educational framework that is mostly concerned with being part of our efforts to create a community of joy, love, justice, and compassion. It is a framework that emerges from an interpretation of contemporary American culture in which we see ourselves at the edge of impending glory or destruction. We see the sources of the problem and resolution in the moral and spiritual realm; more particularly, we see our problems rooted in our inability to deliver on our highest aspirations, a difficulty we believe is at least partly based on confusion and self-deception. As educators we can accept the awareness and thus the reduction of confusion and deception, as a way to legitimately participate professionally in our human responsibilities.

Basic to our difficulty has been our inability to develop a close and enduring sense of democratic community; we are driven by a value system oriented toward individuality, competition, and material success. We have argued, that in spite of our pluralism and diversity we do in fact have the possibility of creating an overarching consensus of general aspirations and moral principles. I have also tried to show that as educators we must be part of the process of forging that vision which can also guide us in our professional policies and practices.

The focal points of such a mythos are those that converge in a vision of democracy, compassion, justice, equality, freedom, and joy. Fundamental to the fulfillment of these commitments is an acceptance of human responsibility for the creation of a culture and environment in which these possibilities can be realized. It is our faith that the educative process is a necessary though not sufficient condition for the development of such a culture. Such an educative process must obviously resonate with the vision and be designed to facilitate the process of constructing it. This means an educative process that affirms and celebrates the vision and consciously adopts its framework, always mindful of the basic professional ethic that mandates free, open, and continuous inquiry. Key to this general vision and the particular ethic is the framework's strong emphasis on criticism and creativity as the interlocking and interdependent hinges of the educational framework.

We are very much aware that the educational process involves a great deal more than theory and visions. There is not only the nature of the profession as described above, there is also the vitally important process of planning, development, and implementation. We deal with these issues in the next chapter, restressing the maxim that the principal ingredients necessary for significant change are the acceptance of the need for significant change and the will to make such changes.

A fundamental tenet of the study of education which we have discussed and affirmed is the intimate relationship between culture and organized education. It is vital then to reiterate this major concern when confronting the issues of educational reform: we must recognize that to make significant educational change requires and means significant cultural change. We cannot continue the myth that educational problems are rooted primarily in professional and technical matters. When we finally give up the process of trivializing education, it will mean that we have taken seriously the propositions that education can make us free and wise, not just rich and smart.

7

Issues of Curriculum Planning, Design, and Implementation

The prophet does not ask if the vision can be implemented for questions of implementation are of no consequence until the vision can be imagined. The imagination must come before the implementation. Our culture is competent to implement almost anything and to imagine almost anything and to imagine almost nothing. The same royal consciousness that makes it possible to implement anything and everything is the one that shrinks imagination because imagination is a danger.

Walter Brueggemann, The Prophetic Imagination

In this chapter we will deal with issues of implementation, of how we might actually make these ideas operational and put them into action so that they actually function in the way they are intended. We fully realize the critical importance of the process of planning and designing a specific and complete educational experience, not only because it is required but because this process is also a vital element in the development of theory. Again, I reject the dichotomy between theory and practice, preferring to see them as dialectical and, hence, continuously dynamic. Indeed, the ideas so far presented represent such an interaction and are presented not as final but as in-process. There is always much more work to be done and this curriculum framework is no exception. In this regard we wish to point out a number of particular issues involving implementation.

ASPECTS OF RESISTANCE

Resistance to Serious Change

We are all aware of the phenomenon of homeostasis, the tendency for people and institutions to seek and maintain continuity and stability. Whether we call this inertia or stability hardly matters in this context since we must recognize the very important impulse in individuals and groups to be wary of the risks that major change entails. As we have pointed out, even the most modest suggestions for educational change are resisted because at some level we realize we are connecting to the possibility of deeper, broader changes in the culture. The proposals sketched in the prior chapter, however, go beyond suggesting the mere possibility of fundamental change.

Our starting point is the necessity for change since we begin in the pain and anguish of the human condition. We are insisting that all curriculum planning focus on the horrors of our time—misery, disease, hunger, poverty, war. We challenge our colleagues and fellow citizens to use these realities of our present state of being as the point of departure when dealing with educational practices. This is to say we need to replace existing points of departure—test scores, college admissions, competition, and the maintenance of the status quo with very different ones, and, indeed, demand that we examine the relationship between existing educational practices and policies and what we as a culture deem to be of ultimate significance. It is time to accept that we are already "in the long run," that there is surely enough data to demonstrate that there is much in our fundamental structure of values, institutions, and organizations that has failed. It is also important that educators speak out not only on the inadequacy of technical aspects of the profession but on the inadequacy of our major cultural institutions. Educators must stop hiding from their responsibility to make clear statements on the moral and spiritual dimensions of various educational policies and practices. Yes, along with many others, I am talking about significant change, and, our ideas will likely be resisted because of this alone, if not for other reasons. Those of us committed to fundamental change challenge other educators to try to demonstrate that there is less risk in not changing. Change is more overtly dramatic, but not changing is just as significant and momentous. Educators must therefore be pressed to go beyond their day to day slogging and engage also in the enormous struggles involved in the fulfillment of our sacred commitments. This brings us to another serious difficulty in following through on these ideas, or on any set of ideas directed at significant liberating change—namely, the differences and divisions in the profession.

Professional Resistance

Stalemates

We have already discussed the problem of paralysis and inaction that emerges from a position of severe caution and reluctance to affirm moral and religious principles. Professional stalemates can result from basic disagreement on more empirical issues (i.e., issues of knowledge, research, strategy). In this context, I particularly wish to focus on the debate over strategies for educational change which usually centers on where the optimum source of change resides. For example, some people argue that fundamental change must result from the slow accretion of gradual and modest reforms at the "practical" level—that is, from teachers and researchers focusing on current practice and work within the existing framework. Others insist that it is a waste of time to attempt to make significant educational changes because that can only happen *after* there are major shifts in other social, political and cultural, institutions. Still others take the position that significant change must be preceded by more high-quality research on the learning/teaching process and much more clarity and precision of critical cultural and educational concepts.

Our answer is yes, yes, and yes. We cannot choose one or even a few reform modes of meeting our responsibilities. For example, it is critically important that teachers and other educators continue to work hard to squeeze as much humanity and sanity as can be found in existing arrangements. That is a critically important task because it is a way of dealing with a concrete reality for very real people and because it helps the process of increasing our critical and creative capacities. When we recognize that we have to make "lemonade from our lemons," we are indicating that we know something about lemons and lemonade.

We need to avoid the unnecessary infighting and competition that comes from differences on which approach is the *most* efficacious. Instead, we can each of us can concentrate on doing what each of us actually *does*, but provided that we have some reason to believe that at minimum what we do does not make matters worse, and even better, can contribute to an improvement in the quality of human life. We need also to affirm the importance of engaging in a struggle which is incredibly complex and profound in a variety of manners and strategies. We need not, and should not, needlessly disparage other strategies in order to validate our own, because when we do so we dissipate valuable energy which has the continuation of the status quo as its unintended consequence. This is not to say, however, that we should not critically attend to what we do, only to suggest that there are a great many battles and skirmishes involved in the war on injustice and oppression. Let us by all means continue to do basic and applied research and be ever mindful of the relationship between research projects and our basic moral commitments. Let us indeed attempt to ameliorate, cope, adapt, and keep bad situations from getting worse, as long as we do not confuse acceptance and coping with validation and legitimation. There can surely be disagreements on strategy, but if we link our strategies to broad common goals, even those strategies that are seemingly contradictory can be productive. We should become less tolerant of certain educational goals (e.g., competition, individual success, amorality, social irresponsibility) and more supportive of strategies designed to meet others (e.g., justice, love, compassion, equality).

Sabotage

Any program, set of ideas, or orientation can be sabotaged. By sabotage I mean those acts that are counterproductive and destructive to the original ideas performed by people uncommitted or only partially committed to them. This, of course, speaks to the power and importance of practice and the futility of trying to develop teacher-proof materials. The whole concept of "teacher-proof" is both a reproach to teachers as well as a recognition of their power. One of the major lessons of the 1960s and 1970s curriculum movement was that teachers who did not participate in the development of curriculum materials were more likely to resist their implementation in one way or another. We note this reality, but we wish to extend our considerations to another dimension of this phenomenon. Sometimes sabotage is actually appropriate, as in the case of trying to undermine policies that are harmful and wrong. We probably would call such acts creative and adaptive rather than subversive. However, there is also the more basic appropriateness to a situation where teachers are treated as objects and instruments. We must not allow ourselves to be used or to consider teachers as another variable, another "resource" to be manipulated and controlled like building blocks. To do so would undermine the basic moral legitimacy of our educational framework, which does not countenance people as a means to an end. In order for a framework such as the one described to become operational, we will need professionals who come to accept its basic validity for themselves. Such a commitment cannot and should not be mandated or taken for granted; it must be the result of conscious and informed choice. This, of course, echoes the signal importance of professional attitudes and ethics described in the last chapter, and I repeat: the profession is itself a major element of the curriculum.

Co-optation

This is by far the most difficult and dangerous form of resistance because it is so seductive and comforting. Schools, mirroring the larger, dominant culture, are not only extremely skilled in taking on changes but also often in assimilating them into their fundamental structures. For example, just as the counterculture's attempt to establish its identity by wearing blue jeans was overcome by "designer jeans," efforts to overcome an arbitrary curriculum resulted in Tylerian lesson planning. The culture and the school are extraordinarily gifted in their ability to absorb changes and pressures without making any significant alternations in basic attitudes and priorities. For example, we sometimes change the grading scheme from A, B, C, to excellent, good, fair, or to excellent, shows improvement, and needs improvement, but it remains hierarchical and summative.

Co-optation is a technique for survival, one that is flexible and tolerant to a degree but ultimately concerned less with change than with continuity. It is a technique for having your cake and eating it and has proven to be remarkably effective. Its danger, of course, is in its deception, in its propensity to give people the illusion and appearance of significant change. It is, therefore, seductive to those who very much want to change but are reluctant or unwilling to deal with the consequences of real change. Co-optation feeds the self-deception that believes, for example, that reducing class size from thirty to twenty-eight is a significant change or that more requirements will result in a more rigorous educational program. The educational system has a definite logic to it, for better or worse, and it will strive, usually successfully, to apply that logic to any suggestion for change. Even when that logic accepts some suggestions, they will likely be substantially transformed by that persistent, fundamental, and everlasting logic. Co-optation represents at least some effort, however, to accommodate to suggestions and pressures. There is, of course, the resistance that takes on the more overt nature of rejection.

Forms of Rejection

There are a number of classic rejections to new ideas, always keeping in mind that it is highly appropriate to closely examine new or difficult ideas and sometimes to reject them. We are here discussing forms of resistance that represent failures of serious reflection or responses of those predictably committed to the preservation of the status quo no matter what alternatives are presented. It is certainly reasonable to assume some validity to existing institutions, and it is not unreasonable for the burden of proof to be on those who are critical. In times such as ours, however, educators should not have to retreat into such a defensive posture and should be able to be affirmative and celebrative about their own beliefs and practices. It is not professional to be defensive, nor is it in the best interests of the culture for educators to wait for someone to try to guess or find out the serious problems of the field. However, our profession and dominant culture do have among them leadership people who instinctively defend what is and who are prone to be suspicious of different formulations. It is to this group that we are addressing issues of resistance, not so much as resistance to serious change but as serious resistance to seriously considering serious change. This group has learned a number of clever responses or reactions that constitute apparently intellectually sound considerations. There are three in particular that need examinations— rejections based on countercharges of "panacea promising," "exaggerated criticism," and "insufficient technology."

Panacea Promising

The charge is often made of suggestions for change (whether they are worthwhile or not is not relevant here) that their supporters are presenting them as a panacea, that they are presented as simple cure-alls for highly complex and perplexing problems. I personally have never seen a proposal for educational change that was ever so presented. I have certainly seen proposals that promised a great deal more than seemed plausible, but never one that promised to be a cure-all. Surely there are proposals that are blind to problems other than the ones which they address, but to label them as promising a panacea is to create a straw man. I certainly do not offer a "panacea"; indeed what is presented here is not so much a cure as a diagnosis. The cure can come only if we accept the diagnosis, and if we do, it will still require an immense amount of hard and complicated work in many areas to develop reasonable responses to that diagnosis.

It is vital to repeat our disclaimer that the schools by themselves cannot solve the problems of the world. We know that they cannot but that they can and should make a significant contribution to the creation of a good and just world. The charge of panacea-pushing is often associated with that of faddism, of which there is quite a lot in education. However, to lump together all critiques of existing forms as passing fads would be self-deceptive and counterproductive to efforts at transcending our current, unpassing fad that is our present educational system. It is vital to remember that our educational organization, policies, and traditions were not revealed at Mt. Sinai or in any other sacred place, but are rather recent and modest efforts by rather recent and modest folks.

Exaggerated Criticism

Another mode of rejection of consideration of serious change is captured by the old folk maxim, "Don't fix it till it's broke." This is to invoke the feeling of pride in our accomplishments and is meant to minimize the validity of the basic premise that structural change is needed. My answer to this criticism would be (and has been in this book) quite simply, "It *is* broke." However, when a system appears on the surface to be functioning, or at worst needs repairs rather than replacement, there is still something comforting to those who are terrified by the implications and suggestion of the destructive quality of the system. An automobile that pollutes the air can still get us to the fair even if such cars eventually destroy the fairgrounds and those who are there.

Educators must avoid the equivalence of the "naturalist fallacy" that confuses "is" with "ought." It is possible to argue that the persistence of our educational institutions means that they have met the test of time. I would argue that their persistence has failed the test of reason. Indeed, the argument that the persistence of the system is in itself evidence of its wisdom breaks down upon examination of the accomplishments of the goals of its own logic.

Insufficient Technology

This failure to deliver on its own promises is reflected in the way this failure is projected on newly formulated proposals. The rejection of change often takes the form of demanding (at least as it has been leveled at some of my colleagues and me) that we should not try to replace the present system until we know what to replace it with. This is another form of automatic support of what we already have as a stubborn and last-ditch type of defense. It is certainly proper to assume a show-me attitude when claims are made, but the criticism should be on the validity of the proposals per se, not on their inherent threat to the status quo. Conversely, it is possible to reject what is proposed as an alternative and still accept the criticism of the existing. We can accept someone as being truthful when he or she tells us that our house is on fire without hiring them to be our architect. Nor does it mean that if an architect's plan is inadequate the house we now live in is habitable.

The truth is that we do not know completely or even mostly how to teach the nature of what we are urging. However, neither do we know any better how to teach the existing goals. The major difference is that the profession has chosen to struggle with the problems inherent in the existing educational agenda. We do not have anywhere near the last word on how to teach people to understand algebra or be a good citizen or a team player. We have, however, applied enormous energies and resources to working on such professional concerns. We have no doubt whatsoever that our educational agenda, however difficult and challenging, can be addressed successfully by a profession committed to its validity. We cannot logically (or morally) withhold its development until it has been developed. What we can do is decide to channel our imagination and energy toward the construction of a practice directed toward a world of peace, justice, love, and joy.

ISSUES OF PLANNING

As we have already noted, current ideas about curriculum planning are heavily influenced by the so-called Tyler model (1949), which stresses an objectivity predetermined by a concern for social needs and an understanding of the learning process that can be made specific enough for its evaluation. There is no question that this model has made a genuine contribution to the field because of its emphasis on rationally determined criteria for how and what to teach. As obvious as this may sound, the Tyler model helped in the struggle against arbitrary and facile thinking about curriculum and instruction. It put boundaries around speculation and conventional theory which did enable serious reflection on instructional issues. The model is a very powerful tool for those primarily interested in efficiency, order, and control. However, it suffers from its pretense to be neutral and objective in two ways: first, the claim of neutrality and objectivity is itself naive and logically impossible, and second, it fails to affirm any principle directly, and the ones that are affirmed indirectly or inadvertently are control, ulitism, and the preservation of the status quo. For educators to posit neutrality is to deny their responsibility as social leaders and to cast doubts on their sophistication as thinkers.

Our framework suggests planning of a very different kind since it puts much more emphasis on a relatively explicit moral and religious framework and has more concern for architecture than engineering. We believe it is imperative that planning not be reduced to the implementation of an already decided set of objectives, but exist as an opportunity for teachers, students, administrators, and community, to participate in praxis—namely, in the dialectic of emerging theory and practice. I have suggested a framework as a significant point of departure for that dialogic process, not as a set of measurable objectives. The planning process itself should not only be functional to developing learning experiences for others but should itself be educational for the planners. Indeed, the concept of "planning" needs to be critically examined, particularly when it is seen as separate from the entire range of educational practice. Planning should be seen as a process and as a dimension of education, not as a separate skill or function. To concentrate on planning in the way the field does (e.g., texts and courses in "curriculum planning," which exists as a separate field for the "curriculum planner") serves mostly to emphasize engineering or applied concerns, brushing aside urgent concerns of architecture or fundamental structure. Curriculum planners want to know the broad goals quickly in order to get on with their job of devising instruction strategies and material, and, hence, they are almost sure to avoid being critical of the more basic goals of the educational system. They see this as something that is beyond their control, or perhaps as simply empty theorizing slowing down the real work of planning for tomorrow's classes.

The more fundamental curriculum planning tends to go on in the realm of big business and government. This planning is done in the context of foreign policy considerations, industrial development, economic considerations, and the needs of the job market. If, for example, there is to be a serious program for space exploration, there will be a concern for the recruitment and training for engineers and physicists. If the government or big business anticipates an expansion of the computer industry, then the schools are asked not only to help in training computer technicians but also to encourage computer consumption by adding computer-oriented materials to the curriculum. When a state goes on a serious campaign to attract industry, it will be sure to do important curriculum planning (e.g., develop community colleges which are responsive to industrial and commercial personnel needs).

ISSUES OF DESIGN

The basic design of the American schools has been set for nearly a hundred years; and through a number of variations, the basic themes are amazingly constant across this time era and our nation. Elementary schools tend to stress the acquisition of basic study skills and attitudes—reading, writing, arithmetic, memorizing, respect for authority and order, etc. At some level there is a transition to a departmental organization. Sometimes this takes the form of areas of learning that suggest their strong connection to traditional disciplines, as is the case of language arts/English and social studies/history. Sometimes the transition is more organizational—students may go to specialized classes in science or art or music. At any rate, sooner or later the conventional secondary school curriculum with its sacred and eternal five subjects will appear. The mighty five are, of course, English, history, science, mathematics, and foreign language. These are usually supplemented by electives and "extracurricular" activities such as music, athletics, and art, but the sacred five are dominant in virtually every secondary school in America.

There is an interesting and important strategic consideration involved with the persistence of this basic design. Of course there is enormous variation within this design, but the hard question is whether to propose an alternative design or an alternative variation. There are several advantages to the option of working within the design, the most attractive one being that it would probably be politically a lot easier than trying to work for total change.

There is the valid argument that this basic design serves an important ritualistic function, one that maintains continuity and tradition. This design, although not really very ancient, does have a great deal of social acceptance, and symbolically it provides an image (however distorted) of rigor, scholarship, universality, and tradition. The argument is that it is prudent, wise, and possible to maintain the design, and that the design is flexible enough to meet the requirements of a variety of educational frameworks and orientations. There is also, of course, a strong educational argument that has been made for at least major elements of the basic design. However, it is very difficult nowadays to find any systematic effort to make sense out of the design as a whole or to feel willing to argue that the basic design makes theoretical and empirical sense as an entity.

The argument that is often made is that students need first to master two sets of basic intellectual skills—first, those often referred to as the three Rs, and second, those conceptual powers contained in major academic disciplines. Mastering these functions is thought to represent the essentials of an education, or at the very least critical prerequisites for "advanced learning." The further argument is that the exposure to major academic disciplines provides an opportunity to learn for the sake of learning and benefit from the pragmatic qualities of the various disciplines. Each discipline is said to have the capacity for inherent value, to provide esthetic satisfaction, as in the love of learning, and to meet certain personal and social needs (e.g., the study of math helps us to be logical, and the study of history helps us to be good citizens).

There are many criticisms that have been directed at the basic design itself, many of which are implied in the preceding chapter of this book. For purposes of this particular section I wish to examine the basic design from the perspective of a single but critical question—namely, should we teach what is interesting or what is important? The intention of this question is to be seen as heuristic; we are interested in probing the claims of the five sacred disciplines to be a major and dominating force of our basic curriculum design. Indeed, we can perhaps sharpen our analysis by examining the claim that necessitates *requiring* students to enroll in these courses.

In effect, the implicit claim is that these courses are interesting *and* important and that the challenge to the instructional program is to develop procedures that will make this potential real. If such a claim were true, it certainly would be not only convincingly persuasive but delightfully attractive. What could possibly be better than a set of experiences that will provide both benefits and satisfaction, have both pragmatic and esthetic payoffs, and unite needs and wants? Let us then examine this claim more carefully than is customary. Let me first clarify what I mean when I make the distinction between "interesting" and "important." When people say they are interested in something, they are reflecting a personal connection and resonance with that something that is of a different order than their relationship with other somethings. Their interest indicates that they are particularly attracted and personally inclined to become more involved and knowledgeable about the source of their interest. Interests are therefore personal and variable in the way that hobbies, tastes, and personal preferences are. To be interested in X is more of an esthetic consideration (i.e., X provides some personal satisfaction on its own terms). We expect enormous individual differences as far as interests are concerned, and our only boundary to them is that our personal interests do not interfere with the pursuit of other people's interest. Apart from that, we are more likely to be amused than threatened when we discover that our friends, colleagues, and neighbors have different interests than our own. We do not take offense when someone finds baseball more interesting than chess and we are not surprised when some people find Hemingway's stories more interesting than those of Updike.

I am using the concept of "important" here in its social sense of what is urgent, required, necessary, and vital. Perhaps it is necessary for individuals to have an interesting life which provides one way of integrating the two concepts. Even in this case, however, we will need to consider the importance of each concept since this involves the important question of how we are to create such a world. As educators, we eternally address the issue of what is important to teach since it involves the classic questions we mentioned in a prior chapter—What knowledge is of most worth? What might be left to chance? When we decide to require or mandate certain experiences we do so because we believe they are vital and important to the culture and to students. We are likely to disagree on what constitutes "important," but we clearly agree that whatever is important should be taught, one way or another. Hence, important in this context should be seen in more social and moral terms in that it involves a statement of value and a hierarchy of values.

To claim that the five sacred disciplines are both important and interesting would seem to be fatuous and self-serving. To even claim that the five subjects are (or, even worse, can be) *made* interesting to all is both arrogant and a denial of the realities of individual differences. There is, of course, a more attractive claim and that is to insist that what is important is interesting. This, I believe, is both wishful thinking and another denial of the human condition. For example, I believe without reservation that the technical aspects of nuclear energy are vitally important and that it would be highly desirable that I become much more informed about them than I am now. Furthermore, I am certainly very interested in many of the social issues that are involved in nuclear energy. However, it is also clear that I am not at all interested in these details—that is, I find them boring in spite of their importance. I very much regret this, for it means either that I will neglect this area of study, probably relying on others to interpret for me, or that I will have to endure the boredom and pain of studying that which I would prefer not to study.

The case is similar for the opposite situation. I find historical details of professional baseball to be very fascinating and compelling. I have also come to know that most of my colleagues and friends find these details to be exceptionally uninteresting, a source of sadness and frustration for me. However interesting I find these data to be, I am still not able to make a case that they are vitally important to the commonweal. As much as I would like people to share my interest, I cannot demand or expect them to do so, although I reserve the right to entice them.

In parallel manner, there is no question that there are people who genuinely and deeply love their disciplines (i.e., find them interesting), and it is quite reasonable to provide opportunities for others to become equally involved. Indeed, a central aspect of our framework is to create a world of joy, where all people could do what really attracted and interested them. Let us by all means expose students to areas of possible interest that they otherwise might not encounter. Why, however, should this be limited to the areas routinely found in the basic design? Why chemistry and not sociology? Why history and not psychology? Why algebra and not astronomy? Why English and not linguistics?

Furthermore, if the school is to provide opportunities to affirm and foster student interests, why limit the population of "interesting" to academic disciplines? Let us, for example, take the matter of chess, a game requiring rigorous, careful thinking, emotional strength, and a sturdy character. Many find the game of chess to be extraordinarily interesting to the point of deep passion and serious commitment. Many math teachers use chess to teach about mathematical concepts. Is it not just as reasonable to use mathematical concepts to teach about chess? A history of chess could give us interesting perspectives on different cultures in different times. Is algebra more or less interesting than chess? This, of course, is a rather silly question since people could be interested in either, or both, or neither. If a curriculum then is to be built partly on the potential interest, it will by necessity have to offer a very wide range of opportunities. If it does not, then the curriculum will have to reflect some criteria or considerations for narrowing the range of potentially interesting phenomenon. Here, we begin to edge into the realm of that which is considered to be "important."

I am personally and professionally prepared to say that we should teach what is important even if it is not going to be very interesting, or not interesting at all. It would be wonderful if we could integrate the two, and we certainly ought to work very hard to do so, but we ought not to sacrifice our sense of what is important on the altar of personal preferences. At the same time we should also make every effort to make the knowledge we consider important meaningful to students. This means linking such knowledge to the stories and experiences that give meaning to students' lives. I am also personally and professionally committed to the proposition that people have a right to live a life of personal joy, play, and excitement. It is vital that schools facilitate this right and nourish the human impulse to develop individual interests. We must, however, guard against another impulse, that of overestimating the significance of one's interest. Sometimes we become so attached and involved with an area of interest that we project that involvement onto others as a way of validating our own attachment. In this way personal interests are transformed into areas of social importance—the hobbies of a few can become the requirements for all. I believe this partly explains the persistence of the sacred five in the basic design; they found their place in the curriculum because the people who designed the curriculum liked them, or found those courses valuable. What's good for the captains of industry, academia, and government must, therefore, be good for the country.

Part of the significance of this analysis turns on different connotations of the word "interesting," and this difference is such that it could be considered a pun. There is "interested" in the sense of that which gives us a certain kind of pleasure and delight and then there is that which is in our interest (i.e., that which serves our own particular purposes). I believe that much of the basic design can be seen as confusion between these two different senses of "interesting." It is to the interests of those in power to convince people that what is interesting to the powerful is in the interest of the weak. Another way to keep the weak under control is to convince them that they are not interested in the truly interesting matters. I believe it to be in the interests of our major moral commitments that we allow individuals to pursue what is truly interesting to them *and* urge the educational community to pursue that which is in the interest of all people.

When it is claimed that certain disciplines are valuable in and of themselves, we are making an esthetic claim, and when we say that they are valuable because they are necessary for the achievement of certain goals (e.g., thinking logically, being a good citizen), we are making an empirical statement. It is this latter claim that we must address as we consider issues of designing a curriculum for social justice and compassion.

In one sense it hardly matters what the form and design are to be, provided that they facilitate and enhance the basic orientation of the framework. It is clear that a basic design which has certain disciplines as its main dimension could be and has been used to reflect a great number of different emphases. To say, for example, that the schools should teach history or math is to say very little, for the teaching of history and math could entail very different orientations. History, for example, can be taught as a structure, as chronology, as epic; it can be taught theoretically, requiring students to read original sources, do originial research, and read critiques of history; it can be taught as intellectual history, political, or social history. Even this attempt to reflect the broad range of orientation inherent in the concept of history as a subject of learning does not begin to deal with the equally broad range of instructional approaches that might be used in the teaching of history (e.g., didactic, critical, mastery). What matters fundamentally is, of course, the choice of orientation, emphasis, and direction. Thus, when one speaks to the pragmatic qualities of discipline or subject, it is clear that we can regard disciplines and subjects as techniques to be used to the degree that they show promise of enhancing the given educational orientation, direction, and emphasis. When we do this, we can cut across the emotion and sentimentality that characterize the passionate and partisan defence of certain disciplines. Those who love their disciplines need not be required to justify their passion, but when these lovers make claims for the potency of these disciplines, they indeed must be prepared to provide evidence for their claims.

Such claims can be examined in the same way we judge the claims of any proposed technique, such as the suggestion that this particular text, film, or learning technique is more effective than another. If a case can be made that the teaching goals can best be reached through the existing basic design as described, then let us by all means use it. Although it is certainly theoretically possible for this to be the case, I remain skeptical and wary about maintaining the basic design because it carries with it a great number of sacred cows and personal pets. It is a design that has been used so extensively and uncritically, and contains so much nostalgia, unverified assumptions, and unchallenged claims, that I doubt that its hegemonic character could be seriously eroded. It is hard for us to think of the study of Shakespeare and Euclid as being questioned and of mathematics and biology as means rather than ends. Teachers have a tendency to identify closely with their subjects and, therefore, tend to make somewhat exaggerated claims for "their" field. It is this sometimes intense loyalty and devotion that clouds the vision of educators, just as any affair of the heart would. However, there must be better ways of sustaining the glory and beauty of a discipline than by exaggerating its importance and imposing it upon the unwilling.

Nonetheless, one must recognize the reality of the power and persistence of the basic design, and so I would not rule out the possibility of using it as a technical support for developing appropriate learning experiences. The key word, of course, is "appropriate," for any design above all else must deeply and thoroughly reflect in all aspects the major sacred, moral, and educational principles contained in our foundations of an orientation toward a society based on a serious and continuing commitment to peace, joy, love, social justice, equality, and community. In my view, it would take enormous work, major restructuring, and significant upheavals if the present basic design was to be the major organizational framework for such an education. Just as it is absurd to believe that the existing educational program is leading us to such a world, I believe it would be an act of self-deception to believe that modest or even major alterations of this program will bring us any closer.

The major difficulty with the basic design resides exactly in its hegemonic character and its sense of inevitability and permanence. The design has been with us so intimately that we find it difficult to imagine any other way of organizing educational experiences than through the medium of courses in disciplines and subjects. Indeed, as I have tried to show, these disciplines have led some of us to an idolatrous posture in which we are prepared to devote our lives to their preservation and continuing existence. Just as it is difficult for us to think about education apart from schools, it is equally difficult for us to think about curriculum without regard to subjects. This, as I have indicated, amounts to another dimension of our technological orientation in that our rhetoric speaks to an educational system focused on the study of techniques and forms. What we often find ourselves doing is engaging in post hoc rationalizations and extended apologies for the inclusion of new forms. Nothing represents the absurdity more than the pretense that we do otherwise. This pretense is in the form of our model of curriculum planning, which presumably tries to overcome irrational and conventional thinking by demanding that we establish objectives before choosing content, method, technique, and evaluation procedures. Establishing goals first would seem at the very least to require education to reflect on the relationship between general goals and specific content. However, in practice teachers are typically *not* asked to state or reflect on their educational goals but rather on the *goals of their subject* (e.g., the purposes, goals, and objectives of teaching history). This is tantamount to giving a potential house builder bricks, mortar, and trowels and urging him or her to decide on what kind of house to build. Such is the persistence of the basic design that these absurdities are not seen as such but rather as rational and critical ways of insuring that goals and objectives inform technique. It is our inability to see subjects and disciplines as techniques that actually inhibits their real power to inform and educate. It is the reification and reductionism of education into the study of disciplines that make them into inert objects of adoration rather than active and vital elements in our liberation.

AN ALTERNATIVE MODEL—QUESTIONS NOT ANSWERS

In addition to the possibility (remote as it may seem) of utilizing the basic design, I would like to suggest an alternative mode of organizing educational experiences to the existing skill/subject mode. This alternative involves organizing an educational program around important and key heuristic and critical questions. Instead of starting with techniques and answers, let us begin with problems and concerns which stir us to seek techniques and answers. Too much of schooling involves giving students answers to questions they do not have or understand, and too many educators are out of touch with many real questions that students do have. It would be far more responsible for teachers to educate students about what constitutes significant problems and questions than to convince them by trying to guess the questions that prompted the answers they are required to learn.

Our orientation toward education is one of active inquiry and research, as opposed to education as passively accepting other people's answers to questions posed by people unknown and at an uncertain time. Inquiry is an impulse generated by need and want (i.e., answers are required to meet needs or to satisfy curiosity). It is our urgent and experienced uncertainties that lead us to inquire, seek, research, and study, and as many psychologists might say, it is important that we "own" the questions before we can accept the validity of the response. As one of my colleagues astutely put it, "It would make a lot more sense if we teachers and students swapped the roles of who asks and who answers questions." Would it not make more sense if schools were places where people could go to get their questions answered, clarified, and refined? We often wonder what happens to the seemingly insatiable curiosity seen in young children who have an endless number of perplexing and profound questions to ask. Parents are familiar with the discomfort that comes from trying to respond to questions like, Where does God come from? Why do I have to go to school if it makes me feel so bad? Why do I have to do what you tell me to do? One way to deal with this discomfort is to shut them off by discounting, sentimentalizing, or ignoring them. This process is strongly emphasized when young people learn very early that school is a place where the teachers and not the students ask the questions. The only exception is questions that students may ask about materials and issues presented by teachers. Schools are places that already have the questions to which they pretend not to have all the answers, but really do.

First, there are the authentic questions that emerge from the experiences of students, and we might arrange schools such that students are encouraged to present their questions and we can help them to respond to them. This may seem cumbersome and inefficient since there is very likely to be significant overlap. Here we once again enter the realm of distinguishing between interesting and important questions. Students have a right to ask and get help on questions that interest them—we call that phenomenon curiosity. In addition, students have a responsibility to engage in questions that the culture's wisdom has determined to be of fundamental significance for the individual and the community.

We have already indicated a number of such questions at different levels of our analysis. There are the questions regarding what it is that has ultimate significance for us, what we hold to be sacred, and to what we are all willing to commit ourselves. There are also other educational questions related to these broad issues: How do we decide these matters? What are proper modes of understanding these questions? How do we deal with uncertainty? And so on.

There are questions of philosophy which are crucial to our culture and to education: What is the nature of knowledge of truth, of the beautiful, and of the good? How do people come to have knowledge and meaning? By what process do we discern reality? There are related questions on the nature of the cosmos—its origin, destiny, and nature. There are parallel questions about humanity and the earth. Mircea Eliade (1959) has written for example of these eternal questions for humanity: What can I know? What can I hope? What ought I to do? A similar and familiar formulation is constituted in the question, Who are we? Where are we? Where do we come from? Where are we going?

On a somewhat less abstract level there are the infinite number of questions that we have about our world: What is the nature of language? What is the origin of sickness? Why do we sleep, dream, forget, remember? What are the causes of wars, depression, creative genius? And so on. The list is literally limitless, as life will continue to spiral in its complexity and richness.

Fundamentally our position is that educators must particularly and concretely respond to the questions of how we can create a culture of abundance, joy, freedom, justice, and peace. That is the central cluster of questions that we as educators must confront and transmit to our students. It would perhaps be more appropriate for educators to transmit the culture's most important questions than their responses, since it seems that our questions are more pertinent and valid than our answers. It is right to ask how to build a culture of abundance, but there is little reason to believe that we have anything like that kind of clarity when it comes to answers. I would also say that we as educators are likely to find greater opportunity for consensus on what are the more important questions than on the answers. We can be united by our questions even as we are divided by our answers.

Education can then be seen as a serious endeavor and struggle to get insight into the questions of social and individual import. People involved in such a process are acting in good faith to work cooperatively on common questions, knowing from the very beginning that there will be enormously different responses to them. By organizing the curriculum around major questions, dilemmas, and issues (e.g., war and peace; equality and freedom; the nature of knowledge), we can also help break down the iron curtains among disciplines. Rigorous, thoughtful, and informed insight into, and understanding of, these problems will require language, concepts, and data from several traditional and nontraditional areas of study. When we study by mode (disciplines), we are forced to study the questions and problems that are illumined by that mode, and, hence, our problems are defined by our modes. It would be far preferable to give the disciplines and areas of study the task of responding to questions that emerge from our experience rather than having them respond to those issues designed at the convenience of existing research methodologies. Let us inquire into what we need and want to learn, not simply learn what has already been studied. The prophetic voice in education reminds us to respond to what is asked of us and to question the adequacy of our answers, while the royal voice in education asks us to think of questions that will match our store of right answers. The royal voice asks us to develop a course on the benefits of the free enterprise system, while the prophetic voice asks us to inquire into the process of creating a society of abundance. The prophetic voice demands that we develop a calculus of social justice, while the royal voice asks us to find the age of Johnny's grandfather. The royal voice speaks of cutoff scores, competencies, tests of cultural quotients, and the knowledge explosion, while the prophetic voice asks us to ask, "If I am not for myself, What am I? If I am only for myself, Who am I?" and "For whom [does] the bell toll?"

To organize a curriculum around such questions, dilemmas, and problems would, of course, mean an enormous amount of complex, delicate, and painstaking work. It would have the advantage (and disadvantage) of giving up the basic design in that it would force us to be more selective and discriminating about content and instruction.

It would also serve to test the strength of our commitment to education as serious inquiry rather than as a ritualistic and instructional process for maintaining our social, political, and cultural institutions.

RESOURCES AND MODELS

Our moral, spiritual, and educational framework is just that, a broad point of departure that focuses on principles, priorities, and orientation. It is our position that important and extensive work is required in order to transform this framework into concrete educational activities, a process which would also serve to inform and enrich the broad framework. Whether there is anything "new" or "original" in these foundations is frankly irrelevant, the more important consultation being the validity, not the age, of the ideas contained in the framework. Clearly this framework is quite different from the mainstream of contemporary educational practice, but the attempt has not been to create something that is different but something that is preferable. What this formulation stresses is its focus on a set of sacred and moral commitments and, hence, speaks to a major shift in our mindset and posture toward curriculum development. However, we are *not* talking about becoming superhuman or changing the nature of our species; we *are* talking about choosing to emphasize a different set of human impulses and about channeling our resources and capacities toward a set of strongly felt but neglected moral principles.

In this spirit we reiterate our faith and confidence in the profession's capacity to meet the challenges of design and implementation inherent in our framework. It is surely not for me to provide the last word on what the broad educational framework ought to be, never mind the absurdity of an expectation that I or anyone else could also provide a detailed blueprint of implementation and practice. This work builds very much on the theory and practice of other educators and theorists; practices of the past and present, if they are of any value, will no doubt be enriched by those of the future. I wish, therefore, to illustrate and indicate (surely not definitely and exhaustively) how works of other theorists and practitioners have already made major contributions to the ideas contained in this book and can be used to guide their further development and implementation.

Clearly, the writings and life of Paulo Freire (1970, 1973) have had a profound influence on the ideas in this book, and, indeed, it can be said that these ideas represent an attempt to focus more sharply the concept of *conscientization* to the specifics of American culture and education. It must be remembered that Freire is not "merely" a theorist but a brilliant practitioner and curriculum developer. His works are not only exhortations and analyses but integrations and synthesis of ideas and practice. His works on adult illiteracy are surely classics of applied educational theory and offer specific and concrete suggestions for action, ideas that are informed by moral and social principles.

There are, of course, other brilliant writers who have made similar integrations of theory and practice and who are oriented toward the human responsibility to create a just and loving world. The genius of John Dewey still shines, and many of his works have as much bite, freshness, and brilliance today as they did decades ago. Maxine Greene (1978) writes eloquently and insightfully of how the humanities can help us become aware of our presence in the world and energize us to make for new possibilities. Henry Giroux offers us more than incisive and trenchant criticisms of the social and economic dimensions of educational practice. He also speaks to alternative practices and has written specifically on how we might more humanely and responsibly respond to the challenges of teacher education, social curriculum, and the teaching of reading. The cumulative works of the late James Macdonald (1974) are a gold mine of practical ideas emerging from an orientation that education provides us with the opportunity to transcend our biological as well as ideological boundaries. The theoretical as well as the applied work of Lawrence Kohlberg (1981) and Ralph Mosher (1979) offers fascinating and provocative examples of serious efforts to engage students in genuine moral discourse. These writers surely differ in substantial degrees on important theoretical matters, but they all are seriously involved in integrating moral concerns, theoretical perspectives, and educational practice. Their work provides insight, exemplars, as well as highly useful conceptual formulations and, if nothing else, demonstrates the possibilities inherent in our profession to develop sound, sensible, and practical educational programs that have moral meaning.

It is important to reiterate that this is presented only as illustrative of existing major resources for those interested in developing a curriculum for justice and compassion. In a similar vein, I also wish to give a number of examples of concrete educational practices which have been actually implemented within the context of real, live, existing conditions of everyday school life. Some of these practices will be familiar, and, indeed, part of the point I am trying to make is that we are not proposing an esoteric or off-the-wall curriculum but rather are suggesting practices that already have a rich tradition in Western and American educational history. Limitations of space and of my own experience will serve to keep the number of these examples to a very few, but there is no question that there are many, many other examples of exciting and provocative practices that represent the work of imaginative, hard-working, courageous teachers who operate under extremely difficult situations.

One of these examples is the ideas contained in the Unified Science,

Math, English, Social Studies Curriculum Projects (USMES) of the 1960s and 1970s. This program synthesized a number of ideas and practices of progressive education, particularly in its stress on dealing with real problems, experiential learning, and a cross-disciplinary approach. The program was designed for students of upper-elementary and junior-high-school ages and had as its focus learning as a function of specific responses to real, concrete, authentic problems. The curriculum materials themselves were simple, direct, and straightforward— a general description of the approach, some sample problems and solutions, and suggestions on developing proper tools. The idea was to engage an entire class (including the teacher) in an as-yet-unsolved problem requiring utilization of a great many skills, ideas, and data. For examaple, a class decided to investigate the need and desirability of installing a traffic light near their school. In order to deal with this issue, the class was confronted with the realities of real inquiry: How does one begin? What do we have to know? How can we get the proper information? What are the dimensions of the problem? And so on. In the course of responding to this challenge, the class had to deal with intellectual issues, scientific concerns, social consideration, and political and economic realities. They learned about sampling and measuring problems involved in traffic flow, demographics, pedestrian habits, etc. It is a curriculum where learning emerges from a real and important problem that has significant consequences. Students learn while and by doing; they also come to share, cooperate, and rely on each other and have the opportunity to experience viscerally the complexities of the search for the truth and the frustrations and rewards of taking social responsibility. Other examples of problems include the design of a student lounge and a nutritious yet tasty soft drink.

This curriculum is a good example of how collegiality and experiential learning can be nourished, providing insight into both the learning process and the nature of knowledge. It also shows how the disciplines can serve the needs and wants of people, rather than the reverse. It is a curriculum of elegant simplicity, straightforward in its approach—it stresses rigor and precision and has built-in, no-nonsense standards of success. Proponents claim that students not only gain in competence, confidence, and self-worth, but in the process they learn the conventional subject matter as well if not better than students in the traditional curriculum design. Given its simple ideas and modest costs, relative to the potential excitement and value such a curriculum promises (and has developed in a number of public and private schools), it is vital that we raise the question of why this curriculum should *not* be more utilized. The question should be pressed even further: In what way is the conventional existing upper-elementary/middle-school/junior-high curriculum *superior* to the USMES formulation? More poignantly, why has this program been allowed to die?

A program similar to USMES, but far more ambitious, daring, and broader in scope, is Fred Newmann's (1975) curriculum for citizenship competence, which he developed and implemented in collaboration with the Madison, Wisconsin, Public Schools. Newman's proposals are rooted in his analysis of traditional citizenship education programs, which he criticizes for stressing understanding rather than competence and for focusing on remote national and international problems rather than more local and immediate issues. The basic purpose of this curriculum formulation is to enrich and preserve democratic traditions by teaching not only the skills of understanding, comprehension, and analysis but also the skills of democratic practice. It is a curriculum that acts on the Jeffersonian notion that democracy requires an active and informed citizenry who participate not just by voting on election day but by being involved in the day-by-day activities of community policymaking as well. Students are taught to be rigorous and thoughtful about the dimensions of a particular policy issue (preferably local, such as a change in the building code or a proposal to build a bicycle path). Eventually they are required, after careful research and intensive deliberation, to take a stand, and are then taught specified skills involved in having that position adopted. Such skills include all the arduous, complicated, and necessary details that go into such efforts—writing letters, knowing how to communicate with various individuals and groups, figuring out which individuals and groups are involved in the issue, organizing, coordinating, making signs, making phone calls, raising funds, etc. In addition, students confront a number of psychological and moral issues that are inherent in such activities—zealotry, frustration, fatigue, stress, overidentification with their particular stand, competition, etc.

As in the case of USMES, students deal with real problems and offer concrete responses that have real consequences for them as well as for the larger community. However, this curriculum is more far-reaching since it represents direct involvement in issues which extend far beyond the school setting. Furthermore, the curriculum explicitly and clearly celebrates a political and moral orientation that involves the dignity of the individual, the principle of government with the consent of the governed, and the responsibility for citizens to participate in good faith and on an informed basis in the decision-making process. The emphasis on developing specific competencies and skills provides a way of taking the goal of nourishing democracy seriously and avoids the conventional lip-service approach involved in stressing learning *about* the system. It is a curriculum of praxis—theory *and* practice— one that recognizes that democracy requires not only reverence and understanding but sweat and detail. It is also a curriculum that specifically affirms the basic framework of American political life as contained in the United States Constitution, meaning rule by law and attention to due process. It is a curriculum that specifically disavows radicalism, violence, and illegality by stressing its faith in the basic legal and constitutional framework and in the educability of people to exercise their democratic right intelligently, wisely, and responsibly.

Newmann has taken his ideas to the point of thoroughly working out the bureaucratic problems that are inherent to implementing such a program in existing school arrangements. He has devised ways of dealing with scheduling, course credit, grading, community involvement, etc., so well that it is impossible to discount the program as "impractical." Given that, and given the curriculum's affirmation of strong traditional American values (democracy, individual dignity, law and order, faith in process, etc.), we must again challenge the profession to justify the superiority of the conventional social studies curriculum over the Newmann curriculum. Do we not want all our citizens to participate fully in the democratic experience? Are we not obliged to pass on to all people all the skills required to have an impact on our community? Are not the schools charged with the responsibility of empowering all individuals with the intellectual, social, and political skills demanded of an informed and active citizenry? This curriculum has been actually implemented within the context of a traditional public high school, so its practicality has been demonstrated. Educators must then confront the challenge that this curriculum poses so powerfully and forcefully. It is an excellent example of a curriculum that does not seek upheaval in the basic design but rather provides a serious and provocative variation of the basic design. It urges students to be thoughtful, careful, precise, and reflective and to utilize the valuable tools and knowledge contained in several disciplines and fields—history, government, sociology, social psychology, English, speech, art, communications, economics, political science. What is most striking for us, however, is its firm moral grounding— that is, its affirmation of the centrality of human dignity.

The concern for providing opportunities for young people to learn about what it means to be responsible has been taken even further in a striking program at Brookline High School, located in suburban Boston. What began as a pilot study in the moral development research programs directed by Ralph Mosher has blossomed into perhaps the most serious effort yet for significant student governance. Although there have been many innovative and promising experiments in this area for several decades, most student governance programs are models of co-optation, trivalization, and impotence. The program introduced by Mosher in the setting of an experimental school-within-a-school involves the notion that students' level of cognitive moral development will increase if they have significant and authentic experience in actually being responsible (i.e., in real student governance). There is wisdom in the old adage that if we want to teach people to be responsible we need to give them responsibility. It is with this spirit that the basic format of the pilot program was adopted by the entire school.

Brookline High School is a large urban/suburban high school (approximately two thousand students) serving a very wide socioeconomic range of people. It is a mostly affluent community of about fifty thousand. Although affluence is certainly there, so are poverty, low-income housing, and urban decay. It is also a community that has maintained, in spite of its size, a representative town meeting of perhaps one hundred people elected at a precinct level, town selectmen, and a town manager. The town meeting has essentially a legislative function but also serves to oversee the management of town services as directed by the town manager. The selectmen serve as a kind of executive committee with special responsibility for making recommendations on the budget and other town policies.

The community has recently applied aspects of this model to the governance of the high school. There is a town meeting composed of fifty people elected from the population of faculty, students, and staff. The principal of the high school acts as the executive officer, much like the town manager. The town meeting has weekly sessions and deals with all the issues that any school administration face—attendance policies and procedures, curriculum requirements, hiring of faculty, discipline, exam schedules. A faculty member designated as friend of the meeting serves as a resource person on matters of existing laws, procedures, precedent, parliamentary matters, etc. The town meeting itself elects a presiding officer called a moderator. In 1984, when I observed the process, forty-four of the fifty who were elected were students, four were teachers, and two were cafeteria workers. The meeting I observed was businesslike, responsible, and sensible and was no less and in some ways more sophisticated and effective than many a university faculty meeting I have attended.

This program acts on faith in young people to be responsible and provides them with a real opportunity to be adult and responsible beyond what is usually expected and required of them. It represents an affirmation of the principles of democracy and a trust in the human capacity to rise to new challenges. This provides a very powerful example of the significance of the concept of the hidden curriculum, since a program like this clearly will have a significant impact on the students, faculty, and staff of the school community *without* any change in course offerings or in the instructional program.

This governance system is currently in operation, and there seems to be general agreement that the administration of the school is as smooth and efficient as it ever was. In effect, this new governance system is hardly noticeable in its technical role but obviously promises to have significant educational meaning to those involved. The members of the town meeting are clearly working within the system; they have not made, nor is it likely that they will seek to make, drastic changes in basic policies. They endeavor to follow legal, professional, and constitutional guidelines just as any other formally constructed group does. Indeed, what is revealing is the perception that such a program is daring and unusual, a reaction which reflects doubt and suspicion of young adults' capacities to be responsible. This program is practical, inexpensive, highly pragmatic, and yet it is rooted in basic human values. It has demonstrated that it can work over a substantial period of time, although clearly there are problems and concerns. It is a program that also cries out for a justification for *not* providing such opportunities at other schools.

The notion of active social involvement takes a somewhat different orientation in the requirement at the Stuart County Day School, a private Catholic girls' school in Princeton, New Jersey. This school is part of a network of schools directed by the religious order of the Society of the Sacred Heart, who have adopted as part and parcel of their stated educational goals a commitment to providing opportunities to connect Christian teaching of love and justice with their academic program.

The programs within the Sacred Heart schools located across the country vary, but the one at Stuart County Day typifies the orientation. Each student at this school is required, as part of the school program, to do a significant amount of community service over a two-year period. Academic credit is given for these experiences, which involve such activities as volunteer work in a soup kitchen, working in low-income nursing homes, and extended internships in areas of Appalachian poverty. Most of these students come from middle- and upper-middle class families, but all are required to feel and experience firsthand the pain and anguish of poverty, misery, and deprivation. The message of this program is clearly that Christian education must perforce include opportunities to learn about the needs of the unfortunate and downtrodden and to learn to serve them.

These examples serve to demonstrate both the possibilities and the difficulties involved in the design of an educational program in a prophetic orientation. The ingenuity and soundness of these exciting programs are used to enhance powerful and meaningful intellectual and moral principles. They represent and mirror, therefore, the professional capacity to respond to the challenge of demands that are based on principle rather than expedience, or on principles that are more exalting than debasing. Yet, there is the harsh reality that these programs, as exciting and promising as they are, also represent the rather severe boundaries that surround our profession.

There is first of all the reality that even when we account for the many programs that we have not mentioned, and those of which we are not aware, we are still speaking of relatively very few in number compared with the overwhelming amount of conventional, mainstream educational practice. The very fact that these programs are unusual, if not unique, reveals a great deal about the norms of what happens in schools. Secondly, even these programs are essentially isolated and tangential to the overall educational program. They represent special aspects, not pervasive themes, of the curriculum; they are easily separated and distinguishable and, hence, fragmented. All of these schools still maintain the basic design: they all have grading and concern themselves with examinations, college admissions, and competition. These are programs that supplement the usual diet, not ones that transform or replace it. Their isolation or quarantine not only prevents their growth and permutation, but their co-optation can lead to a deluded sense that serious change has taken place.

The modesty of the scope of these exemplary programs is not just within the parameters of the school program. Ultimately, such programs fall far short of the kind of commitment that we are suggesting— that is, a determination to transform our society into a just, loving, compassionate, and peaceful one. All of these exciting and imaginative programs implicitly accept or explicitly do not challenge the structure that sanctions basic cultural values such as materialism, competition, individual success, and hierarchy. They all represent an ameliorative rather than a transformative approach to the problems of our culture.

Let me be understood. I am not *against* such efforts. Indeed, I have presented them in praise and admiration, and I hope these and others like them flourish. Those who have developed and implemented such programs are to be congratulated for their imagination, integrity, and courage. The criticisms that I raise do not reflect on their ability or commitment but rather on the severe restrictions and pressures that prevent them and others from going further. These people deserve encouragement, support, and affirmation for their heroic efforts to extend the limits that our culture and profession have imposed.

I do not believe that such admiration and support is in any way diminished by realizing that these limitations, even when extended, are still too restrictive. We celebrate the achievement of our more courageous and imaginative colleagues and share with them the resolution to go beyond those achievements. Let us hope that there will be more celebrations for such achievements and for even greater ones. These achievements are great and significant when measured by the standards of the existing and conventional, but they are modest by the profession's and culture's highest and noblest standards. Indeed, one of the painful aspects of professional duty is establishing standards that are valid but very difficult to meet. In education this translates to working very hard to accomplish that which is very unlikely to be accomplished in one's lifetime. This requires discipline, endurance, patience, and above all else hope, or, in negative terms, the avoidance of despair.

There is, to be blunt, plenty of reason to be in despair over the prospects of an educational program that focuses on the creation of a just world. Our history bulges with war, holocaust, poverty, greed, and barbarism. Our future contains real possibilities of disasters emerging from a present reality that contains pollution, suspicion, nuclear armament, and hatred. We seem to be in a race and are feeling more and more that we cannot control events. In the meantime, day-to-day life continues in its relentless pressures—there is anxiety, fear, and frustration on issues of mundane survival. There is also the strong issue of disillusionment and cynicism about our leadership, and with it the sense that little or nothing can really change—the absence of hope, which is what despair means.

Although I have encountered many people who reject the assumption that fundamental change is necessary, I have met many more who agree that it is necessary but believe that it is not possible. Part of the reason for this despair lies in the difficulty of being able to continue to knock one's head against stone walls. As indicated above, it is natural to want and expect to achieve substantial accomplishments. There are, however, two risks involved in such expectations. First, we may redefine what is "major" by limiting our expectations to what is easier to achieve. We can believe that the educational millennium has arrived, for example, by believing that it will be marked by the reduction of class size to twenty. The second risk is almost the opposite of the first: we will be frustrated and paralyzed by our failure to achieve our truly major goals. I believe that as professionals the first risk is far more dangerous and that taking the second risk has more possibility for a life of meaning and integrity.

We must in taking this risk utilize a different time span than is customarily used. In order to dwell in a profession which has universal and eternal dimensions, we must not be trapped by the narrow boundaries of the short or even medium run. We must recognize, whether we like it or not (and I do not), that there is such a tremendous amount of very difficult work to do that it perforce must take a very long time to accomplish it. Indeed, one way to keep this work from being accomplished is to expect that it can be done soon. It is a very significant accomplishment when we make a modest contribution to a profoundly significant goal. It is, on the other hand, counterproductive to make a profound contribution to a very modest goal. Better to fail in a worthwhile project than succeed in a vulgar one. A large share of time and a large perspective can make this orientation less painful. When Buckminster Fuller was ridiculed about the astronomically high cost of his proposed plastic bubble around the earth, his answer was that the bubble would probably extend the life of the planet for a million years, and hence the cost was ridiculously low.

Human history is barely of a ten-thousand-year duration, and the concept of justice, love, and compassion is perhaps four thousand years old. The fact that those ideas have been developed and affirmed is in itself miraculous, and the related fact that we have not nearly accomplished other commitments is not at all surprising. If it took millions of years to go from stone to energy (as in the example of coal), what would be a reasonable expectation for a people to go from an-imal-like to God-like? The unit of such expectations clearly cannot be months, years, or even decades. We are talking about individuals mak-ing lifelong commitments to age-long goals, so we must see the minor effort of our major efforts as part of a very long process. The basic way to make this meaningful is to be clear that the direction is of ultimate significance and is one that can be called sacred. We as a people have taken several of the first steps, and our successors will need to take several more in order to reach the end of our "ten-thousand-mile journey." What can sustain us on this trip is hope and a faith in the direction of our path. I am not talking of starting but continuing; not of returning to a land that never was, or of creating a world that can never be, but of insisting that we nourish and enrich that which is best in us. Our responsibility as educators is to remind us of this commitment, to help us become what is our best, by pro-viding our students and ourselves with the knowledge, skills, imagi-nation, energy, and hope that are required.

Bibliography

Ackermann, Robert J. 1985. *Religion as Critique*. Amherst, Mass.: University of Massachusetts Press.

Aronowitz, Stanley, and Henry A. Giroux. 1985. *Education Under Siege: The Conservative, Liberal, and Radical Debate over Schooling*. South Hadley, Mass.: Bergin & Garvey.

Bellah, Robert N. 1975. *The Broken Covenant: American Civil Religion in a Time of Trial*. New York: Seabury Press.

Bellah, Robert N., et al. 1985. *Habits of the Heart: Individualism and Commitment in American Life*. Berkeley: University of California Press.

Bercovitch, Sacvan. 1978. *The American Jeremiad*. Madison: University of Wisconsin Press.

Berger, Peter L. 1961. *The Precarious Vision: A Sociologist Looks at Social Fictions and Christian Faith*. Garden City, N. Y.: Doubleday.

Brueggemann, Walter. 1978. *The Prophetic Imagination*. Philadelphia: Fortress Press.

Brueggemann, Walter. 1982. *The Creative Word: Canon as a Model for Biblical Education*. Philadelphia: Fortress Press.

Buber, Martin. 1960. *The Prophetic Faith*. New York: Harper & Row.

Cox, Harvey G. 1984. *Religion in the Secular City: Toward a Postmodern Theology*. New York: Simon & Schuster.

Croatto, J. Severino. 1981. *Exodus: A Hermeneutics of Freedom*. Trans. Salvator Attanasio. Maryknoll, N. Y.: Orbis Books.

Cuddihy, John Martin. 1978. *No Offense: Civil Religion and Protestant Taste*. New York: Seabury Press.

Desroche, Henri. 1979. *The Sociology of Hope*. Trans. Carol Martin-Sperry. London: Routledge & Kegan Paul.

Eliade, Mircea. 1959. *The Sacred and the Profane*. Trans. William R. Trask. New York: Harcourt, Brace & Company.

Fingarette, Herbert. 1969. *Self-Deception*. New York: Humanities Press.

Fowler, James William. 1981. *Stages of Faith: The Psychology of Human Development and the Quest for Meaning*. San Francisco: Harper & Row.

Fox, Matthew. 1979. *A Spirituality Named Compassion and the Healing of the Global Village*. Minneapolis: Winston Press.

Fox, Matthew. 1983. *Original Blessing*. Santa Fe: Bear & Co.

Freire, Paulo. 1970. *Pedagogy of the Oppressed*. Trans. Myra Bergman Ramos. New York: Herder & Herder.

Freire, Paulo. 1973. *Education for Critical Consciousness*. New York: Seabury Press.

Gaylin, Willard, et al. 1978. *Doing Good: The Limits of Benevolence*. New York: Pantheon Books.

Greene, Maxine. 1978. *Landscapes of Learning*. New York: Teachers College Press.

Gunn, Janet. 1986. "Flannery O'Connor and the Religious Function of Displacement," unpublished paper, presented at UNC at Greensboro, November.

Harrington, Michael. 1983. *The Politics at God's Funeral: The Spiritual Crisis of Western Civilization*. New York: Holt, Rinehart & Winston.

Herberg, Will. 1960. *Protestant, Catholic, Jew: An Essay in American Religious Sociology*. Garden City, N. Y.: Anchor Books.

Heschel, Abraham Joshua. 1962. *The Prophets*, 2 vols. New York: Harper & Row.

Kohlberg, Lawrence. 1981. *Essays on Moral Development*. San Francisco: Harper & Row.

Kozol, Jonathan. 1985. *Illiterate America*. Garden City, N. Y.: Anchor Press.

Lasch, Christopher. 1979. *The Culture of Narcissism: American Life in an Age of Diminishing Expectations*. New York: Norton.

Macdonald, James. 1974. "A Transcendental Developmental Ideology of Education," in *Heightened Consciousness, Cultural Revolution, and Curriculum Theory*. Ed. William Pinar. Berkeley: McCutchan Publishing.

Miranda, José P. 1974. *Marx and the Bible: A Critique of the Philosophy of Oppression*. Trans. John Eagleson. Maryknoll, N. Y.: Orbis Books.

Mosher, Ralph (ed.). 1979. *Adolescent's Education and Development: A Janus Knot*. Berkeley: McCutchan Publishing.

Newmann, Fred M. 1975. *Education for Citizen Action: Challenge for Secondary Curriculum*. Berkeley: McCutchan Publishers.

Niebuhr, H. Richard. 1960. *Radical Monotheism and Western Culture*. New York: Harper & Row.

Niebuhr, Reinhold. 1935. *An Interpretation of Christian Ethics*. New York: Harper & Brothers.

Niebuhr, Reinhold. 1960. *Moral Man and Immoral Society*. N. Y.: Charles Scribner.

Nisbet, Robert. 1974. *The Sociology of Emile Durkheim*. New York: Oxford University Press.

Plato. 1985. *The Rebublic*. Trans. Richard Sterling and William Scott. New York: Norton.

Porteous, Alvin G. 1966. *Prophetic Voices in Contemporary Theology: The Theo-*

logical Renaissance and the Renewal of the Church. Nashville: Abingdon Press.

Richard, Mary Caroline. 1964. *Centering*. Middletown, Conn.: Wesleyan University Press.

Sartre, Jean-Paul. 1956. *Being and Nothingness*. Trans. Hazel Barnes. New York: Philosophical Library.

Segundo, Jan Luis. 1976. *Liberation of Theology*, Trans. John Drury. Maryknoll, N. Y.: Orbis Books.

Sennett, Richard. 1977. *The Fall of Public Man*. New York: Knopf.

Silberman, Charles E. 1970. *Crisis in the Classroom: The Remaking of American Education*. New York: Random House.

Smith, Wilfred Cantwell. 1963. *The Meaning and End of Religion*. New York: Macmillan.

Soelle, Dorothee. 1974. *Political Theology*. Trans. John Shelley. Philadelphia: Fortress Press.

Thomas, Lewis 1983. *Late Night Thoughts on Listening to Mahler's Ninth Symphony*. New York: Viking Press.

Tyler, Ralph. 1949. *Principles of Curriculum and Instruction*. Chicago: University of Chicago Press.

Walzer, Michael. 1985. *Exodus and Revolution*. New York: Basic Books.

Welch, Sharon. 1985. *Communities of Resistance and Solidarity*. Maryknoll, N. Y.: Orbis Books.

Winter, Gibson. 1985. "Community and Education," in *Schools and Meaning*, David Purpel and H. Svi Shapiro, Eds. Washington, D. C.: University Press.

Index

Acculturation: and education, 10–11, 18–20, 46–47, 122–23, 130; and religious ideals and symbols, 74

Achievement, as cultural value, 9, 32, 40, 43. *See also* Worth and achievement

Ackermann, Robert J., 26

Affirmation of commitments, as necessity for educators, x, 11–13, 57, 93–98, 105, 115–17

Alienation, 55–56; and commitment, as value conflict, 56–57, 83, 111–12; and fear of education, 7

Ambivalence toward education. *See* Fear of education

Anti-intellectualism, x, 6–7, 54–55, 126

Apple, Michael, x, 19

Arguelles, José, 92–93

Aronowitz, Stanley: on intellectualism and teaching, 102–3; on play, 134

Arrogance and humility: and the Puritans, 97–98; as value conflict, 52–56, 57, 112

Art, 17, 133–36; and creation theology, 91–93

Athletic programs, 32, 52

Authority, power, and coercion, 45–48, 120; in the prophetic tradition, 81. *See also* Indoctrination.

Bakunin, Mikhail, 65

Bellah, Robert N.: on civil religion, 74; on individualism and well-being, 16, 31, 33, 42; on Lincoln, 71

Bennett, William, xv

Bercovitch, Sacvan, 73, 96–98

Berger, Peter L., 74, 112

Biblical prophets, 108–9. *See also* Prophetic tradition.

Brueggemann, Walter: on confusion and self-deception, 61; on criticism and grief, 28; on prophecy, xi, 1, 83–85, 110, 138

Buber, Martin, 108-9

Caring: compassion and sentimentality, 40–44, 89, 95. *See also* Creation theology; Liberation theology; Prophetic tradition

"Cheating," 32, 40

Coercion. *See* Authority, power, and coercion

Commitment and critical consciousness, 95–98. *See also* Affirmation of commitments; Alienation and commitment

Community, 16; and common knowledge, 129. *See also* Individuality

Competition: and arrogance, 52; and community, 35; and dignity, 36; and grading, 9, 61; and individualism, 16–17, 31–32; and liberation theology, 86; and sentimentalism, 43. *See also* Equality and competition

Complacency. *See* Displacement and complacency

Confusion. *See* Value paradoxes and conflicts.

Conscientization, 84, 131–32, 156–57

Constitution of the United States, 71, 73, 129

Control and democracy, 48–50

Co-optation, as form of professional resistance, 141–42

Counts, George S., xiii, xv

Cox, Harvey G., 26, 86

Creation theology, 88–93

Crisis, cultural, enormity of, ix–x, 1–3, 12–13, 15–17, 21–23, 48, 54, 111–13, 164

Critical and creative consciousness: and creation theology, 91–93; as educational goal, 20, 26–27, 28, 115, 126, 128, 130–34, 137, 140; and humility, 95–98, 130–31; and liberation theology, 85–86; and prophetic tradition, 84–85; and Socratic tradition, 78–80

Croatto, J. Severino, 26, 125

Cuddihy, John Martin, 74

Culture, American, 15–17, 21–64; unease in, 21–23, 26, 68. *See also* Crisis, cultural, enormity of

Curriculum change, resistance to, 138–44; co-optation of, 141–42; exaggerated criticism of, 143–44; and forms of rejection, 142–43; insufficient technology, 144; panacea promising, 143; sabotage, 141; stalemates, 69, 139–41

Curriculum design, 146–53; alternative model, 153–56. *See also* Curriculum implementation

Curriculum implementation, 156–65

Curriculum, model programs of: Mosher program, 160–62; Newmann, 159–60; Sacred Heart, 162; USMES, 157–59

Curriculum planning, 145–46, 152–56

Declaration of Independence, 71, 129
Democracy. *See* Control and democracy
Democratic heritage. *See* Heritage
Desroche, Henri, 77
Dewey, John, 4, 49, 125, 157
Dialectic ground of education, 111–13; and curriculum
    planning, 145–46
Dickens, Charles, 12, 40
Disciplines, basic five, 146–50; and hegemonic character,
    52–53, 150–53
Displacement and complacency, 57–58
Douglas, Ann, 42
Durkheim, Émile, 75–76

Economic uncertainty, 2, 15–17, 39–40
Educability of humanity, faith in, 10, 160
Education profession, 5, 100–4. *See also* Curriculum
    change, resistance to
Educational credo, xi, 113–19
Educational reform movement, ix, xiv–xv, 14–27. *See also*
    Trivialization of education
Eliade, Mircea, 75, 76, 154
Empowerment. *See* Liberation/empowerment
Equality and competition, as value conflict, 37–40
Ethnocentrism, 50–52
Evil: and affirmation, 98; and confusion, 30, 60; and
    prophetic tradition, 83, 113
Exaggerated criticism, as form of professional resistance,
    143–44
"Excellence" in education, 3, 17–19, 36–37, 50
Expectations of schools, 4–5, 122

Faith and reason, 58–61
Fear of education, x, 5–8, 20, 22–23, 55, 101–2, 107
Fingarette, Herbert, 62–63
Finn, Chester, Jr., xv
Fowler, James William, 59–60
Fox, Matthew, 42–43, 88–92, 121
Free expression and inquiry, faith in, 10–11
Freire, Paulo, x, 22, 30, 111; on human freedom and
    critical literacy, 19–20, 84, 124, 131–32, 156–57
Freud, Sigmund, 54, 58, 111

Gandhi, Mohandas K. (Mahatma), xvii, 71, and the
    prophetic tradition, 82–83, 86, 105, 135
Gaylin, Willard, 40
Gettysburg Address, 71, 129
Giroux, Henry, x, 19, 157; on intellectualism and teaching,
    102–3; on play, 134
Grading, 8–9, 32, 47, 61, 120, 142, 163

Greene, Maxine, x, 19, 132, 135, 157
Guilt. *See* Responsibility
Gunn, Janet, 57–58

Harrington, Michael, 58, 65, 77
Herberg, Will, 74
Heritage, 7, 11, 47–48, 70–75, 97, 117–18; intellectual, 71–73;
   moral, 71; political, 71; religious, 25, 73–75, 97
Heschel, Abraham Joshua: on caring, 41, 44; on evil, 113;
   on prophecy, xi, 80–83; on responsibility, 119
Hidden curriculum, 20–21, 24, 101, 161
Historicity, as educational goal, 126–27, 132
Holt, John, 128
Humility, as goal of educational practice, 113 14, 123–24,
   130–31. *See also* Arrogance and humility

Imagination: and play, as educational goal, 27, 133–36;
   prophetic, 83–85
Individuality: and alienation, 56; and community, as value
   conflict, 23, 31–34, 35; and economic uncertainty,
   15–17; and sentimentalism, 43. *See also* Equality and
   competition
Indoctrination, 119–20
Insufficient technology, as form of professional resistance,
   144
Intellectual ferment within culture, 2, 112, 135–36
Intellectual processes and forms, knowledge of, as
   educational goal, 125–26
"Interesting"/"important" curriculum question, 147–50,
   154

Jesus, xvii, 26, 71, 85–90, 105, 111

King, Martin Luther, Jr., xvii, 8, 71; and the prophetic
   tradition, 82–83, 86, 105, 111
Knowledge: assimilation of, as educational goal, 128–30; as
   cultural value, 72
Kohlberg, Lawrence, 157
Kozol, Jonathan, 19, 20

Language, religious, moral, and mythic, 25, 27, 65–68, 88,
   96
Lasch, Christopher, xv, 31, 42
Liberation theology, xi, 26, 85–88
Liberation/empowerment: as educational goal, xvii, 20,
   29–30, 84, 120, 124–26, 131–33, 134, 153, 160; of the
   poor and powerless, 29–30
Lincoln, Abraham, 8, 71

Macdonald, James, x, 19, 157
Marx, Karl, 4, 54, 58, 86, 111

Middle class: and cultural transformation, 29; and "excellence," 36; focus of analysis, x, xvi–xvii; and military draft, 38–39; in the 1960s, 38; and religion, 74; value choices, 30; views on self and group, 33
Miranda, José, 112
Moses, 71, 84–85, 105, 111, 125, 135
Mosher, Ralph, and student governance program, 157, 160–62
Mythic traditions in culture, 70–77
Mythos of meaning, need to develop, x, 27, 54, 68–70, 91, 93–99, 136–37. *See also* Educational credo; Prophecy and education

"New age" thinking, 88–89
New Right, xiv–xvi, 25–26
Newmann, Fred, curriculum for citizenship competence, 159–60
Niebuhr, H. Richard, 59
Niebuhr, Reinhold, 14, 65, 100
1960s and educational reform, 14–17, 37–38, 50, 141
Nisbet, Robert, 75–76

O'Connor, Flannery, 57–58

Panacea promising, as form of professional resistance, 143
Paradoxical traditions and values. *See* Value paradoxes and conflicts
Pinar, William, x, 19
Pinon, Nelida, xiii
Plato, 4; and Socrates, 46, 78
Play. *See* Imagination and play, as educational goal
Porteous, Alvin G., 82
Power. *See* Authority, power, and coercion
Prophecy and education, 103–11, 134–35; in curriculum planning, design, and implementation, 155, 162–63
Prophetic tradition, x, 80–85. *See also* Creation theology; Liberation theology; Prophecy and education
Puritans, 73, 96–98

Reason. *See* Faith and reason
Rejection, as form of professional resistance, 142–43
Religion, as social criticism, 26–27, 79–93. *See also* Heritage; Sacred and profane
Resources to support education, 5–6, 101, 106, 122
Responsibility: and guilt, 40–41, 44–45, 119; in the face of oppression, 118–19; and prophetic voice, 81
Revisionist criticism, 19–21, 22
Right, and educational reform movement, xiv–xv, 24–26, 56

Sabotage, as form of professional resistance, 141

Sacred Heart programs. *See* Society of the Sacred Heart community service school programs

Sacred and profane, 75–77; as distinction educators should make, 77–78, 94, 117; and prophetic tradition, 80

Sartre, Jean-Paul, 61

Scholarship, 59, 60–61, 72, 123, 147

Segundo, Jan Luis, 26

Self-deception: and professional responsibility, 61–63, 130, 136; as response to fear and confusion, 8, 13, 22, 68, 98

Shaull, Richard, 132

Silberman, Charles E., 19, 22

Skills, development of, as educational goal, 127–28

Smith, Wilfred Cantwell, 59–60

Society of the Sacred Heart community service school programs, 162

Socrates, 86, 105, 111; and Socratic tradition, x, 78–80, 88, 130; trial of, and paradox of education, 7–8, 9

Soelle, Dorothée, 26, 63, 65

Stalemate, as form of professional resistance, 69, 139–41

Testing, standardized, 17–18, 32, 35, 50, 105–6

Thomas, Lewis, 53

Tillich, Paul, 82, 111–12

Traditions, cultural. *See* Heritage

Trivialization of education, ix–x, xvi, 2–13, 19, 22, 137

Tyler model of curriculum planning, 49, 142, 145

Unified Science, Math, English, Social Studies Curriculum Projects (USMES), 157–59

Universalism. *See* Ethnocentrism

Values paradoxes and conflicts, x, xvi, 11, 30–40, 51, 56, 57, 61, 68, 93, 117, 136; equality/competition, 37–40; individuality/community, 31–34; worth/achievement, 34–37

Vision of meaning. *See* Mythos of meaning, need to develop

Voltaire, 65

Walzer, Michael, 125

Welch, Sharon, 95

Winter, Gibson, 133

Women's movement, 135

Working conditions of educators, 5–6, 20, 101–3, 106–7

Worth and achievement, as value conflict, 34–37, 93